SAINT PATRICK RETOLD

Saint Patrick Retold

THE LEGEND AND HISTORY OF
IRELAND'S PATRON SAINT

ROY FLECHNER

PRINCETON UNIVERSITY PRESS
PRINCETON & OXFORD

Published by Princeton University Press
41 William Street, Princeton, New Jersey 08540
6 Oxford Street, Woodstock, Oxfordshire OX20 1TR

press.princeton.edu

Library of Congress Control Number: 2018962693
ISBN 978-0-691-18464-7

British Library Cataloging-in-Publication Data is available

Editorial: Ben Tate, Hannah Paul, and Charlie Allen
Production Editorial: Karen Carter
Jacket Design: Faceout Studio, Derek Thornton
Production: Erin Suydam
Publicity: Tayler Lord and Katie Lewis

Jacket Credit: St. Patrick Climbs Croagh Patrick, 1932 (oil on canvas),
Clarke, Margaret (1888–1961) / Dublin City Gallery, The Hugh Lane,
Ireland / Bridgeman Images

This book has been composed in Arno

Printed on acid-free paper. ∞

Printed in the United States of America

10 9 8 7 6 5 4 3 2 1

CONTENTS

List of Illustrations and Maps vii

List of Abbreviations ix

Preface xv

Introduction: Patrick of Legend and of History 1

1 Patrick's Britain 29

2 Patrick's Ireland 61

3 Captivity 94

4 Religion in Britain and Ireland 119

5 The Missionary Life 154

6 Imagining Patrick in the Middle Ages 183

Epilogue: Remembering Saint Patrick 218

Cited Scholarship and Further Reading 237

Index 261

ILLUSTRATIONS AND MAPS

Illustrations

1. The four Evangelists from the Book of Armagh. 8
2. Remains of Roman villa at Great Witcombe (Gloucestershire). 39
3. Littlecote Roman villa (Wiltshire), Orpheus mosaic. 40
4. Irish penannular brooch. 70
5. Reconstruction of Ptolemy's map of Ireland (2nd century AD). 75
6. Maiden Castle hillfort (Dorset). 139
7. Neolithic passage tomb at Newgrange (County Meath). 143
8. Map of Saint Patrick's Purgatory on Station Island. 225
9. Shrine of Saint Patrick's Bell, National Museum of Ireland. 227

Maps

1. Some population groups, provinces, and significant places in late antique Ireland.   xii
2. Some Roman towns, settlements, and population groups in Britain.   xiii

ABBREVIATIONS

BCLL M. Lapidge and R. Sharpe,
*Bibliography of Celtic-Latin Literature
400–1200* (Dublin, 1985)

Bede, *HE* Bede, *Historia Ecclesiastica Gentis
Anglorum*, Bertram Colgrave and
R.A.B. Mynors, eds. and trans., *Bede's
Ecclesiastical History of the English
People* (Oxford, 1969)

Bieler, *Patrician Texts* Ludwig Bieler, ed. and trans.,
*The Patrician Texts in the Book of
Armagh* (Dublin, 1979)

CCSL Corpus Christianorum Series Latina
(Turnhout, 1953–)

Chronicle of Ireland T. M. Charles-Edwards, trans.,
The Chronicle of Ireland, 2 vols.
(Liverpool, 2006)

CLH D. Ó Corráin, *Clavis Litterarum
Hibernensium: Medieval Irish Books
and Texts (c. 400–c. 1600)*, 3 vols.
(Turnhout, 2017)

Codex Iustinianus Paul Krüger, ed., Fred Blume et al.,
trans., *The Codex of Justinian: A New
Translation with Parallel Latin and
Greek Text*, 3 vols. (Cambridge, UK,
2016)

Codex Theodosianus Theodor Mommsen and P. M.
Meyer, eds., *Theodosiani Libri XVI
cum Constitutionibus Sirmondianis*
(Berlin, 1905); C. Pharr, trans., *The
Theodosian Code and Novels and the
Sirmondian Constitutions* (Princeton,
NJ, 1952)

Confessio Patrick, *Confessio*, in *Libri
Epistolarum Sancti Patricii Episcopi*, 2
vols., ed. Ludwig Bieler (Dublin,
1952), 1:56–91; Allan B. E. Hood,
trans., *St. Patrick: His Writings and
Muirchu's Life* (Chichester, 1978),
41–54. Bieler's edition available at
http://www.confessio.ie

CSEL Corpus Scriptorum Ecclesiasticorum
Latinorum (Vienna, 1866–)

Digesta Theodor Mommsen and Paul Krüger,
eds., Alan Watson, trans., *The Digest
of Justinian*, 4 vols. (Philadelphia,
1985)

Heist W. W. Heist, ed., *Vitae Sanctorum
Hiberniae e Codice Salmanticensi*
(Brussels, 1965)

Hibernensis	Hermann Wasserschleben, ed., *Die irische Kanonensammlung* (Giessen, 1874; 2nd ed., Leipzig, 1885); Roy Flechner, ed. and trans., *The Hibernensis,* Studies in Medieval and Early Modern Canon Law (Washington, DC, 2019 [forthcoming])
Letter	Patrick, Letter to the Soldiers of Coroticus, in Ludwig Bieler, ed., *Libri Epistolarum Sancti Patricii Episcopi,* 2 vols. (Dublin, 1952), 1:91–102; Allan B. E. Hood, trans., *St. Patrick: His Writings and Muirchu's Life* (Chichester, 1978), 55–59. Bieler's edition available at http://www.confessio.ie
PL	Patrologia Latina, ed. J.-P. Migne, 221 vols. (Paris, 1844–64)
Plummer	Charles Plummer, ed., *Vitae Sanctorum Hiberniae,* 2 vols. (Oxford, 1910)

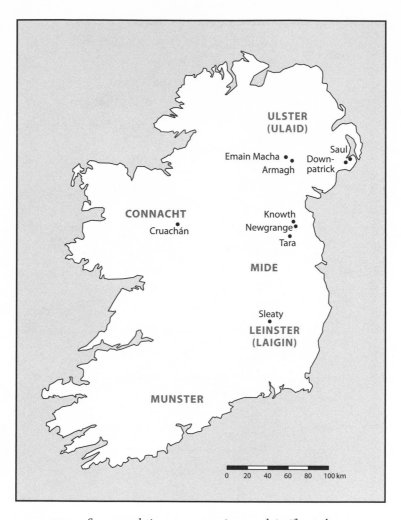

MAP 1. Some population groups, provinces, and significant places in late antique Ireland

MAP 2. Some Roman towns, settlements, and population groups in Britain

PREFACE

THIS BOOK IS as much a biography of Saint Patrick as it is a history of the late antique insular world as seen through Patrick's eyes and as he might have interpreted it through the many facets of his cultural identity: as a Briton, as a Roman, and as an immigrant to Ireland who could comment on Irish society with both an insider's and outsider's perspective. Straddling, as he did, late Roman Britain and late Iron Age Ireland, Patrick would have experienced a world that went through far-reaching political, economic, and religious changes. The fourth and fifth centuries were a time of great flux in the Roman world: from the conversion of Emperor Constantine in 312/313, to the Gothic triumph over Emperor Valens at Hadrianople in 378, to the retreat of the remaining Roman forces from Britain in 410, to the abdication of the last emperor of the western Roman Empire in 476. Patrick was there to experience the consequences of these proverbial 'interesting times'.

Patrick's testimony is of crucial importance because he is the *only* contemporary witness (whose writings survive) to the goings-on in Britain and Ireland at the turn of the fifth century. But the uniqueness of his testimony does raise challenges for the modern biographer, who risks circularity when trying to understand Patrick primarily within a historical context that Patrick himself describes. In order to overcome this risk, a biographer must piece together as many sherds of independent details as possible by revisiting the usual (albeit meagre) sources about the period and by drawing on analogies with other places that are better attested in the contemporary record, but also by introducing new forms of evidence, which in this book consist primarily of Roman law and archaeology. The new evidence inevitably invites new interpretations, some quite provocative, and indeed certain hypotheses that I constructed have made headlines worldwide when they were first published in article form in 2011. Some readers agreed with them, others did not, but this is the way it should be: informed disagreement is the lifeblood of academic research. Although I revisit, and occasionally revise, some of these hypotheses in the chapters that follow, this book was not written in order to provoke. Rather, it challenges the reader to contemplate different images of Patrick that emerge from the different kinds of available evidence but also from the internal ambiguities of individual sources. We will see Patrick as he is depicted in his own words, Patrick as inferred from the circumstances of his immediate historical contexts, Patrick as a figure of veneration whose saintly image developed in different ways over a millennium and a half, and Patrick as a figure who, by his own account, was regarded as controversial by some of his contemporaries. In the course of expounding each image, I also tell the reader about the methodological difficulties that historians experienced in interpreting the evidence and how these difficulties may (or may not) be overcome.

Saint Patrick Retold is based on original research, but it also includes a good deal of synthesis of scholarly publications. It endeavours to offer a broad perspective of the development of historiographical debates on key issues such as religion in Britain and Ireland and what it meant to be 'Celtic'. Although the book is not strictly academic and was written with a wider popular appeal in mind, some discussions are nevertheless denser in detail in order to satisfy a more specialist readership but also inform nonexperts. Most chapters contain a core of original research, and all references to primary sources are given in endnotes. However, for the most part, the book is written in nonspecialist language, assumes no background knowledge, and mentions the historiography only in bibliographic essays corresponding to each chapter rather than in footnotes. Certain themes, like servitude, missionary work, and Celtic identity, are revisited in different chapters and reexamined from different angles. Some degree of repetition was therefore inevitable in order to allow each chapter to be read as independently as possible from other chapters.

In the course of writing this book, I have been fortunate to receive expert comments and criticisms from friends and colleagues who kindly made time to read draft chapters. I cannot thank them enough from saving me from many errors and for teaching me much that I did not know. They are Elizabeth Dawson, Matthias Egeler, Elva Johnston, Shane Lordan, Charles Ivar McGrath, Thomas Pickles, Ulrike Roth, Helle Vogt, and the anonymous readers for Princeton University Press. All remaining errors are, of course, my own.

SAINT PATRICK RETOLD

Patrick of Legend and of History

SAINT PATRICK WAS never formally canonised. Nor, for that matter, were the other two saintly luminaries of early medieval Ireland, Colum Cille and Brigit. It was only in 1190, twenty years after the papacy assumed exclusive authority over canonisation, that Ireland received its first papally sanctioned saint, Archbishop Malachy (d. 1148) of Armagh. Yet, unlike Patrick, Saint Malachy is far from being a household name. Patrick's renown, on the other hand, has long since extended beyond the confines of Ireland as his fame grew in tandem with his continual association with myths and legends, from the tale of his ridding Ireland of snakes to that of his unlocking an entrance to purgatory. His greatest claim to fame, however, always lay in an achievement that was not supernatural but equally astonishing: being the apostle of the Irish, the man who brought Ireland into the fold of the Christian faith. Although some modern historians of earlier generations did indeed believe that Patrick single-handedly converted Ireland to Christianity, with one historian, George Stokes, going as far as to style his mission 'the national conversion of Ireland', it is nowadays clear that whatever Patrick actually accomplished, he could not have effected a 'national conversion' all by himself. Nevertheless, he did make an enduring contribution to the formation of Ireland's religious identity. Assessing the extent of this contribution and separating the historical Patrick from the Patrick of myth are two objectives of this book, while a third objective is to reconstruct the wider historical context in which he lived.

Commonly depicted with green robes, a mitre, and a crozier, Patrick is recognised internationally as an iconic Irish symbol, an ambassador of Ireland's postcard-perfect rolling hills and green meadows, ever flowing with sheep and shamrocks. But it is not to be taken for granted that Patrick should be regarded as quintessentially Irish, because he wasn't. Born in Britain, he was recently styled an immigrant, even the 'patron of immigrants', by then-taoiseach Enda Kenny in his Saint Patrick's Day address on 17 March 2017, delivered in the company of the American president, Donald Trump, whose immigration policies he was parabolically criticising. Patrick, it seems, continues to be topical even in the world of current international politics.

Patrick is first and foremost a historical figure. That he originates from Britain is an undisputed fact, and so is his long sojourn in Ireland, where he most likely died. As a native of Roman Britain or of Britain in the period shortly after the Roman legions left in 410, he is unique for straddling two cultures, the Romano-British and Irish, forming a live link between them. As such, he is an important bridge connecting the late antique culture of the empire, with its sophisticated political, social, and intellectual attributes, to the more rural- and kin-based society of Ireland, an island sometimes described as 'barbarous' by contemporaries writing with a Roman bias, and even by Patrick himself, who spoke of dwelling among barbarians (*inter barbaras itaque gentes habito*).[1]

Although the exact years of Patrick's birth and death are unknown, the mere fact of his existence is unequivocally confirmed by his own writings, two of which survive. One is the *Confessio*, an apologetic text containing a large number of autobiographical anecdotes that he wrote towards the end of his life, framed— to an extent—as a response to accusations against him. The other text is the Letter to the Soldiers of Coroticus, essentially a public condemnation of a British warlord and slaver who captured some of Patrick's recent converts and killed others.

Yet, apart from being attested in genuine writings that he himself penned, Patrick is also a figure of legend, or indeed legends. These took shape over time through a combination of oral traditions and edifying reverential biographies belonging to the genre of saints' Lives or, by another name, hagiographies. As an imagined persona, Patrick's identity was further augmented through centuries of folklore and popular tales, which crafted an ideal portrait of him as a miracle worker, church founder, and all-round saintly role model. The image that hagiography constructed for Patrick endured in popular culture despite the best efforts of scholars to attenuate it by concentrating on the historical and more human features of his personality, insofar as these are discernible from the rather scant biographical material available. Anyone who has ever attempted to redress historical misconceptions knows how challenging and—all too often— frustrating this can be.

Writing the biography of a late antique figure is invariably a different exercise from writing about a modern personality. The paucity of sources is a perennial obstacle, but even when sources are available, their testimony is moderated by their stated or unstated biases, the subtleties of their rhetoric, and the absence of corroborating material. All these hamper our ability to make use of them in an uncomplicated manner. Consequently, the detail that we are able to glean about the life of the historical Patrick is rather patchy, and there is much that is entirely obscured from view, especially the most mundane and trivial details, which remain hopelessly irrecoverable. We will never know, for example, what he looked like. Nor will we know exactly when he was born and when he died. Likewise, it is unknown whether he was ever married or had children, even though (as has recently been revealed) eighteenth- and nineteenth-century folkloric traditions from Ireland venerated a certain Sheelah as his wife and even commemorated a feast day in honour of this imagined lady, a day after Patrick's own. And, finally, it is unknown where exactly he was buried, although, as we shall see in the following chapters, medieval hagiographers laid claim to having 'identified' the whereabouts of his remains.

Speculations and fanciful interpretations flourish when accurate information is scant or ambiguous. But one would like to minimise the need to resort to imaginative fiction to make up for the gaps in the story. An alternative way of compensating for the evidential deficit, and of reconciling ourselves with it, is to accept that in Patrick's case we can only hope to be able to draw the outline of a figure whose subtle features will forever remain obscured from view. This outline comes into focus when we concentrate not so much on the person himself but rather on his background. This is, by analogy, the sort of exercise to which a painter may refer as painting 'negative space': it is the exercise of concentrating on, say, the wallpaper around a blurred figure or the shadow that the figure casts, rather than the figure itself. In doing this, the contours of a figure do eventually emerge, albeit faintly in some places, but nevertheless visible, unique, and recognisable. To a large extent, this is the method that the present book follows: it outlines the figure of Patrick by reading his own writings in the context of surviving contemporary sources, as well as early medieval sources and archaeology, which can shed light on the conditions of Patrick's time. A reading of this kind will allow us to make educated guesses about certain obscure aspects of Patrick's life—for example, the standard of living he enjoyed in Ireland, the type of dwelling his family had in Britain, and even the extent of his education. This book is by no means the first to take this approach, but it is the first to do so by examining how Patrick's own words chime with Roman law and how they should be interpreted with recourse to both the Roman rhetorical tradition that he imbibed in his education and the biblical exegetical conventions that were the staple of a literate cleric's training. Helpfully, the past couple of decades have witnessed a shift in the critical approach to interpreting late antique texts: previously advocating a predominantly philologically driven approach confined to the positivist binary of true versus false, currently the historiography in the field has become more refined, more theoretically aware, and just as concerned with investigating the rhetorical methods and posturings of late antique authors as it is with the facts of their accounts. This study has also benefitted from several recent publications, both historical and archaeological, that led to important advances in our understanding of contemporary Britain and Ireland. Here I attempt to make the most of these contributions while fully acknowledging a debt to the works of past scholars on whose shoulders any modern biography of Patrick inevitably stands. These include, in chronological order, J. B. Bury's *Life of St. Patrick and His Place in History* (1905), Ludwig Bieler's *Life and Legend of St. Patrick* (1948), R.P.C. Hanson's *Saint Patrick: His Origins and Career* (1968), James Carney's *Problem of St. Patrick* (1973), E. A. Thompson's *Who Was Saint Patrick?* (1985), David N. Dumville and contributors' *Saint Patrick: A.D. 493–1993* (1993), and the works of many other eminent scholars who, while they did not publish monographs on Patrick, contributed to the study of his biography through articles or book chapters, many of which are cited in the pages of the present book. Apart from scholarly works about Patrick, there has been a constant trickle of popular books, like Philip Freeman's insightful *St. Patrick of Ireland* (2004); more discursive, yet perceptive, interpretations of Patrick's biography written with subtle confessional leanings, like Eoin MacNeill's *Saint Patrick: Apostle of Ireland* (1934, for which MacNeill sought an imprimatur from the auxiliary bishop of Westminster) or Thomas O'Loughlin's *Discovering Saint Patrick* (2005, which says in the preface that reading Patrick is a means by which Christians can discover their identity); and new translations of Patrick's works, listed in the bibliographic essay for this chapter. There have also been and continue to be more speculative publications in print and online that sport hypotheses that range from the plausible to the outright barmy. Though, in fairness, it must be acknowledged that any radical departure from the received wisdom on Patrick runs the risk of being dismissed as fatuous, and this risk applies to some of the hypotheses that I shall advance here. Bearing in mind this risk, I set out to write a biography that falls somewhere in between the academic and the popular: written in non-specialist language accessible to both experts and the wider public, this is a work by an academic historian that showcases the findings of original research and offers an up-to-date synthesis of the historiography. The chapter plan is systematic, beginning with two chronological chapters that follow Patrick's journey from Britain to Ireland, and continuing with thematic chapters concentrating on major themes in Patrick's biography and its historical background: captivity, religion, and missionary work. The book concludes with a chapter on the building of Patrick's saintly image in the Middle Ages, followed by a discursive reflection on the manner in which Patrick's memory has been framed since the early modern era and the impact of his legacy on more recent historical events, both in Ireland and abroad.

But before we can rethink Patrick's biography, we must first have an idea of the received wisdom to which this book responds. In the remainder of this introduction, therefore, I shall give an overview of the standard narrative of Patrick's biography—which is largely informed by his own writings—and draw attention to a number of problems that it raises and that this book will address. Our starting point will be Patrick's writings, the *Confessio* and the Letter, which are the two central texts that underpin this (and indeed every) study of Patrick's life and career. I shall ask how best to interpret them in their historical, but also their literary, context, taking into account both Patrick's Christian intellectual background and his Roman one. This discussion will set the scene for the questions that will be debated throughout this book and give the reader a sense of the methodological approach taken here.

Let us therefore begin by revisiting the chief sources for Patrick's biography, his two genuine writings: the *Confessio* and the Letter to the Soldiers of Coroticus. The earliest copy of the Letter is preserved among a collection of saints' Lives in a tenth-century manuscript, now Paris Bibliothèque nationale de France Ms. latin 17626; and the earliest copy of the *Confessio* is found in the famous Book of Armagh, a small manuscript measuring 195 × 145 mm, which has been kept at Trinity College Dublin's library since 1892 (TCD 52; see Figure 1). The manuscript was written mostly by the scribe Ferdomnach (d. 846), who signed his name in five places, although two more hands, according to Richard Sharpe, can be discerned. It was compiled under the patronage of Abbot Torbach, 'Patrick's heir' (*comharba*) at Armagh, whose death in 808 is commonly treated as an upper limit for the manuscript's date. In 937 the manuscript was

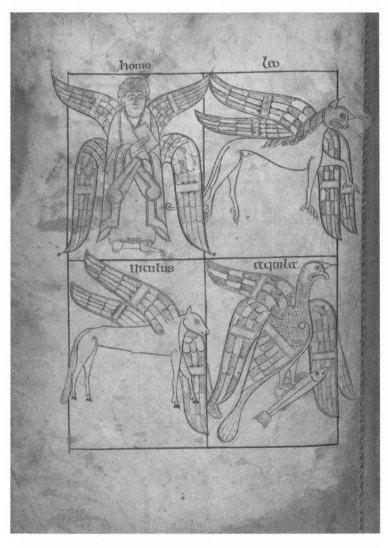

FIGURE 1. The four Evangelists from the Book of Armagh (Trinity College Dublin, MS 52 fol. 32v), by permission of the Board of Trinity College Dublin

enshrined in a casket (*cumdach*) by Donnchadh, son of Flan Sinna, High King of Ireland. This was not unusual for a time when manuscripts were venerated as relics on the belief that they were written by saints. I shall return to this topic in chapter 6 on hagiography. On a visit to Armagh in 1005, King Brían Bórama (Brian Boru) signed his name on folio 16v of the manuscript and added the outlandish epithet *Imperator Scottorum* as he placed twenty ounces of gold on the altar, a token of his patronage. By the twelfth century the manuscript passed into the hands of a hereditary keeper (*maor*).

The texts contained in the manuscript are diverse: the earliest (nearly) complete copy of the New Testament in Ireland, Sulpicius Severus's Life of Saint Martin, Patrick's own *Confessio*, and seventh-century material relating to Patrick consisting of a Life by Muirchú, the *Collectanea* by Tírechán, the *Liber Angeli*, the so-called *Additamenta*, and various abbreviated notes commonly known as the *Notulae*. In addition, there are extracts from Pope Gregory the Great's *Moralia in Iob*. This combination of texts forms the codicological context in which the *Confessio* can be found. The group of texts relating to Patrick in the Book of Armagh is sometimes referred to by scholars—and in the present book—as the 'Patrician dossier'. This dossier will be discussed further in chapter 6.

Returning now to the *Confessio* and Letter. Close textual correspondences confirm that the two were indeed written by the same author. The author of the *Confessio* was based in Ireland and wrote for an Irish audience. His whereabouts are specifically given in the concluding chapter, which states that he 'wrote in Ireland' (*Hiberione conscripsit*), and his intended audience is designated clearly in an earlier chapter in which he says, 'You know, and so does God, how I have lived among you from my youth in the faith of truth and in sincerity of the heart'.[2] His familiarity with the Irish landscape is reinforced by his use of an Irish place-name, 'the forest of Voclut by the western sea' (*silva Focluti quae est prope mare occidentale*).[3] As for the Letter, in the form that we have it, it is said to be the second letter to the soldiers of Coroticus, who is depicted as a British leader who was Christian, albeit a ruthless and depraved one.

Like many a late antique letter, it is difficult to determine whether the version of the text that has come down to us is faithful to the original that was (or, at least, purports to have been) sent to the soldiers, or whether it is a reworking of the original that was meant to proclaim the author's condemnation of Coroticus and his men to a wider contemporary audience or to posterity. Interestingly, very few details are repeated in both the Letter and the *Confessio*, and never the crucial details: for instance, the *Confessio* makes no mention of the capture of Patrick's converts by Coroticus. The differences suggest that Patrick chose what to say and how to say it based on the audience for which each text was intended. For example, the Roman administrative office that Patrick's father held, the decurionate, only appears in the Letter, which was addressed to a group of self-proclaimed Roman citizens whom Patrick sought to impress by flashing his own Roman credentials. In the *Confessio*, on the other hand, the father's only epithet is 'deacon'.

What do the *Confessio* and Letter tell us about Patrick's life and career? According to the *Confessio*, Patrick's family owned a *villula* near a *vicus* called Bannavem Taburniae, which has never been securely identified. Patrick's father, Calpornius, was a deacon and his grandfather, Potitus, a *presbyter* (priest). Around the age of sixteen, Patrick's life changed suddenly when he was taken captive 'with so many thousands of people' (*cum tot milia hominum*). After six years of servitude near the Wood of Voclut (County Mayo), during which he grew more steadfast in the

Christian faith, he deserted his master and was reunited with his kinsfolk in Britain, who welcomed him with open arms. Although no other sources about slavery in Ireland at this period survive, we may nevertheless query Patrick's version of events, not least because of what he himself says about the perils facing a foreigner travelling alone in Ireland: according to him, when he returned to Ireland later in life, he had to be accompanied by a costly retinue and also needed to secure his protection by paying off kings.[4] This testimony seems at odds with the prospect that an unredeemed slave could escape captivity, travel two hundred miles or so from the west to the east coast of Ireland, and then cross the Irish Sea to Britain without being captured or harmed. Whereas Patrick's version is not impossible, to a sceptic it is nevertheless improbable. But it has the virtue of possessing the quality of verisimilitude, which I shall return to shortly when discussing Patrick's debt to classical rhetoric. It is clear, however, that Patrick was aware that some of his contemporaries found his story fanciful, since he himself admits in the *Confessio* that there were those who called him out for leaving Britain of his own free will (see chapters 1 and 3 on the Romano-British background and on captivity).[5] And even if his readers or hearers believed him, they could nevertheless have considered him to be unfree because he was not formally freed by his master. It would appear that doubts about his free status even dogged his posthumous reputation, until by the seventh century we witness traditions that sought to put things right by claiming that Patrick retrospectively attempted to redeem himself and convert his former master.[6]

   If Patrick was indeed titivating the record, he could easily have found justification for doing so in the tradition of classical rhetoric that he would have been exposed to as a young boy who received a literate education within the bosom of elite

Romanised society. Patrick's early education would, at the very least, have consisted of a combination of subjects that would later be known as the 'trivium' (in Cassiodorus's sixth-century coinage)—namely, the study of grammar, logic, and rhetoric. Certainly by the seventh century Ireland became a prominent European centre for the teaching of grammar, the primary requisite for acquiring proficiency in biblical exegesis, and attracted swarms of students bent on a future as Christian clerical scholars.[7] But all this was still a while away from Patrick's time.

Although he may not—as he himself admits—have been trained for a shining career in the courts or for holding high political office, he would nevertheless have had an introduction to the rudimentaries of the subject of rhetoric.[8] Our best guides on the fundamentals of the subject are Cicero (d. 43 BC) and Quintilian (d. AD 35), whose instructions and observations were at the heart of the 'textbook manuals' for late antique rhetorical training. And, indeed, some scholars, like Daniel Melia, have argued that Patrick shows familiarity with Quintilian. In the classical tradition, all rhetorical creations, be they speeches or texts for public performance like Patrick's own, were understood to contain a narrative. In Cicero's treatise on rhetoric, *De inventione*, the term 'narrative' (*narratio*) is defined as comprising three subcategories: *fabula, historia*, and *argumentum*.[9] The *fabula* is defined as a 'term applied to a narrative in which the events are not true and have no verisimilitude'. This, in short, could be a myth, a legend, or a fantasy of any kind that makes no pretence for having the appearance of anything real. The category of *historia* is then defined as 'an account of actual occurrences remote from the recollection of our age'. In other words, events narrated by *historia* are such that actually happened but were not experienced by the author or his or her contemporaries. And the final category, *argumentum*, is 'a fictitious narrative which nevertheless could have occurred'. Hence, unlike *fabula*, the *argumentum* possesses verisimilitude.

Quintilian, whose didactic works articulated some of the fundamentals of classical rhetoric, made allowance for an *argumentum* that deploys falsehoods in stating cases, provided that the occasion required it. An occasion of this kind would have been rather frequent since, as Quintilian conceded, humans have never lived in a perfect world in which the truth is always valued and in which the truth could, by itself, convince audiences, particularly not in the Roman courts or at political assemblies. Too often an audience is itself biased or given to misconceptions and cannot be expected to show unflinching commitment to the truth. Hence, an *argumentum* that contains falsehoods is a legitimate strategy so long as it has the quality of verisimilitude and so long as it is employed in service of a good and higher cause.[10] When, in court or the assembly, the gloves are off and ruthlessness is the order of the day, one would be irrational to choose a more mild rhetorical course than a sharp *argumentum*. We will soon see how, in addition to being pursued by various allegations in his youth, Patrick also had to contend with being put on trial, a situation in which even the most righteous were advised to resort to shrewd rhetorical tactics in order to be heard and to prevail. In such a confrontation, the righteous could be excused for deploying a creative *argumentum* in the service of a good cause. And Patrick could also have been justified in doing so in the defence that he mounts in the *Confessio* against his detractors, who would not have shied away from falsehood themselves. This defence, addressed both to his contemporaries and to posterity, could certainly count as a good cause. How so? Because unless he redeemed his reputation, the readers' or listeners' attention would be distracted from the higher purpose of hearing about his religious mission and his vision for the formation of a Christian society. There was, therefore, a higher truth that Patrick was aiming for, but the malicious blathering clutter around it needed to be silenced for it to be heard properly.

We rejoin Patrick's narrative as he tells of his release from captivity, following which he remained in Britain for a number of years and was ordained deacon. However, the *Confessio* goes on to say that he experienced a vision that had persuaded him to return to Ireland, which he did, taking with him sufficient funds to enable him to pay Irish kings and judges. Indeed, he devoted himself to the missionary life, baptised thousands, converted nobles and sons of kings, and trained clerics who could succeed him. He also endured many hardships, including a two-week imprisonment, during which his property was taken away from him but later restored. At no point does he say what his property consisted of, nor does he say of what value it could have been in Ireland's nonmonetary economy, where wealth was based primarily on the ownership of land and cattle, neither of which Patrick could transport across the Irish Sea from Britain.

Patrick was to return again to Britain later in his life, when he was already bishop. It was then that he was put on trial by his *seniores* (elders) on a charge that is not specified. According to Patrick, the trial was only an *occasio* (pretext) that his elders used to settle an open score with him: 'After thirty years they found a pretext for their allegations against me in a confession which I had made before I was a deacon. In a depressed and worried state of mind I mentioned to a close friend what I had done as a boy one day.'[11] The offence for which he was charged had therefore been committed thirty years earlier, before Patrick reached the age of fifteen, and the friend to whom he confessed it later betrayed his trust. We are not told what punishment he was given, if any, only that he subsequently returned to Ireland, where he wrote his *Confessio*.

The Letter to the Soldiers of Coroticus, to which we now turn, adds nothing to the *Confessio*'s account concerning the trial or the nature of the offence, which remains a mystery. But it does shed light on episodes from Patrick's later life and allows us to augment his biography with important details. At the outset we learn that Patrick was already bishop when he wrote the Letter.[12] As such, he was in a position to excommunicate the soldiers, who are understood to be Christian. From the fact that he says that he refuses to address them as his 'fellow citizens' or 'citizens of the holy Romans' because of their wickedness, one may surmise that they were in fact Roman citizens, or at least self-proclaimed citizens.[13] Alternatively, as suggested by David Dumville, one can interpret this passage metaphorically and take 'citizens of the holy Romans' to mean 'Christians'. Later in the Letter we learn that in addition to being a Roman citizen himself, Patrick was *ingenuus* (free-born) and that his father was a decurion, and not just a deacon as he was styled in the *Confessio*. In the same sentence Patrick says that he sold his own nobility and declares that he is not ashamed of this.[14] Eventually, according to his own account, Patrick was stripped of his freedom when he was abducted from Britain. His captors, we are told, 'harried the male and female slaves of my father's house' (*devastaverunt servos et ancillas domus patris mei*), which can be taken to mean that they were either killed or dragged away by force to a worse servitude overseas.

Being a teenager at the age at which he says he was taken captive, he would already have been steeped in Roman culture and, therefore, can be assumed to have achieved a certain proficiency in Latin. Nevertheless, some modern readers have relished finding fault with the standard of Patrick's Latin prose, regarding it as rather mediocre. To some extent, disparaging judgements about his Latin are owed to Patrick's own deprecatory statements—for example, his admission in the *Confessio* that he was untaught and that, unlike his more erudite contemporaries, his first language was not Latin but—one may guess—a British dialect.[15] And then there is the curious revelation that his language had been corrupted: 'I have changed my language and my speech for a foreign tongue, as may easily be proved from the flavour of my writing' (*nam sermo et loquela nostra translata est in linguam alienam, sicut facile potest probari ex saliva scripturae meae*).[16] By playing down his linguistic abilities, Patrick may simply have been rehearsing a trope of humility that was common among contemporary authors. Indeed, in recent years scholars have begun to look beyond Patrick's 'stumbling barbarous Latin' (as Daniel Binchy put it) and have grown more aware of his unique yet carefully crafted rhetoric, which exhibits a sophisticated use of biblical allusions and metaphors. Consequently, one no longer accepts that all of Patrick's narrative can be taken at face value, nor that he speaks the entire truth, despite his insistence that he does.[17] The narrative he offers is widely acknowledged to be defensive, apologetic, replete with rhetorical tropes, employing evasive language, and deliberately obfuscating uncomfortable truths, such as the nature of the offence or sin of which he was accused. This is not to say that Patrick's sole objective in the *Confessio* was to rewrite his life story by concocting falsehoods. Rather, in the spirit of classical rhetoric that was described earlier, he was simply writing to promote an agenda to which the factual details were subservient: they could be bent or obscured as the circumstances required. What exactly this agenda was, what he might have tried to hide, and how he crafted his narrative to suit his objectives are the subject of chapters 1–3 and 5 of this book. Curiously, Patrick was not the only missionary to modify his biography in this way. If we take a huge leap forward in time, we find an analogous example of a 'revised' missionary narrative in the legacy of the famous nineteenth-century missionary and adventurer David Livingstone (d. 1873). The eventful autobiographical tale he penned of his time in Africa was judged as misleading by some of his biographers, but others have stressed the importance of considering it within the contemporary conventions of its genre. To his apologists, Livingstone was simply telling his readers what they expected to hear in an account about a missionary adventure in a faraway land. By the same token, Patrick should not be thought of as either honest or dishonest, because accuracy and comprehensiveness were not the main objectives of his literary project. He was writing within certain literary and rhetorical conventions that allowed the author a degree of poetic license. This authorial freedom was justified by the understanding that visible reality and the plain wording of texts are both open to interpretation and can have multiple meanings. In other words, the truth may lie not only in what we see and read but also in what lies behind the text. This proposition could easily be justified by principles of classical rhetoric of the sort that we have seen Quintilian advocating. In Patrick's time such classical principles continued to hold currency but acquired a Christian twist. They were now complemented by an epistemological theory that enabled the stretching of the boundaries of what could be perceived as the truth and how this 'truth' ought to be communicated. This theory drew on foundations from classical antiquity, rooted in the idea that the truth may be found outside visible reality, ultimately going back to Plato. The proposition that the truth may lie beyond what we see forms the core of Plato's theory of 'ideas', which (through later Platonic apologists and Neoplatonists) exerted a strong influence on the development of Christian theological thought in late antiquity. It also informed one of the most influential approaches to Christian biblical interpretation: allegorical biblical exegesis. This form of biblical interpretation was so pervasive and so deeply ingrained in the curriculum of an educated Christian that for many a Christian scholar it began to frame not only his or her approach to reading the Bible but also his or her perception of the world at large. This perception may conveniently be called the 'exegetical reflex', and it can also be detected in Patrick's approach to biographical writing. It is this 'exegetical reflex' that I wish to expand on now.

Acknowledging the significance of biblical exegesis to the late antique Christian curriculum and to the Christian scholarly mind-set is key to a contextual understanding of the message of many an early Christian text. The Bible—consisting in this period of the New Testament and parts of the Old Testament, especially the prophets—was the core text that defined a Christian education and laid the preamble for virtuous Christian living. But only rarely could the biblical text be followed at face value. Interpretation was necessary first and foremost in order to distil rules of conduct from the New Testament, which, unlike the Pentateuch of the Old Testament, did not contain a code of law. Second, interpretation was necessary for making sense of obscure and ambiguous biblical verses. Third, interpretation provided an essential tool for extracting and following the prophetic message of the Old Testament concerning the end of times. And fourth, it was indispensable in vindicating the truth of Christian providential history, which shows how events and personalities of the New Testament had been foretold in the Old Testament by means of prophecy. This foretelling, or foreshadowing, was achieved through 'types', each type prefiguring (to use the technical term) something in the New Testament. For example, Melchizedek's offering bread and wine to Abraham in Genesis 14:18 prefigures the Last Supper and also the Christian priestly ministry, and Moses's raising his arms in the battle against Amalek in Exodus 17:11–12 prefigures Christ's passion. The foundations for the method of identifying types were understood to have been laid by Saint Paul in his letters to the Colossians and the Galatians, both of which are quoted in Patrick's *Confessio*. In Colossians 2:16–17 we read, 'Let no man therefore judge you in meat or in drink, or in respect of a festival day, or of the new moon, or of the Sabbaths, which are a shadow of things to come, but the body is of Christ'. In other words: the law of the letter of the Old Testament need not be followed any longer, for it is merely a prefiguration of the body of Christ. And in the letter to the Galatians 4:21–31, we read the following parable, which, once more, stresses that Christians are dead to the old law and should, instead, submit to a new spiritual law:

Tell me, you that desire to be under the law, have you not read the law? For it is written that Abraham had two sons: the one by a slave-woman, and the other by a free woman. But he who was of the slave-woman, was born according to the flesh: but he of the free woman, was by promise. Which things are said by an allegory. For these are the two testaments. The one from mount Sinai, engendering unto bondage; which is Agar. For Sinai is a mountain in Arabia, which hath affinity to that Jerusalem which now is, and is in bondage with her children. But that Jerusalem, which is above, is free: which is our mother. For it is written: 'Rejoice, thou barren that bearest not: break forth and cry, thou that travailest not: for many are the children of the desolate, more than of her that hath a husband'. Now we, brethren, as Isaac was, are the children of promise. But as then he, who was born according to the flesh, persecuted him, who was after the spirit; so also it is now. But what says the scripture? Cast out the slave-woman and her son; for the son of the slave-woman shall not be heir with the son of the free woman. So then, brethren, we are not the children of the slave-woman, but of the free: by the freedom wherewith Christ has made us free.

Here Paul explicitly sets out the principle of allegorical exegesis, choosing to interpret the son of Hagar as servile, representing the Old Testament law of this world, and the son of Sarah (Isaac is not mentioned by name) as free, representing the liberating New Testament gospel of the spirit. Matching types to their analogues in the New Testament was the main business of allegorical exegesis (also known as figurative exegesis), as distinct from literal exegesis (also known as historical exegesis), which concerned itself with the plain wording of the text. The two approaches are conventionally identified with two distinct exegetical schools: the literal with the 'Antiochene school' and the allegorical with the 'Alexandrian school', which could trace its roots through Origen (d. 245) to Philo (d. 50), a Hellenistic Jewish scholar who incorporated contemporary Platonism into his teachings. Literal and allegorical exegesis were not mutually exclusive but could be treated as complementary. For example, one can read Christ's healing miracles literally and at the same time follow Origen in interpreting them allegorically as representing the healing of a disorder in the soul.[18]

As for Patrick, his use of the Bible is exemplary, despite his claim that he did not receive formal training in *sacrae literae*.[19] It is the only source in his works that can be identified with certainty, and passages from the Bible, or allusions to it, are often used in order to add eloquence to the author's own thoughts, much as someone in the modern era may cite a poem to embellish one's own words. In particular, Patrick drew inspiration from Paul's defence of his own ministry in the Second Letter to the Corinthians, from which (as Joseph Nagy cogently argued) 'Patrick derives the thematic framework for the *Confessio*'. A comprehensive list of Patrick's biblical references in both his texts was compiled by Ludwig Bieler. Altogether there are 319 references, of which 80 are direct quotations and the remainder are allusions to the Bible or modified biblical passages. The majority of references, 244, are to the New Testament, and 75 to the Old Testament. Most of the biblical references, 245, are in the *Confessio*, with only 74 in the Letter. Nevertheless, the ratio of direct quotations to allusions is higher in the Letter (43 percent) than in the *Confessio* (20 percent). Perhaps the gap in the ratios suggests something about the different audiences for which each text was intended. Thus, the recipients of the Letter, the soldiers of Coroticus, could not be expected to pick up on subtle biblical allusions as much as the readers of the *Confessio*, a text that exhibits Patrick's literary ingenuity and was aimed, perhaps, at a better-educated readership.

Biblical quotations are sometimes used as a means of garnishing Patrick's prose, but they may also serve to give deeper meaning to his account, signalling to the readers to keep an eye open for an additional dimension beyond the trivial descriptive level of the text. A case in point is Patrick's unusual exclamation that, while preparing to sail to Britain, he refused to 'suck the breasts' (*reppuli sugere mamellas eorum*) of the pagan sailors.[20] Apart from being, perhaps, a contemporary colloquial expression for denoting deference, or apart from alluding (as some scholars wrongly believed) to an obscure Irish ritual of homage, Patrick appears to be echoing a biblical verse, Isaiah 60:16: 'And you shall suck the milk of the gentiles, and you shall be nursed with the breasts of kings' (*Et suges lac gentium, et mamilla regum lactaberis*).[21] How he deploys this as a metaphor for conversion, when contrasted with the nourishment that he himself provides them, we shall see when this episode is considered in detail in chapter 3 (on captivity). Another example of a biblical allusion hinting at a hidden meaning, also discussed at length in the same chapter, is Patrick's description of his emancipation after six years of captivity.[22] Commenting on this, an exegetically aware scholar of the eighth century, whose comments are preserved as glosses in a manuscript, pointed out that Patrick's release after six years was 'after the manner of the little jubilee of the Hebrews' (*fo intamail na hiubile Ebreorum*). This is a reference to Exodus 21:2 (repeated in Jeremiah 34:14): 'If you buy a Hebrew servant, six years shall he serve you, but in the seventh he shall go free without owing anything.'[23] For this particular glossator, the biblical allusion was self-evident and suggested that Patrick was not necessarily intending his readers to take him literally but, rather, was consciously invoking a biblical text. Why he would choose to do so will be examined in chapter 3.

Two other frequent uses that Patrick makes of the Bible are as a prescriptive text—namely, a source of divine command that prompts him into action—and as a store of prophecy that either is continually fulfilled throughout history (also in his own time) or anticipates future events. I shall take these two in turn. As a prescriptive text, Patrick crucially attributes his calling to embark on a mission to the Bible. In chapter 40 of the *Confessio*, he incorporates a series of biblical quotations, principally from the New Testament, urging the spread of the Gospel, among them Matthew 4:19, 'And he said to them: "Follow me, and I will make you to be fishers of men"', and Matthew 24:14, 'And this gospel of the kingdom shall be preached in the whole world as a testimony to all nations, and then shall the consummation come'. The latter verse also highlights another motif in Patrick's prose— namely, its eschatological hue—which is closely tied to Patrick's

motivation to evangelise in expectation of the 'imminent coming' of Christ (*expectamus adventum ipsius mox futurum*),
which will bring with it a terrible judgement.[24]

Patrick's use of the Bible as a prophetic text is closely linked
to his extraordinary ability to receive prophecy directly and to
communicate with angels, as well as other divine apparitions.
Before escaping his captivity, for example, he heard a voice
prophesying, 'You do well to fast, since you will soon be going
to your homeland'.[25] When he is tested by the devil, he is able
to call on Christ and in response hear God speak to him, but also
have God speaking prophetically *through* him.[26] And in an art-
ful description of his closeness to God, he says, in the spirit of
Proverbs 10:1 ('A wise son is his father's pride'), that he is the
pride of the Father for having succeeded in his mission.[27] God
appeared to him and strengthened him in his quest to evangelise,
a quest he follows in fulfilment of a number of biblical prophe-
cies, which he cites, beginning with a paraphrase of an eschatological prophecy from Joel 2:28: 'And it shall come to pass in the
last days, says the Lord, that I will pour out my spirit upon all
flesh: and your sons and your daughters shall prophesy, and your
young shall see visions'.[28]

The frequent references to the Bible in Patrick's prose are a
reminder to the reader that Patrick's words and the Bible's are
often inseparable. One complements the other with the effect
of mutually enhancing the sense of either. Following from this,
I would argue, the text of the *Confessio* as we have it (and, to some
extent, that of the Letter too), can be understood on different
levels, in the same manner that the Bible can be interpreted according to different senses, be it allegorical, literal, moral, or
spiritual. Patrick's prose style is an invitation to the readers to
engage in exegesis of the *Confessio* itself. And the present book
rises to this challenge.

To some extent, an informed 'exegesis' is what this very book aims to offer. Let me give one example in anticipation of several others that will be discussed in the following chapters. Take the phrase 'harried the male and female slaves of my father's house' (*devastaverunt servos et ancillas domus patris mei*).[29] This is what Patrick says in describing the deeds of the slavers who raided his home and captured him. But when examined from another angle, the phrase can be interpreted metaphorically by taking *servos et ancillas domus patris mei* to mean 'fellow Christians'. Metaphors of this kind, which portray Christian believers as slaves of the Father, were used by other late antique authors. For instance, in his commentary on Paul's letter to Titus, Jerome says that 'the apostle, who was not a slave to sin, is rightly called the slave of God the Father and Christ' (*apostolus igitur, qui peccati non fuit servus, recte Dei patris vocatur servus et Christi*).[30] This is not to say that Patrick has read his Jerome, but rather that such slavery metaphors, helpfully collected by Isobel Combes in her *Metaphor of Slavery in the Writings of the Early Church*, were common in late antiquity. They echoed similar metaphors found in the Bible, often embedded in parables in which Christ invokes slavery, such as the parable of the faithful servant, in which Christ asks, 'Who then is the faithful and wise slave, whom the master put in charge of his household, to give them their food at the appropriate time?'[31] Here, as in the example from the *Confessio*, the literal and metaphorical meanings of 'slave' are not mutually exclusive.

Where do interpretations of this kind leave the plain meaning of Patrick's own account? When the literal and allegorical are consistent with one another, there is no problem. But what happens when our 'allegorical exegesis' replaces a literal understanding? For example, if we take Patrick's six years in captivity strictly as an allusion to the book of Exodus (as our eighth-century glossator suggested that we should), does this mean that Patrick was not taken captive? This is a possibility, although the proposition that his captivity was merely an alibi also rests on other, firmer evidence, outlined in chapters 1 and 3.

Patrick's prose can be interpreted in a range of ways. Like any late antique text with an agenda, it cannot be read simply as a factual account of his career and of the historical circumstances in which he lived. That Patrick wrote with an agenda, which included redeeming his own reputation, does not diminish the fact that he had other, higher motives, such as conveying a didactic message about the impending end of times, the need for a mission in anticipation of it, the ideal course of a mission, the righteous way of Christian living, and the behaviour expected of the newly converted. Nevertheless, it cannot be ignored that a central objective of his *Confessio* was to mount a defence against accusations that pursued him, the details of which will be considered in the following chapters of this book. In combining all these different objectives, we see Patrick employing rhetorical tactics that, as I have attempted to argue here, drew on principles of classical rhetoric and of biblical exegesis that gave him license to depart from a factual account.

A famous example of the exegetical recognition of the gap between text and reality comes from the giant of Christian theology, Saint Jerome, whom we have already encountered in another context. In his *Adversus Hilvidium*, written in the 380s, he observed in regard to the question of Christ's paternity in the New Testament, 'Therefore, except Joseph, and Elizabeth, and Mary herself, and a few others besides—if we can believe that we hear them from these [words]—everyone believed that Jesus was Joseph's son, so much so that even the Evangelists, expressing the common opinion (*opinio vulgi*), which is the true rule of narration (*vera lex historiae*), said that he is the Saviour's father.'[32]

The question that vexed Jerome was the difficulty of reconciling the idea of Mary's virgin birth with the text of the genealogies of Christ in both the Gospel of Matthew and Luke, according to which Joseph was Christ's father. Jerome's solution was that the Gospels were merely expressing a 'common opinion' (*opinio vulgi*). But does this not imply that the Gospels are being deliberately mendacious? Not according to Jerome, who explains that their narrations are framed according to what he styles the 'true rule of narration' (*vera lex historiae*), an enigmatic expression that attracted considerable attention from scholars (especially for the way in which it was employed in the eighth century by the Northumbrian historian Bede), which I take to mean that an author can claim to have been operating in good faith so long as he or she faithfully reiterated a received narrative, irrespective of whether it was true or false. By the seventh century the idea will have developed such that an Irish biblical exegete could even say that the six days of creation should not be understood literally, but that 'the *narrator historiae* ("biblical narrator") afterwards divided in his account that which God did not divide in the perfection of his work.'[33]

Patrick cannot be shown to have followed Jerome directly. However, both examples from Jerome (on the metaphor of slavery and the virgin birth) illustrate a central feature of the Christian exegetical mind-set—namely, that a text can be made to convey different meanings to different readerships, who may be distinguished from one another by such criteria as their level of learning, religiosity, partisanship with the author, or proximity to the events that are being described. Following principles of interpretation of the kind that Jerome applied to the Gospels, Patrick was at liberty to address his words to different readerships simultaneously and to position his narrations at varying degrees of separation from the truth. This was not deceit, but a way of tightly controlling what was being said and of directing the reader towards what the author believed to be a higher truth.

Notes

1. Letter § 1.

2. *Confessio* §§ 62, 48.

3. *Confessio* § 23.

4. *Confessio* §§ 52, 53.

5. *Confessio* § 10.

6. Muirchú, Life of Patrick I.11(10), in Bieler, *Patrician Texts*, 76.

7. Aldhelm, Letter 5, to Heahfrith, in D. R. Howlett, ed. and trans., 'Aldhelm and Irish learning', *Bulletin de Cange* 52 (1994): 50–75, lines 59–70.

8. On the deprecatory reflection on his own education, see *Confessio* § 13.

9. This and the following quotations are from Cicero, *De Inventione* 1.19.27, trans. H. M. Hubbell (Cambridge, MA, 1949), 54–57.

10. See especially Quintilian, *Institutio Oratoria* 2.17.19–29, 36; 3.8.63, trans. Donald Russell, in *Quintilian: The Orator's Education*, 5 vols. (Cambridge, MA, 2001), 1: 384–90, 392; 2: 146.

11. *Confessio* § 27.

12. The account that follows is based on Letter §§ 1, 2, 10, 21.

13. Letter § 2: 'Non dico civibus meis neque civibus sanctorum Romanorum' (I do not say to my fellow citizens, nor to the citizens of the holy Romans).

14. Letter § 10: 'Vendidi enim nobilitatem meam, non erubesco' (For I have sold my nobility, I am not ashamed [of it]). The expression 'fellow citizens' in Letter § 2 implies, by association, that he himself was Roman.

15. See, respectively, *Confessio* §§ 12, 9.

16. *Confessio* § 9. Translation is by Jean-Michel Picard, 'The Latin language in early medieval Ireland', in *The Languages of Ireland*, ed. Michael Cronin and Cormac Ó Cuilleanáin (Dublin, 2003), 44–56, at 46n17.

17. E.g., *Confessio* §§ 44, 54, 61.

18. Origen, 'Commentary on the Gospel of John', 13:3, in *Commentary on the Gospel according to John*, trans. Ronald Heine (Washington, DC, 1993).

19. *Confessio* § 9.

20. *Confessio* § 18.

21. *Confessio* § 18.

22. *Confessio* § 17.

23. The scholar was a glossator of Fiacc's Hymn, an edition and translation of which is W. Stokes and J. Strachan, *Thesaurus Palaeohibernicus*, 2 vols. (Dublin, 1901–3), 2:307–21. The gloss is on p. 309, lines 13–14.

24. *Confessio* §§ 4, 8.

25. *Confessio* § 17.

26. *Confessio* § 20.

27. *Confessio* § 47.

28. *Confessio* §§ 34, 36, 40.

29. Letter § 10.

30. Jerome, *Commentarii in iv epistulas Paulinas*, in PL vol. 26, cols. 307–618, at col. 592.

31. Matthew 24:45.

32. Jerome, *Adversus Helvidium*, in PL vol. 23, cols. 183–206, at col. 187: 'Denique excepto Ioseph, et Elisabeth, et ipsa Maria, paucisque admodum, si quos ab his audisse possumus aestimare, omnes Iesum filium aestimabant Ioseph, intantum, ut etiam Evangelistae opinionem vulgi exprimentes, quae vera historiae lex est, patrem eum dixerint Salvatoris'.

33. Augustinus Hibernicus, *De mirabilibus sacrae scripturae libri tres*, PL 35:2149–2200, at 2151: "post namque historiae narrator diuisit in sermone, quod Deus non divisit in operis perfectione."

1

Patrick's Britain

THE GROWTH OF CHRISTIANITY was among the most conspicuous changes that the Roman Empire experienced between
the early fourth century and the birth of Patrick towards the end
of that century or in the early fifth century. Beginning in 325, the
year in which Emperor Constantine presided over the first ecumenical church council at Nicaea, a process of state-sanctioned
religious change was set in motion that transformed the religious
lives of the empire's inhabitants and integrated the church and
its clergy more firmly into local as well as imperial government.
Religious change seldom happens in isolation, and in this case
too it was accompanied by social, economic, and cultural
changes: communities began to embrace a new set of moral val-
ues, they congregated around new pastors based in churches
(initially urban but gradually also rural), the churches themselves
prospered as the wealthy and the well-to-do made them a new
focus for ostentatious philanthropy under the banner of almsgiving, new forms of literature emerged with the Bible at their
core, and gender relations in some societies were being recon-
ceptualised with the gradual phasing out of polygamy and an
unprecedented degree of (relative) independence that some
women were able to attain in the monastic life. Following on

from Constantine's successful gambit at the Council of Nicaea, emperors were keen to assert themselves as the champions of the church and of Orthodox belief, while gradually marginalising public pagan rituals until these were eventually outlawed by Emperor Theodosius (d. 395). Laws were routinely passed to safeguard the interests of the church and its personnel with the aim of guaranteeing a sustainable and mutually beneficial modus vivendi between churches and the state. This transition towards an ever-more-Christian empire was still very much an ongoing process in Patrick's day, and he is likely to have been alive to experience the last days of Roman Britain and their aftermath. The continual growth of the church and the vibrant atmosphere of religious change may, perhaps, have contributed to his choice to undertake missionary work in Ireland and spread the Christian faith beyond the westernmost boundaries of the empire.

As we attempt to examine where Patrick himself stood within this reality of religious and political transformation in the late imperial era, we may turn to some autobiographical details, mainly from the *Confessio* but also from the Letter to the Soldiers of Coroticus. Of the details relating to Patrick's 'Romano-British phase', the aspects that scholars have seized on the most have been his pedigree and place of origin. His pedigree does indeed anchor him firmly in the cultural environment that historians commonly characterise as Romano-British, which was, by the late Roman period, overwhelmingly Christian. This much is clear from the opening of the *Confessio*, in which he introduces himself as the son of the deacon Calpornius and the grandson of the priest (*presbyter*) Potitus. In the Letter, he adds that his father was also a senior Roman administrator who held the office of decurion (*decorione patre nascor*).[1] As a decurion, Calpornius would have sat on a Roman town council and would have had specific duties to discharge, such as managing the community's finances, organising votes, seeing to the maintenance of roads, administering the public post, recruiting soldiers for the army, and communicating with the provincial governor or emperor. But the chief obligation of decurions was the collection of imperial taxes, an ungrateful task that did not always endear them to the communities they served. Patrick himself identified as a Roman citizen; he says in the Letter, with reference to Coroticus's soldiers, 'I do not say to my fellow citizens, nor to the citizens of the holy Romans' (*non dico civibus meis neque civibus sanctorum Romanorum*).[2] Patrick therefore emerges as the product of a solidly Romanised and solidly Christian background.

As for his place of birth, we are told in the *Confessio* that the family hailed from the town of Bannavem Taburniae and that his father also owned a small villa (*villula*).[3] The exact whereabouts of the town and villa are unknown, although they occasioned much speculation in both medieval and modern times, ranging from Thomas O'Rahilly's identification of Bannavem Taburniae with Glastonbury to Charles Thomas's suggestion that it may have been Birdoswald (Banna), towards the western end of Hadrian's Wall, approximately twenty kilometres east of Carlisle. One of the more curious identifications draws on a tradition that was first committed to writing in the seventh-century Irish hagiography of Muirchú and by the eighth century was treasured in the hymn *Génair Patraicc in Nemthur* (Patrick was born in Nemthor).[4] The tradition developed until, before the year circa 1000, Nemthor became identified with a place in Strathclyde. Although an origin in western Scotland has very little to recommend it apart from local-patriotic wishful thinking, historians tend to agree that the town and villa of Patrick's family lay somewhere along the west coast of Britain because of Patrick's testimony that he was abducted from his home to Ireland. A western origin would place him in the territory of the Demetae, or the

Ordovices, or the Deceangli, or the Brigantes, or the Carvetii, population groups of which little is known, save the checkered record of initial resistance and later subjection to Roman rule, with some achieving a degree of political autonomy as client kingdoms (see Map 2). If Patrick's idea of a *villula* was in any way like the modern catch-all definition of *villa*—namely, 'a site consisting of a rural building of Roman aspect' (in David Mattingly's coining)—then his *villula* is unlikely to have been situated north of the river Tees in the Pennines, where no such site is known to have existed. Faced with these contingencies and uncertainties, the best we can hope for in locating Patrick's villa and hometown is educated guesswork. Patrick's reference to Bannavem Taburniae as a *vicus* may suggest it was a small town. But given that Calpornius was a member of a *curia*, one may infer that there was a larger public town nearby, in which an administrative bureaucracy was active and where Calpurnius would have fulfilled his obligations as decurion. An attractive identification, proposed by Charles Thomas, is Carlisle (Luguvalium), although, being north of the zone of Roman villas, it does not correspond perfectly to the landscape that Patrick describes.

As for the church or churches in which Patrick's father and grandfather would have served, these could have been located either in a town or in the countryside. Christianity is assumed to have been widespread, initially implanting itself among those of low to middle status. Consequently, as this hypothesis goes, churches were rather modest, and of the buildings that have tentatively been identified as churches, none actually contains Christian symbols. Such symbols occur only in high-status contexts, in buildings whose purpose might not have been exclusively to serve as a church. Indeed, it is very possible that Christian ritual was conducted in private residences (a possible candidate is a villa at Lullingstone in Kent containing distinct Christian symbols like the Chi-Rho and the alpha and omega) and in converted Roman public buildings, *basilicae* (for example, Calleva in Hampshire, Saint Paul in the Bail in Lincoln, and Verulamium, by Saint Albans), only some of which became distinctly identifiable as churches, usually following generations of architectural adaptation that lasted into the post-Roman period. These factors complicate the job of identifying the church or churches of Patrick's elders. We are not better informed in regard to the question of how exactly these churches or residences were served by priests—for instance, whether the priests were itinerant or permanently based. Only a few names of clerics from the period survive, and these tend to be senior members of the clergy, such as bishops who could be identified with specific sees. For example, we know of three British bishops who attended the Council of Arles in 314: Eborius, bishop of York; Restitutus, bishop of London; and Adelphius, bishop of Colonia Londinensium, a corrupt rendering of, perhaps, Colonia Lindensium, which was the Roman name for Lincoln. Unlike such lofty clergy, priests at the coalface do not receive mention in our sources.

The extent to which Patrick might have experienced life under Roman occupation is a contested issue. His self-identification as a Roman citizen does not necessarily mean that the empire still held Britain when he described himself in this way, towards the end of his life. By analogy, one can think of present-day refugees who identify as citizens of a certain state, even though that state no longer controls the area in which they were born. Territories formerly held by Syria and Iraq are two grim topical examples of this. However, the office of decurion, which his father had held, offers the strongest point of reference for dating Patrick's life in relation to the Roman occupation of Britain. Since the occupation officially came to an end in 410 following decades of political and economic decline (a date corroborated by the cessation of Roman coinage in the second quarter of the fifth century), then Patrick's father must have held office before this crucial year. Patrick could therefore not have been born long after 410, but may well have been born earlier. It has become commonplace in scholarship to date Patrick's life mainly to the fifth century, with little or no overlap with Roman rule. In the first place, this dating rests on the two contradictory obits given to Patrick by the Irish annals, both of which are in the second half of the fifth century: 457 and 493.[5] However, since these obits are retrospective (they were written in the mid-sixth century at least), they offer no reliable dating criterion. Only rarely has his career, or the bulk of it, been dated before the fifth century. But to my mind there is no decisive argument for rejecting a dating before the fifth century. To understand why the objections to a pre-fifth-century date are not compelling, it is necessary to get a little technical. The strongest objection to a pre-fifth-century date was raised by David Dumville, drawing on previous work by Ludwig Bieler. Dumville holds that Patrick must have been writing after 404, but not too soon after, because in this year Jerome completed his translation of the Bible into Latin, the Vulgate, which is cited in the *Confessio* and Letter. He rejects the possibility that readings from the Vulgate were interpolated into Patrick's writings in the course of their medieval transmission: 'The untidy distribution of Vulgate-readings in the Psalter, Gospels, and Epistles, the absolute dominance of the Vulgate Acts of the Apostles, and the clearly Old Latin nature of the remainder are, in their very inconsistency with one another, as good a guarantee of general authenticity as could be wished for'. However, this common-sense argument is called into question by Bieler's own finding that at least four surviving copies of Patrick's *Confessio* 'frequently correct Old Latin quotations according to a standard text, generally the Vulgate'. In other words, medieval scribes who copied Patrick's *Confessio* replaced quotations from the Old Latin version of the Bible with quotations from the Vulgate. Hence one need not assume that a copy of the Vulgate was available to Patrick, and the Vulgate must therefore be dismissed as a dating criterion.

In addition to this rather technical argument for accepting that Patrick's career might have—in whole or in part—spanned the fourth century, we may also entertain a dating on historical grounds, which underscores the extent to which we lack secure dating criteria. The main difficulty is identifying something in Patrick's writings that can serve as a precise point of reference for dating. But there are no mentions of historical events that are attested elsewhere, and the attempt to date with reference to general phenomena is futile. For example, the mention in the Letter of 'pagan Franks' and the subsequent inference that this must refer to a period before the conversion of the Frankish king Clovis in 496 only provide an upper limit for the dating range, and (unhelpfully) only after Patrick is likely to have been dead.[6]

Another attempt to date Patrick on historical evidence, this time from the *Confessio*, can be made on his own admission that unlike other educated contemporaries, he could not claim Latin as his first language, that he was not brought up to use language to perfection, and that he did not study either law or scripture (*iura et sacra literas*).[7] Apart from suggesting that Patrick's first language was probably a dialect of British, this deprecatory admission appears to be his way of telling his readers that he was not trained as a professional rhetor with a view to acceding to a political career or a career in the church. But, as we shall see later, he may nevertheless have been expected to perform a role in provincial politics and he definitely did become a cleric, eventually assuming a senior position in a church that he himself had founded in Ireland. What he describes as his modest education can be contrasted with the more accomplished education of the readers of the *Confessio*, whom he refers to as *dominicati retho-rici*, an expression translated by Bieler as 'men of letters on your estates'. Patrick also styled them *sapientes* and *legis periti et potentes in sermone*, translated by Bieler as 'wise and expert in law and powerful in word', although *legisperiti* can also be translated in its narrower technical sense, meaning simply 'lawyers'.[8] Here Patrick is giving us an important glimpse of what sort of education was considered elitist in his own time. It also raises the possibility that Roman law still carried force, either because Roman rule had not yet ceased or because certain communities continued to practice it voluntarily after the end of Roman rule. It is not unreasonable to assume that some communities in Britain did indeed continue to adhere to Roman law and to Roman patterns of education for some time after Roman occupation ended, perhaps to be identified with communities in places like Cadbury Congresbury (Somerset) or Wroxeter (Shropshire), which consciously retained Roman material culture into the fifth century. Such a continuity does not necessitate the observance of a pure form of Roman law, but perhaps a law combined with local custom, something for which the Roman legal system made allowances even in places in which its grip was firm—for example, Egypt and the Romanised eastern Mediterranean, where we have good evidence for different forms of law being practised concurrently in Roman times. All this suggests a date for Patrick during the Roman occupation of Britain (perhaps even in the fourth century) or not too long after.

This dating broadly corresponds to the prevailing scholarly view that Patrick spent at least his early years in a region in which Roman rule still held sway. Let us therefore accept this view as a tentative working premise, which will allow us to sketch a hypothetical background for the circumstances of his child-hood. His father's office suggests that the family belonged to the Romano-British elite, for which the ownership of a dwelling in both town and country would not have been unusual. Towns were a common feature of the British landscape, consisting of both well-planned public towns, which were centres of government and administration set up mainly in the first century, and small towns, like Bath, Water Newton, or Catterick, which developed organically from the third century, usually on the vast network of Roman roads (there were around eighty in the late Roman period). In the hierarchy of Roman towns, *colonia*, which were colonies of Roman citizens, were at the top of the pyramid. The earliest such towns in Britain were Gloucester, Colchester, Lincoln, and York. Below them in the hierarchy were the *municipia*, sometimes incorporating provincial communities that were rewarded for military service. And below these were the *civitates*, regional capitals usually corresponding to traditional territorial divisions of indigenous peoples. There were approximately fifteen such capitals, each of which included a town council, such as the one on which Calpornius served, most likely in the west of Britain. The westernmost among the *civitates* were (from south to north) Caerwent, Carmarthen, Kenchester, Wroxeter, and Carlisle.

Towns of all kinds had satellite villas, and some public towns in late antiquity sprang villas of their own within their walls. The appearance and function of villas are among the primary examples of things that were undergoing significant transformations in late third- and early fourth-century Britain, and that show the growing assimilation of native elites into the inner circles of Roman society. The decades after the era known as the third-century crisis, the end of which is usually dated around the ascendency of Diocletian in 284, are regarded as the apogee of

Roman culture in Britain. This was a time in which the native Britons were aligning themselves with the trappings of Roman culture in the same way as other native populations had been doing elsewhere in the empire, especially in Gaul. Architecture, vessels, dress fashions, and manners all took after Roman models, though often with a native twist.

That Calpornius was a member of a town council (*curia*) suggests that the administrative network in and around his town was still functioning, at least to some extent, in the mid- to late fourth century or even into the early fifth. A town of his period would have been a far cry from the Roman towns of second- and early third-century Britain, with their thriving commercial centres, lavish public spaces, grand public buildings, monumental temples, and extravagant baths. The persistent military threats and relentless political fragmentation that characterised the third-century crisis had all taken their toll on Britain, just as they had on the rest of the empire, transforming the economy, the military organisation, the imperial government, and, in many cases, the core structure of society. However, whereas the crisis struck a nasty blow to the old imperial aristocracy, especially the senatorial class, there were others who benefitted from the mood of change. Among them were the Romanised British elites, who rose in prominence, achieving a social standing equal to that of members of the shrinking Roman settlement. Among the conspicuous expressions of this assertive native class of new wealth was the rise of lavish villas. Such can be found in the fourth century at sites including Great Witcombe, Eccles, Woodchester, North Leigh, and Chedworth (see Figure 2). Apart from Calpornius, no other villa owner from this period is known by name. Around five hundred villas are known to have been built by the British elite in late antique Roman Britain, most of which were in the vicinity of towns that were originally established as

FIGURE 2. Remains of Roman villa at Great Witcombe
(Gloucestershire). Available from Geograph. © Copyright Jonathan
Billinger and licensed for reuse (CC BY-SA 2.0)

administrative centres but decreased in importance in the twilight years of the Roman colony. These villas displayed private wealth in the most ostentatious manner, with large rooms, baths, and ornate mosaic floors bedecked with scenes from classical mythology. The display of pagan scenes in the Christian era signalled the owners' predilection for Roman culture, which, like their ancestors, they were appropriating and fusing with their own native culture (see Figure 3). Historians have tended to interpret mosaics of this kind as a means through which a pagan elite asserted itself vis-à-vis a mostly Christian class of tenants. Kenneth Dark, for example, believes that distinctions in wealth and status were mirrored and reinforced by religious differences. This hypothesis gains support from the proximity— to which Timothy Potter and Catherine Jones drew attention— of villas and pagan temples that were still active into the fourth century.

FIGURE 3. Littlecote Roman villa (Wiltshire), Orpheus mosaic.
Available from Geograph. © Copyright Ken Ripper and
licensed for reuse (CC BY-SA 2.0)

But villas, as country estates, were not solely places of dwelling and entertainment. They could also be places of agricultural
production. At the villa of Gatcombe, for example, near Bristol,
grain storage, milling, and baking are all attested on a large scale,
and so too are the processing of meat and iron working. Even
when not supported by agriculture and when the display elements were few, a villa remained, as Potter put it, 'a country

residence designed to impress'. They were not merely elite dwellings but also displayed an aspect of monumentality. A Romano-British villa, even a modest one, could have contained houses consisting of not one but two stories, as well as structural features that were intended to be ostentatious, like stone carvings. There was, however, one significant way in which such late Roman villas were different from earlier Roman settlements: these were strictly private dwellings with no public function, open only to the owners and their circle of friends and clients, who could feel both pride and awe at being associated with such luxury. Villas in and around the time of Calpornius's tenure on a Roman town council also offer a convenient measure for tracing the eventual decline of *romanitas* in Britain and the loosening of Roman control more generally. By the 360s, villas reached a low ebb, with archaeological evidence showing that many fell hopelessly into disrepair while others were abandoned or destroyed.

The dramatic and apparently sudden decline is usually attributed to an increase in the frequency and intensity of invasions. The Scotti 'Irish' of Ireland and Argyll, as well as the Picts, the native population of the territory corresponding to present-day Scotland, are often regarded as the main culprits. Irish and Pictish raiding expeditions were not uncommon throughout Roman times, but from the early 340s they intensified and were amplified by further raids from mainland Europe. The Roman response was to reinforce defences along Hadrian's Wall, the barrier that separated Roman Britain from the Picts, and to increase military outposts along the island's east coast. Raiding resumed in the early 360s after a hiatus, until in 367 Britain faced what the pagan Roman historian Ammianus Marcellinus described as the 'barbarian conspiracy' (*barbarica conspiratio*), an event in which Picts, Scotti, Attacotti (an insular group), and Saxons from the Continent all attacked Britain at once.[9] The Roman defences were not able to withstand the onslaught, and even Hadrian's Wall was breached. Another invasion that took place between 396 and 398 once more saw simultaneous assaults by Picts, Scotti, and Saxons. In Ammianus's account, these successive attacks were leading to a state of near hopelessness: 'But in Britain, during Constantius's tenth and Julian's third consulship, the wild tribes of the Scotti and Picts broke their undertaking to keep peace, laid waste the country near the frontier, and caused alarm among the provincials, who were exhausted by the repeated disasters they had already suffered'. He continues, 'The Picts, Saxons, Scotti, and Attacotti were bringing continual misery upon Britain'.[10]

In an attempt to restore the peace, the general Stilicho, arguably the de facto ruler of the Western Roman Empire, arrived in Britain at the head of a military force. However, while he was in Britain, news arrived of the Gothic incursions into Italy, and in response, armies were diverted towards Rome's defence. Political struggles at the highest levels of imperial government took their toll as well: in 407 the usurper Constantine III assumed command of the imperial troops in Britain, leading them into Gaul in a failed attempt to depose Emperor Honorius, and all remaining troops were gone by the time of the Gothic sack of Rome in 410 (but see the bibliographic essay for this chapter for a hypothesis that some troops remained). Constantine's coup was not the only time that Roman forces in Britain were implicated in bids to rival central imperial power. Between 383 and 388 the commander of the Roman armies in Britain, Magnus Maximus, set himself up at the head of a rival empire with its capital at Trier. This echoed an earlier such episode, at the height of the third-century crisis between 260 and 274, when Britain fell within another rival empire, the so-called Gallic empire founded by the Roman commander Posthumus (d. 269), which encompassed the provinces of Britain, Gaul, and Germania. Honorius's rescript of 410, which called on the Britons to defend themselves following what is commonly assumed to have been the final withdrawal of the remaining legionaries from Britain, marks a watershed in the fortunes of late antique Britain.[11] Thereafter the demography of Britain experienced far-reaching changes, as there was no serious military obstacle to prevent migration from Continental Europe, mainly by Angles, Saxons, and Jutes, who arrived sporadically or in larger, organised groups.

But even before this period of relatively unchecked migration, the population of Britain was not ethnically homogenous. Among the best sources for establishing the degree of ethnic diversity in Britain are inscriptions, of which some 2,400 have been catalogued. There are approximately 250 Christian inscriptions from western Britain from before 700. Many of the Christian inscriptions have traditionally been interpreted as reflecting Gallic influence or even Gallic presence, as inferred from the names and formulae inscribed on them, although recent studies have contested the extent to which they testify to a wide Gallic impact. The earlier inscriptions are more telling of the multiculturalism of Britain, with seventy-six of those commemorated in funerary inscriptions being newcomers from Athens, Noricum, Syria, Vienne, and North Africa.

The ethnic diversity of the island included not only the Romans, the Britons, the Picts, and the occasional Gallic or North African newcomer but also the Irish, who began to form their own polity in south Wales during the course of the fifth century. What would later become known as the kingdom of Dyfed started as an Irish colony of immigrants, the earliest phase of which has been argued by Thomas Charles-Edwards to date not before the 'barbarian conspiracy' of 367.

Another important driver of ethnic diversity was slavery. A very common form of slave in antiquity was the captive, who was captured either during war or in raids by slavers. In the context of Patrick's biography, slaving is known in the first place because of Coroticus, the British leader who, despite being Christian himself, captured some of Patrick's new converts in Ireland and transported them to Britain. Patrick's main regret was that these newly converted Christians would be sold to Pictish masters, who were not Christian, but there is no indication that Patrick was opposed to slavery per se as an institution.[12] Coroticus's assault will be considered at length in a later chapter on captivity (chapter 3). However, he is also of interest in the present context because the episode concerning him allows us to explore some issues relating to the construction of Roman identity and to the culture of slave raiding in Roman and post-Roman Britain. The Roman features of Patrick's Letter, which we saw in the introduction, were carefully chosen to impress Coroticus, who was a self-styled Roman citizen. Thus, Patrick stresses the fact that he himself is the son of a decurion, that he is a Roman citizen, and that the Roman Christians of Gaul are in the habit of redeeming captives.[13] Whether Coroticus was an actual Roman citizen or not is impossible to determine. He appears to be among the warlords who would have become more prominent either in the period of insecurity preceding the collapse of Roman occupation in Britain or shortly after, when power was up for grabs. According to a later source, an eighth-century table of contents interpolated into Muirchú's Life of Patrick in the Book of Armagh, Coroticus was *rex Aloo*, a place interpreted as Ail Chluathe, which is an Old Irish rendering of Dumbarton, the fort that served as the political centre of the British kingdom of Strathclyde, in the northwest of Britain.[14] It is impossible to say whether the epithet in the Book of Armagh reflects an old tradition or a tradition closer to the scribe's own time. Either way, it is of questionable historical value.

Presumably, Patrick believed that in declaring that he refuses to address Coroticus and his men as Roman citizens, but instead prefers to refer to them as 'citizens of demons', he could cause them a certain embarrassment. It follows that being acknowledged as a Roman citizen was considered honourable, whereas the converse may not necessarily have been. Yet Coroticus's self-identification as a Roman citizen might not have been entirely bogus. Possibly, he was a British auxiliary who gained Roman citizenship on his retirement from the army (and might later have become king of Strathclyde, if one believes the Book of Armagh). Such people, especially the higher ranking among them, would have been able to use their military training and connections to their advantage once Roman rule in Britain collapsed. While in the army, he might also have been among those frontier soldiers who were profiting from the slave trade. This practice was sometimes denounced, as was the case in the tenth oration of Themistius (d. 390), prefect of Constantinople, in which he berated military captains serving on the frontiers for neglecting their military duties as they preoccupied themselves too much with slave trading.

Among those who would purchase slaves from slavers like Coroticus were people like Patrick's father.[15] These slaves would then become an integral part of the economy of the Roman household. Some would be burdened with heavy labour and exercise minimal or no autonomy, while others could hold positions of trust as teachers, foremen, or even administrators.

Often described by historians as a 'slave economy', the Roman economy relied heavily on servile labour for domestic chores, craft production, agriculture, urban building projects, and the maintenance of its road network, which enabled vital communication and essential transport of goods and people. The gradual adoption of Christianity by the empire did not change much in the manner in which servitude was perceived or practiced. Although redemption from captivity was praised by the church as an act of Christian charity and masters were urged to treat their slaves humanely, neither the church nor the converted

Roman state forbade the ownership of slaves, be they Christian or non-Christian, by the ordinary Christian faithful, by individual clerics, or by churches (though there were restrictions on Jewish ownership of Christian slaves). Even aristocratic hermits and monks were known to keep slaves, and they were sometimes praised if they were content with owning only a single slave. Therefore, Patrick's father and grandfather, both of whom were clerics, experienced no contradiction between the ownership of slaves and the holding of religious offices. Rather, to have slaves was part and parcel of being a Roman of sufficient means, so much so that even noncommissioned officers of the lowest rank (*circitor*) are known to have owned at least one slave. So when Patrick describes 'the slaves and slave-women of my father's estate' (*servos et ancillas domus patris mei*), he is describing an ordinary household that possessed domestic slaves who would be owned even by Romans of modest means.[16] However, Patrick's reference to both male and female slaves in the plural suggests a household that was more affluent than average.

As abhorrent as the practice of owning a human in order to serve another is, it must be acknowledged that in certain societies (indeed, to this day), a person can be treated as a commodity, and commodities have a price tag. The prices of slaves in the empire could vary. The most famous document to tell us about the prices of slaves in the late empire is Diocletian's Prices Edict from 301, which gives a maximum tariff for slaves according to their gender and age: males between the ages of sixteen and forty were the most expensive, while females under the age of eight or over the age of sixty had the lowest value.[17] The price of skilled slaves was higher but negotiable. Another detailed record for the cost of slaves, although one that does not differentiate between male and female slaves, comes from a later period than Patrick's: the reign of Justinian (527–65).[18] Whereas the absolute value of slaves would have changed between Patrick's time and the sixth century, one may assume that the relative rates for different kinds of slaves would broadly have stayed the same. Thus, among the most expensive were castrated boys, valued at three times as much as an ordinary young slave, and skilled slaves were also more expensive than unskilled ones, with clerks and doctors topping the list. In terms of actual records of the slave trade, available figures show that slaves sold in provincial areas such as Britain were usually cheaper than slaves in Italy.

Contemporary Christian thinkers were divided on the reasons for the existence of slavery, but they did not oppose it on moral grounds. The following are two examples of the manner in which Christian scholars rationalised slavery. In the first, we find Basil (d. 379) of Caesarea arguing that servitude was not innate to individuals but could be justified by certain social circumstances:

> Do they not realize that even among men, no one is a slave by nature? Men are brought under the yoke of slavery either because they are captured in battle or else they sell themselves into slavery owing to poverty; as the Egyptians became the slaves of Pharaoh. Sometimes, by a wise and inscrutable providence, worthless children are commanded by their father to serve their more intelligent brothers and sisters. Any upright person investigating the circumstances would realize that such situations bring much benefit, and are not a sentence of condemnation for those involved. . . . That is why Jacob obtained his father's blessing and became Esau's master: so that this foolish son, who had no intelligence properly to guide him, might profit from his prudent brother, even against his will. . . . And even though one man is called a master, and another a slave, we are all the possessions of our Creator; we all share the rank of slave.[19]

In contrast, Saint Augustine (d. 430) of Hippo believed that the free and unfree were separated by a fate determined by God rather than human contingency: 'The first cause of slavery, then, is sin, whereby man was subjected to man in the condition of bondage; and this can only happen by the judgment of God, with whom there is no injustice, and who knows how to allot different punishments according to the deserts of the offenders.'[20]

Authors like Basil and Augustine would have been closely familiar with instances in which the New Testament mentioned—with no hint of disapproval—followers of the new faith who owned slaves, like Mary, the mother of John, who owned Rhoda, and more famously Philemon, who owned Onesimus.[21] Paul's letter to Philemon is in fact a key text that shaped the construction of Christian attitudes to slavery in the early Christian centuries, and it is also central to the modern scholarly understanding of Paul's approach to the Christian ownership of slaves. Written on behalf of the escaped and recently baptised slave Onesimus, Paul urges his Christian master, Philemon, to receive him graciously, as a brother rather than a slave. Interpretations of the texts vary, with a recent study by Ulrike Roth arguing (with reference to Greek law) that the slave was owned jointly by Paul and Philemon. Philemon is said to have presided over a church, some of the members of which were slaves, perhaps owned jointly by free members of that church. Indeed, the teachings of the Gospel urged such slaves to be respectful towards their Christian masters, but they also encouraged masters to show restraint in their treatment of slaves.[22]

The ownership of slaves more generally by the church in late antiquity and the early Middle Ages is well documented, and clerics themselves were not always free men or indeed women, as attested in a letter by Pliny the Younger, governor of Bithynia and Pontus, which mentions slave women serving as deacons.[23]

Nevertheless, throughout the early Christian centuries, pre-scriptive ecclesiastical texts can be seen to have restricted the admittance of slaves into the ranks of the clergy.[24] It is not until Justinian that one finds legislation granting manumission (free-dom) to slaves joining the clergy, and then only with their mas-ters' permission.[25] A later settlement, allowing slaves owned by monasteries to be freed once they had taken monastic vows, was severely limited by Pope Gregory the Great in 595.[26]

The topic of slavery takes us back to the matter of Patrick's family's wealth, which was—in part—invested in slaves. Hints as to the extent of his family's wealth and the wealth that he him-self had in Ireland are scattered throughout his writings. In the *Confessio* he tells of presents that he gave to Irish kings and their sons who travelled with him. He also paid judges in different places (*per omnes regiones*) 'the price of fifteen men at least' (*non minimum quam pretium quindecim hominum distribui illis*).[27] What exactly he meant by this expression is unclear, and I shall return to it in the next chapter. Then there is, of course, the ref-erence to the slaves and slave women of his father's estate.[28] As I have already argued, the mention of servile persons in the plu-ral signals a high level of wealth, compatible with landowners who commanded servile farm labour. And the slaves themselves were also an investment, a means of accumulating wealth. By the end of his life, however, Patrick admits to having had no wealth at all, although the means by which he was separated from it (generosity? misfortune?) is not specified.[29]

The possession of wealth in the Roman Empire played a cru-cial role in determining a person's capacity—and sometimes obligation—to undertake a senior administrative role. Thus, any individual who possessed enough property to qualify as a decu-rion was obliged to serve on the council if nominated. Decuri-ons, also known as *curiales*, after the local administrative councils (*curiae*) of which they were members, made up the great bulk of aristocratic landowners in the late empire. What counted as property for the purpose of being appointed to a council was normally land, but from 383, those whose wealth was invested primarily in slaves could also enrol in the councils.[30] And Patrick's family, as we are well aware by now, owned both land and slaves.

Membership in the *curia* was not only obligatory but also de facto hereditary, because the heirs of decurions possessed the necessary property qualification by default. From 390 the hereditary aspect was also enshrined in Roman law.[31] Sons of decurions were nominated as soon as they came of age, in their eighteenth year, but in practice children as young as seven or eight are known to have been nominated when necessity required. Certain wealthy individuals could claim exemption from serving on the council—for instance, if they held senatorial rank or, from 313, if they joined the clergy.

Like other members of the rural aristocracy, Patrick's father would have held, in addition to his country estate (the *villula*), an urban residence in the town where he discharged his obligations as a decurion on the town council. Since there is no reason to assume that the decurionship in Britain was fundamentally different from the decurionship elsewhere in the empire, there are a few general observations that can be made about Calpornius's office. Decurions, as we have seen, were expected to fulfil a variety of roles, the most important of which was the collection of taxes. By late Roman times, taxes in Britain consisted mainly of payment in kind of foodstuffs. This was a time when the staple crop for the majority of the inhabitants of Britain was bread wheat (*Triticum aestivum*), which the Romans had introduced. Throughout the duration of Roman rule in Britain, the collection of taxes remained the single most onerous duty of the decurions, because they were expected to make up for any short-fall in tax revenues from their own pockets. This inconvenience was believed to have contributed to a surge in *curiales* seeking to escape their position on councils. During the fourth and fifth centuries, emperors showed a growing concern with what has come to be known as the 'flight of the *curiales*'. The exact scale of the phenomenon is difficult to assess, due to imprecise and rhetorically exaggerated figures provided by contemporary sources. For instance, the fourth-century Antiochene master of rhetoric Libanius says in one oration that numbers decreased locally from 1,200 to 12, but in a different oration the decrease is said to be less extreme but nevertheless substantial: from 600 to 60.[32]

From 313, a favourite escape route for *curiales* was to join the clergy, which also accounts for their predominance in the epis-copate. But approximately fifteen years later, when it became evi-dent that many decurions adopted the religious life only to avoid the councils, Constantine restricted the clergy's immunity from curial charges. However, the restrictions were soon relaxed, and *curiales* were allowed to take holy orders, provided that they proved their sincerity by surrendering either all or two-thirds of their property to their sons or other relatives who would re-place them on the *curia*. Between 361 and 452, emperors some-times tightened and sometimes relaxed the restrictions they imposed on *curiales* who wanted to take holy orders.

Among the challenges that decurions faced in the late empire were arbitrary lawsuits. These were a persistent menace, and de-curions in Britain seem to have been just as susceptible to them as were their colleagues elsewhere in the empire. Indeed, in 332 an imperial official based in Britain found it necessary to issue a decree restricting the circumstances under which a decurion could be sued.[33] The decurions' discontent with the obligations of their office and the refuge that many of them sought in the clergy provide the background for the dual career that Patrick's father had as decurion and deacon. Historians, including J. B. Bury, Eoin MacNeill, Richard Hanson, David Howlett, and M. B. De Paor, have long speculated that Calpornius sought relief from certain burdens associated with the decurionship by swapping his place on the council for a deaconate. What seems to have escaped notice, however, is that Calpornius's tenure in the imperial office would also have affected his heir. The heir, as we have seen, was obliged by his property ranking to enter the council, but he was also obliged to do so by law if his father took clerical orders. As already mentioned, the need to fill the curial ranks had even led to children as young as seven being nominated, despite the age barrier formally being eighteen.

That Patrick was heir to his father is a reasonable inference from the fact that he was a wealthy man. Since he was not a soldier or a merchant, the only legitimate path open before him to become rich was to inherit the family fortune. The hypothesis that Patrick held an imperial office gains further support from his own admission that he sold his nobility (*vendidi enim nobilitatem meam*).[34] Nobility in imperial Rome was conferred through wealth and the participation in government by holding an office. Therefore, if Patrick was speaking of nobility in the Roman sense, then he must have held an imperial office. He adds that he was not ashamed to admit that he sold his nobility, and nor should he have been, because trafficking in imperial offices was ubiquitous and a thriving business in the fourth century. All this raises the intriguing speculation that Patrick himself was a part of the phenomenon known as the 'flight of the *curiales*', and that he set himself up in Ireland in order to evade curial responsibilities, such as the collection of taxes, and to avoid certain associated risks, such as defaulting on tax collecting. In order to sustain this hypothesis, it is necessary to posit a late fourth- or early fifth-century date for the early part of Patrick's career, which has already been shown to be possible. The hypothesis of a 'curial absconder' would also cast doubt on Patrick's own testimony that he was taken captive from Britain, suggesting that he may have willingly—and perhaps with the support of his father, who himself appears to have shunned curial responsibilities— set himself up in Ireland as soon as he was about to be nominated to take his father's place on the *curia*. Ireland then became his adoptive home, but his British past would eventually catch up with him and aspersions would be cast on his character.

Whatever the reason that brought (or took) Patrick to Ireland in the first place, Britain did not cease to play a part in his adult life. He eventually returned (or, by his account, escaped) to Britain 'a few years later' (*post paucos annos*), where he rejoined his relatives and attempted to reinstate himself.[35] However, twenty-four years after his arrival, when he was already bishop, he had an inexplicable falling-out with his elders (*seniores*), following which he sailed back to Ireland. I shall return to this incident soon. But first, I must address a more mundane but crucial issue relating to his Irish sojourn.

In order to sustain his operations in Ireland—at least as an adult, if not as an adolescent who fled his curial chores—Patrick would have needed an effective way of liquidating wealth and transporting it across the Irish Sea. The selling of noble status was one way in which he could raise funds for his life in Ireland, but there might have been other ways. For instance, he could, hypothetically, have sold the family land, or parts of it. But he could only do this while Britain still had an active land market. From what we know of the land market in Roman Britain, it owed its existence primarily to major absentee landowners like the famous Melania the Younger, who owned vast lands in Africa and

Europe, including Britain, but gave up her wealth for the benefit of the church. Once the legions began to depart from Britain, no imperial armed forces were left to protect the landed estates of the absentee landowners. Consequently, it is difficult to imagine that Britain could continue to attract new investors from outside. In all likelihood, then, the land market would have collapsed around 410 if not before, during the long years of political unrest. Hence, if Patrick did in fact sell land, he is likely to have done so before 410. Another way in which Patrick could have secured the funding he needed was by selling the family slaves or by bringing them with him to Ireland.

And so, we return to his conflict with his elders and ask whether it may be connected in some way to his Irish venture. This conflict took place, you will remember, a quarter of a century after he first returned to Britain from Ireland. According to Patrick, his elders were eager to find a pretext to undermine him. The most convenient pretext they found was to confront him with an accusation for which he had once been put on trial.[36] The exact charge is not specified and the chronology is hopelessly confused (or perhaps deliberately fudged), making this one of the more frustrating episodes in the *Confessio*, all the more so since it is pivotal to the progress of the narrative. All we are told is that he was accosted for an offence he committed at the age of fifteen, and that he later confessed to a friend when he was a young deacon:

> And when I was attacked by a number of my elders, who came and brought up my sins against my arduous episcopate, certainly that day I was struck a heavy blow. . . .
>
> After thirty years they found a pretext for their allegations against me in a confession which I had made before I was a deacon. In a depressed and worried state of mind I mentioned

to a close friend what I had done as a boy one day. . . . I do not know, God knows, whether I was fifteen years old at that time. . . .

. . . But how did he take it into his head afterwards, publicly, before everyone, good and evil, to discredit me for something which he had previously been glad to pardon of his own accord, as had the Lord too, who is greater than us all?[37]

The offence, which Patrick claims to have committed because he was not yet immune to temptation, might have been perceived by some as being related to his initial departure to Ireland, because immediately after he mentions it, he emphasises that he did not go to Ireland of his own accord (*Hiberione non sponte pergebam*).[38] This apologetic statement was presumably made in response to allegations that he *did* leave for Ireland of his own free will and that he was not taken captive.[39] Indeed, in the *Confessio* he says in no uncertain terms that some will continue to disbelieve him even if he repeats his story over and over.[40] Later we learn that when the accusation was first brought against him and a trial was conducted in his absence, he was in fact away from Britain, which suggests that he returned to Britain twice: once after his alleged captivity and a second time after the trial, when he was already bishop, though no word is said about where and by whom he was ordained.[41] Patrick then went back to Ireland after (or because) his elders rejected him, using the old trial as an excuse. Before his departure, however, he saw a vision in his sleep in which a document appeared before him. He does not say what the document contained, but adds that it was accompanied by a prophetic voice reassuring him that the verdict against him was unfair and that he was nevertheless among the elect: 'Therefore, on the day on which I was rejected by the aforementioned and abovementioned, that same night I saw in a vision a document opposite my face, without honour, and meanwhile I heard a divine prophecy saying to me: "We were grieved to see the face of our elect stripped of his good name"; and He did not say: "You were grieved to see", but "We were grieved to see", as though He included Himself with him, just as He said: "He that touches you is as he that touches the apple of My eye"'.[42]

The closing sentence in this quote is taken from Zacharias 2:8, in which God reassures the exiled Israelites of his protection. As for the phrase 'my face without honour' (*faciem meam sine honore*), this appears to echo Christ's rebuke to detractors who mocked his humble origins: 'A prophet is not without honour, save in his own country and in his own house' (*Non est propheta sine honore, nisi in patria sua et in domo sua*), in Matthew 13:7 and Mark 6:4. To his readers, Patrick wants to appear as the paradigmatic persecuted prophet, suffering the same predicament as Christ. Like Christ, he was able to assert himself despite his critics and persecutors, and to embark on a mission to bring a new faith to the uninitiated. Despite the fuzzy chronology of his account, it appears that Patrick started his missionary work in Ireland in the period between his visits to Britain. And it is Ireland that we shall turn to in the next chapter, after reflecting briefly on the foregoing discussion.

This chapter, which has concentrated on the Romano-British background to Patrick's upbringing and subsequent mission, highlighted the vicissitudes of Roman occupation in Britain, which experienced different forms of settlement, different configurations in its economic regime, different religious transitions, and different rates of integration of the indigenous population into its social texture, such that—at least at the higher echelons—local elites could gradually be seen to play a more important part. An ostensible upward trajectory towards increasing stability and prosperity seems to have given way in the course of the fourth century to a conspicuous decline, eventually leading to a collapse of much, but by no means all, of what could be identified as distinctly Roman. That certain strains of Roman culture continued into the fifth century despite the political disintegration is not disputed, nor is the fact that certain groups or individuals, like Patrick and Coroticus, continued to define themselves as Roman citizens. The idea of *romanitas* endured, although one would imagine that it meant different things to different people who held on to it.

Patrick's own life in Britain experienced its fair share of upheavals. He talks of committing a grave sin, a trial, an abduction to Ireland, return trips to Britain, betrayal by a close friend, rejection by his own community, and a humiliating expulsion. In Patrick's account, which is disappointingly imprecise and perhaps deliberately ambiguous about the order of events, his travails are depicted as the misfortunes of an individual rather than as a consequence of the political circumstances in which he lived. But a historian would be curious to explore the link between Patrick's biography and his historical context, and this is precisely what this chapter sought to do as it brought the Romano-British background to bear on Patrick's own personal story. The more we tried to place the individual into context, the more necessary it was to resort to speculation to correlate episodes from Patrick's own life with chapters from the history of Roman Britain. Ultimately, our aim was to answer questions that his account leaves open: Why was it that some of his contemporaries believed that he left Britain for Ireland of his own free will? How was Patrick able to support himself in Ireland? What did he stand trial for? And what was that offence that he committed as a youth? The alternative narrative offered here, dotted by speculation, attempted to fill in the gaps by explaining his actions with recourse to the happenings in his contemporary Britain and to the cultural and administrative Roman background that defined (at least) Patrick's family history and his early years. This alternative narrative cannot, admittedly, be corroborated, and it is clear that there is more to the story than we have been able to recover. It must be remembered, however, that it is Patrick himself who scattered clues about the evidence of a rival narrative that differed from his own. These clues come in the form of salient inconsistencies, throwaway comments, and the repeated admissions that he was regarded as a controversial figure. It is the historian's duty to heed Patrick's implicit invitation to dig beneath the surface of his account, as we shall continue to do in the next chapter.

Notes

1. Letter § 10.

2. Letter § 2.

3. *Confessio* § 1.

4. W. Stokes and J. Strachan, eds. and trans., *Thesaurus Palaeohibernicus*, 2 vols. (Cambridge, UK, 1901–3), 2:312–13.

5. Chronicle of Ireland 457.3, 493.4.

6. Letter § 14.

7. *Confessio* §§ 9, 12.

8. *Confessio* § 13. For Bieler's translation, see his *Works of St. Patrick* (London, 1953), 24.

9. Ammianus, *Res Gestae* 27.8, ed. Wolfgang Seyfarth, 2 vols. (Leipzig, 1978), 2:47.

10. Ammianus, *Res Gestae* 20.1, 26.4, ed. Seyfarth, 1:19, 2:9; trans. Walter Hamilton, *Ammianus Marcellinus: The Later Roman Empire (A.D. 354–378)* (London, 1986), 185, 318.

11. The rescript is related by Zosimus, *Historia Nova* 6.10.2, in *Zosimi comitis exadvocati fisci Historia Nova*, ed. L. Mendelssohn (Leipzig, 1887), 291–92; trans. R. T. Ridley, *Zosimus: New History* (Canberra, 1982), 130.

12. Letter §§ 13, 15.

13. Letter § 10.

14. Book of Armagh (Trinity College Dublin, MS 52), fol. 20v: 'De conflictu sancti Patricii adversum Coirthech regem aloo'; edited in Bieler, *Patrician Texts*, 66. For Ail Chluathe, see, e.g., Chronicle of Ireland 870.6.

15. Letter § 10.

16. Letter § 10.

17. Benet Salway, ed. and trans., 'MANCIPIVM RVSTICVM SIVE VRBANVM: The slave chapter of Diocletian's Edict on Maximum Prices', in *By the Sweat of Your Brow: Roman Slavery in Its Socio-economic Setting*, ed. Ulrike Roth (London, 2010), 1–20, at 19–20.

18. *Codex Iustinianus* 7.7.

19. Basil, On the Holy Spirit § 20, trans. Peter Garnsey, in *Ideas of Slavery from Aristotle to Augustine*, by Peter Garnsey (Cambridge, UK, 1996), 45.

20. Augustine, City of God 19.15, in *Augustine: City of God*, trans. David Knowles (New York, 1981), 875.

21. Acts 12:12–16, Epistle to Philemon.

22. I Timothy 6:2; Colossians 4:1.

23. Pliny the Younger, Letter 10.96.8 to Emperor Trajan, in *Pliny the Younger: Complete Letters*, trans. Peter G. Walsh, Oxford World's Classics (Oxford, 2006), 278.

24. Apostolic Constitutions 8.47.82, in *The Work Claiming to Be the Constitutions of the Holy Apostles, Including the Canons*, trans. Irah Chase (New York, 1848), 256; Council of Chalcedon 451, Canon 4, in *Acts of the Council of Chalcedon*, 3 vols., trans. Richard Price and Michael Gaddis (Liverpool, 2005), 3:94–103, at 95–96.

25. *Novellae* 123.17, in *Corpus Iuris Civilis*, 4th ed., ed. Rudolph Schoell and William Kroll, vol. 3 (Berlin, 1912); Fred Blume and Timothy Kearley, trans., *Annotated Justinian Code: Justinian's Novels*, available at http://www.uwyo.edu/lawlib/blume-justinian/ajc-edition-2/novels/index.html.

26. Roman council of 595, canon 6, in *Monumenta Germaniae Historica: Epistolae 1*, ed. P. Ewald and L. M. Hartmann (Berlin, 1891), 362–67, at 365.

27. *Confessio* §§ 52, 53.

28. Letter § 10.

29. *Confessio* § 55.

30. *Codex Theodosianus* 12.1.96 (AD 383).

31. *Codex Theodosianus* 13.5.19: 'Manebit vero in ordine curiali et ei filius in officium curiale succedat' (He shall remain in the curial order and his son shall succeed him in the curial office).

32. Libanius, Orations 48.4, 49.8, in *Libanius: Selected Works*, 2 vols., ed. and trans. A. F. Norman (Cambridge, MA, 1969–77), 2:424, 468.

33. *Codex Theodosianus* 2.7.2.

34. Letter § 10.

35. *Confessio* § 23.

36. *Confessio* §§ 26, 27.

37. *Confessio* §§ 26, 27, 32.
38. *Confessio* § 28.
39. As implied in *Confessio* § 10.
40. *Confessio* § 10.
41. *Confessio* § 32.
42. *Confessio* § 29.

2

Patrick's Ireland

TO SOME ROMAN ONLOOKERS from Britain, Ireland was of
strategic importance. Tacitus reports that Agricola (d. 93), the
Roman general who commanded the conquest of Britain, had
contemplated an invasion and often exclaimed that the Romans
could capture it with a single legion if they wanted. In the event,
Agricola's plans came to naught and the Romans never established a military presence there. Nevertheless, there seems to
have been a degree of political contact between the Romans of
Britain and the Irish, for Agricola himself is said to have given
shelter to an exiled Irish king.[1] Further connections between
the two islands during the Roman occupation of Britain can be
demonstrated by other forms of evidence, especially archaeology. It is the archaeology and the Roman sources that are the
best windows on contemporary Ireland, and they compensate
for the absence of any Irish written source from the period. Together with other classical accounts of Ireland, they will form
a central strand of the present chapter, although, as we are about
to see, they are not without their ambiguities, especially when
it comes to shedding light on the identity of the island's
inhabitants.

Before the Romano-British had made any noticeable impact on the neighbouring island, Ireland experienced much earlier influences that led to the formation of a culture that, by Patrick's time, was already considered indigenous. That culture and the ethnic identity with which it is (rightly or wrongly) associated are often referred to by the shorthand 'Celtic'. The argument for placing Ireland within the ambit of Celtic culture is made primarily on linguistic grounds, because the Irish language belongs to the Celtic family of languages. Consequently, the study of Iron Age Ireland has traditionally been premised on the assumption that it would exhibit similarities with Continental Celtic material culture, known in the archaeological jargon as 'Hallstatt C and D' and 'La Tène I–III' cultures. The terms 'Hallstatt' and 'La Tène' are derived from sites in Continental Europe in which distinct artefacts were found that came to be identified with the Celtic Iron Age: an Austrian village southeast of Salzburg and a site beside Lake Neuchâtel in Switzerland, respectively.

However, there are very few finds from Ireland that can be described either as Hallstatt or La Tène. Arguably, there are some Hallstatt-like ironworking artefacts, dating from the seventh century BC, among them from the Rathtinaun crannog (County Sligo) and Aughinish (County Limerick). Ostensible traces of La Tène culture are attested at two sites only, Emain Macha (Navan Fort, County Armagh) and Dún Ailinne (County Kildare), both royal hilltop ritual sites. All these artefacts were imported rather than produced locally. From a methodological point of view, the near absence of Hallstatt or La Tène objects in Ireland and the wholesale absence of locally produced objects of these kinds expose the weakness of identifying an ethnic group by its material culture. For if we were to go by the archaeology alone and omit the linguistic argument, we would not be able to infer that Ireland had a 'Celtic' culture along Continental lines. Another methodological point is that the expectation of finding 'Celtic' artefacts in Ireland betrays an a priori assumption about the presence of a Celtic culture there, irrespective of the existence of supporting evidence for it. The absurdity of such a preconception can be illustrated by the circular question, How is it that Ireland's Celts have no Celtic material culture? We see here the hazards of placing too much store in the evidence of linguistic similarities and making assumptions about a common ethnic origin for the inhabitants of Ireland and Gaul. Indeed, already in antiquity there were authors, like Strabo (d. AD 23), whom we shall meet again later, who drew a distinction between the Celts and the Irish. For these reasons, some modern scholars prefer to exercise more caution when defining the peoples settled in Ireland and refer to them noncommittally as 'Celtic speaking' rather than 'Celtic'.

The question of Celtic identity is a vexed issue in scholarship and cannot be considered separately from a discussion of the historiography on the topic itself. The historiography for Ireland, as indeed elsewhere, can be argued not only to *describe* conceptions of ethnic identity but also to *construct* them. The observer, in other words, affects the results of the experiment. In what follows, I shall address certain aspects of Celtic identity, leaving the matter of Celtic religion for a later chapter concerning cult and religion (chapter 4).

The notion of a common Celtic identity in Iron Age Europe and, more specifically, in Ireland has traditionally been premised on an idea of continuity of cult and myth from a common Indo-European origin via Continental Celtic society. For example, the matriarchal protagonist of the Ulster Cycle, Queen Medbh, has sometimes been perceived as a distant echo of the ancient Indian princess Madhavi, who reached the Irish literary tradition through a presumed role as a sovereignty goddess in prehistoric Celtic culture. Apart from the name, the different incarnations of this figure throughout history are believed by some to be connected by a common role as a king's consort who contracted her partner by means of a ritual of offering him drink. Such views on shared aspects of Celtic culture that cut across geographical and temporal boundaries ultimately go back to hypotheses emanating from nineteenth-century comparative linguistics and philology that posited a common cultural heritage for peoples whose languages were closely related or derived from a common parent language. The ancestral Indo-European language was thus identified with an original Indo-European culture whose vestiges are said to be traceable among the ancient Gauls, the Irish, and the Continental and insular British.

The extent to which there might have been overarching similarities between the political order in Iron Age Ireland and in other societies that have been deemed Celtic continues to be a hotly debated topic. The debate is hampered by the usual absence of contemporary evidence, although some scholars have been comfortable using later, even much later, sources to fill the gaps. These later sources consist primarily of written mythological accounts from the Middle Irish period (tenth to twelfth century). They tell of kings and heroes living on an island that was divided between different dynasties and peoples, sometimes connected and sometimes separated by alliances or conflict, observing clear hierarchies within each political entity, and occasionally going into battle on foot or on agile chariots. Scholars of earlier generations believed that mythological tales from Ireland are, to a certain degree, euhemeristic, which is to say that they draw on the memory of bygone times and should ultimately be understood to portray actual events and political

structures from those times. Among the scholars who advocated a euhemeristic interpretation were Henry Chadwick,
Nora Chadwick, Kenneth Jackson, Eleanor Knott, and Gerard
Murphy. The title of Jackson's 1964 Rede Lecture on the historical background to the Middle Irish Ulster Cycle is especially
telling of his approach: *The Oldest Irish Tradition: A Window on
the Iron Age*. He championed the view—now associated with
'nativist' scholars—that tales of events in the Iron Age were
transmitted orally into the early medieval period, a view opposed by James Carney, who dismissed the possibility of a long
oral tradition and argued that early Irish saga is a mix of written
sources, some oral traditions (but not such that go as far back
as the Iron Age), and contemporary imaginative additions influenced by Christianity. Later, more refined hypotheses, for
instance by Tomás Ó Cathasaigh, argued for an oral tradition
continuing to exist alongside a literate tradition in the Christian
era, with the two cross-fertilising each other. And in a recent
monograph, Elva Johnston endorsed this view, arguing that
'early Irish literacy functioned within a secondary-oral environment, an environment in which the oral and written were in
continual interaction'.

The notion that an 'oral' tradition preserves a more authentic
'voice' or a pan-Celtic 'voice' can, to a certain extent, be argued
to owe something to the legacy of an Irish medieval literary
trope of religious conversion, which, as Joseph Nagy has shown,
consciously framed the interaction between Christian and
pagan in the context of a dialogue, both oral and public, between saints and figures that predate Christianity. This resilient
trope, which equated orality with authenticity, has been continually challenged for over half a century. At the same time, the
value of saga as a window onto the *actual* happenings in the Iron
Age has gradually been eroded. Nevertheless, even as late as the

1970s scholars could still be found who tried to justify a 'nativist' reading against the growing tide of revisionism. For example, F. J. Byrne went as far as to argue that 'our use of literature as a valid historical source is to some extent imposed upon us by the literary bias of the Irish historical tradition'. This contention does not have much purchase nowadays, but some may be tempted to follow it nevertheless because it holds true for places other than Ireland. Indeed, in the literary traditions of certain other cultures, a euhemeristic reading can be a rewarding exercise if done prudently. For example, in Icelandic saga tradition, many a tale is euhemeristic, at least in the sense that it draws on a kernel of historical fact involving historical personalities, even if such a factual core is then obscured by layers of fanciful detail. It is also the case that saga literary tales, like that of the Norwegian king Ólaf Tryggvason, or Saint Olaf, written between 1180 and 1220, can have an earlier and more fanciful version as well as a later and more probable version— for example, Snorri's thirteenth-century rendering.

It is a commonplace of scholarship to divide Irish tales into cycles, although identifying how many there are can seem like a somewhat arbitrary exercise in taxonomy. One well-known division, which has late nineteenth-century roots and is described by both Ó Cathasaigh and John Carey as simply 'convenient', talks of (more or less) four cycles: a Mythological Cycle, the Ulster Cycle, the Finn Cycle, and the Cycle of Kings, which sometimes also relates the contributions of poets and saints. The earliest identifiable strata of these date from around the seventh or eighth century, but they certainly do not go back to Patrick's time or before. The heroic deeds of warriors, such as Finn mac Cumaill and his *fían* (warrior band), are the staple of many a tale and are sometimes punctuated by supernatural intervention, more so in the Finn Cycle than the Ulster Cycle.

Nevertheless, both have their share of powerful figures, who can be identified as deities and demigods, interfering in human affairs. Neither attests a coherent pantheon or the practice of cults devoted to specific deities. The different elements that compose the Cycle of Kings are an eclectic accretion of tales concerning various kings, some historical but others—and this is especially true of the earliest ones—spurious. Any hope of using it to detect even a distant echo of the Iron Age is doomed to be frustrated.

One would have hoped that Patrick's contemporary testimony would add something more concrete to the fanciful picture that myth and saga paint of the political realities of late Iron Age Ireland, but in fact it offers only a few selective glimpses. The most important of these is that the prevalent form of government in Ireland was kingship. In his description of the conversion of sons and daughters of petty kings (*reguli*), he tells how these royal offspring became monks and nuns of Christ (*monachi et virgines Christi*): 'And how has it lately come about in Ireland that those who never had any knowledge of God but up till now always worshipped idols and abominations (*idola et inmunda*) are now called the people of the Lord and the sons of God, and sons and daughters of Irish *reguli* are seen to be monks and virgins of Christ'?[2]

His reference to petty kings may be to the lowliest rank of king, known from medieval Ireland as *rí*. A king of this rank would rule a *túath*, a petty kingdom comprising a farming community. Early Irish law tracts on rank and status define two higher ranks of king: the *rí buiden* (king of war bands) and the *rí ruirech* (king of great kings). Aside from kings, the mention of the worship of 'idols and abominations' would make us wonder about other divisions in contemporary society, perhaps into a priestly class that oversaw the religious worship of such 'abominations' and enjoyed a special status vis-à-vis kings. Such a class has often been inferred by analogy to the druids in Celtic societies, which were described by Caesar or by the later—admittedly ahistorical—accounts from Irish hagiography that posit a clear division of responsibilities between the legendary king Lóegaire and his druids. Caesar would have us believe that there were common cultic functions that cut across different communities in Gaul, the most conspicuous of which was the role accorded to druids as a priestly caste. Caesar believed that the druidic art originated in Britain and thereafter was adopted in Celtic Gaul.[3] Patrick says nothing of druids in Ireland, but one may nevertheless make an argument for the existence of pagan priests or for familiarity with pagan priests on the evidence of links between Ireland and cultic sites in Britain, where classical sources report the existence of druids. A site at Anglesey, which, according to Tacitus, the Romans destroyed in AD 61, offers a tangible link between cult practice in Britain and Ireland:[4] Irish artefacts that were recovered from the Llyn Cerrig Iron Age hoard of metalwork, dated between 150 BC and AD 60, are commonly interpreted as votive offerings that Irish pilgrims deposited in a sacred lake, which might have been under druidic oversight. But more on religion and druids in Ireland in chapter 4.

While contemporary political organisation continues to be a topic for speculation, we are on a more secure footing when it comes to some of the mundanities of life in Ireland, such as forms of settlement. Most settlements would have been constructed of wood—this at a time when Ireland was densely covered by forests—and only rarely left a trace. However, some were made of stone or exploited prominent features in the landscape and are therefore more conspicuous in the archaeological record. These tend to be high-status settlements, defensive settlements, or ritual sites with (one assumes) adjacent settlements. Of these categories, there are settlements that can be securely dated between the fifth century BC and the fifth century AD We find a few hillforts and promontory forts, which is the technical name for defensive structures on the edges of cliffs. There are around 250 crannogs, which are dwellings on small islands in lakes or other water features. And there are souterrains, underground passages that appear chiefly to have had a ritual purpose, but archaeologists often infer from them the existence of nearby habitation. Most hillforts tend to be early medieval, but there are some that can be dated earlier: Freestone Hill (County Kildare) is fourth century, Cathedral Hill (Downpatrick) starts in the Bronze Age and continues into the Iron Age, and Rathgall (County Wicklow) has late Bronze Age occupation as well as an Iron Age phase. Some hillforts continued to be occupied from the Iron Age into the early Middle Ages.

The indigenous archaeological evidence from Ireland can be complemented with material finds from Roman Britain that can shed light on the Irish situation and also with written sources by authors who observed Ireland from afar. The archaeological material that connects Ireland and Roman Britain is of great value. Roman objects from Britain and objects produced under Roman influence in Ireland are in evidence from the first to the fifth century, suggesting a continuous chain of (more or less) uninterrupted links. Sherds of late Roman amphorae (LR, also known as B-ware) have been excavated from twenty-seven sites throughout the island. Other types of Roman items found in Ireland consist of brooches and pins. Of the objects made under Roman influence, the Irish penannular brooch is the most elaborate (see Figure 4). Its style, which came to be associated with the Irish elite, could be the result of an arbitrary artistic preference or a conscious choice by the aristocracy in Ireland to mimic the trappings of its Romano-British neighbours—a

FIGURE 4. Irish penannular brooch: Tara brooch
at the National Museum of Ireland. Based on a
sketch by William Frederick Wakeman in
his *Handbook of Irish Antiquities: Pagan and
Christian*, 3rd ed. (Dublin, 1903), 360

kind of late antique equivalent of keeping up with the Joneses.
Roman artefacts deposited on political and territorial boundaries, such as a statuette of a *Lar*, a Roman guardian deity, found
in the Boyne River, may suggest that Roman notions of ritual
were incorporated into the symbolic idiom of political power
in Iron Age Ireland. These were, perhaps, thoughtful attempts
to respond to Roman culture in a more profound way or to in-
troduce elements from Roman cult into vernacular cosmology;
although it must be admitted that the exact significance of these
depositions is beyond our present understanding.

Roman coins have also been found in Ireland, dating from
the first to the fifth century. These may evidence trade, but also

raiding. The Ballinrees hoard of the late fourth or early fifth century, from Coleraine (County Derry), has been argued to have been obtained from Irish raids on Britain. It even features on one of its silver ingots the name Patricius, a common name at the time, in this case probably the owner of a private workshop that produced it. Approximately three centuries later, from the eighth century at the very latest, such precious metal objects, especially of silver (which was rare in pre-Viking Ireland), would be used as a form of currency, especially in exchanges between persons of high rank. Nevertheless, there have been attempts to argue that some of the surviving coins were used as a form of payment in earlier times, but these are inconclusive. For example, Jacqueline Cahill Wilson raised the possibility that coins from the late fourth- or early fifth-century Balline hoard (County Limerick) of Roman silver were the payment received by an Irish soldier in the Roman army. However, the most common explanation for the presence of Roman coins in Ireland in the early centuries of the first millennium—especially at sites with cultic associations—is that they were votive offerings or ritual depositions. Among the best-known sites at which supposed votive offerings have been found are the prehistoric monumental site of Newgrange (County Meath) and the Rath of the Synods in Tara (County Meath). Apart from Roman coins, the finds at Newgrange consist of jewellery dating between the third and fifth centuries. These are discussed further in chapter 4, on religious practice. At the Rath of the Synods, there are high-status goods such as second-century British and Gallic pottery, Roman glass, copper-alloy pins, rings, a grinding stone, and pebbles. This assemblage has recently been shown by Seán Daffy to have parallels with shrines in Roman Britain, reinforcing their Roman connection.

As for trading activity, some findings may point in this direction, although the scale of trading appears to have been small, and the surviving evidence meagre: fifth-century potsherds from amphorae that might have contained wine or olive oil. What the Irish traded in return for these goods is unknown, and although the material evidence for trading is rather patchy, we know that trading between Britain and Ireland must have taken place as early as the first century AD, for Tacitus says that 'thanks to commercial contacts we know most of its [Ireland's] harbours and approaches.'[5] Some borrowings into Irish from Latin also appear to bear testimony of commercial activity with the empire, as noted by (among others) Jean-Michel Picard: *fín*, from Latin *vinum* (wine); *screpul*, from Latin *scripulum* (scruple, which is one-twenty-fourth of an imperial ounce); *ampaill*, from Latin *ampula* (flask); and *libern*, from Latin *liburna* (gallery or ship). Although it stands to reason that the trading activity that resulted in some of these borrowings (at least) took place directly with Britain, it cannot be ruled out that other provinces of the empire could have been involved.

Since the trade—insofar as it is attested—appears to have been mainly in high-status goods, one assumes that it was localised and infrequent, rather than regular and intensive. It cannot be said, for example, that Irish peasants were regularly cultivating crops for export to a market in Roman Britain, but some commodities from Ireland must nevertheless have been gathered on an ad hoc basis to be exchanged for the Roman imports. One such commodity, which would have been fitting for elite-focused trade, is slaves. There are only two contemporary attestations of slaving on Irish soil, both of which are known, thanks to Patrick. The first is of slave women who underwent conversion and, consequently, are said to have suffered tribulations, perhaps owing to their masters' objections, although this is not explicitly stated.[6] The second is of the exploits of Coroticus's war band. This is not so much a case of 'exporting' slaves but rather, to put it crudely, one of 'stealing' people. The international exchange of valuable objects and goods could happen for reasons other than trade—for example, as the result of ceremonial gift exchange among aristocrats. Johnston has recently raised this possibility in connection with what appears to be a form of gift exchange that Patrick mentions in the *Confessio*.[7] I shall return to the matter of reciprocal gift giving later in this chapter.

A Roman import of another kind, to which no monetary value can be attached, is literacy. The earliest expression of Irish literacy is to be found in the ogam inscription. Inscriptions in ogam rendered the Irish language, but the script was influenced by Latin, a language that can be assumed to have reached Ireland from Roman Britain. The majority of ogam inscriptions are commemorative. There are over three hundred surviving inscriptions from Ireland, with new inscriptions continuing to come to light. Around forty inscriptions are found in Wales, and a handful in Argyll, the Isle of Man, Devon, and Cornwall, in places where there were Irish settlements. The inscriptions from Ireland stand out not only for their large number but also for the fact that nearly all are exclusively in the vernacular. By contrast, inscriptions in Britain tend to be bilingual, comprising both Latin and the vernacular. The dating of the earliest inscriptions continues to be a vexed issue. Traditionally, the earliest inscriptions have been dated (mainly on linguistic grounds) to the fifth century, though a date in the late fourth for some of them has also been envisaged. They are, however, generally believed to be a phenomenon of the Christian era. This view has been challenged in a recent study by Anthony Harvey, who argues that ogam script need not necessarily be thought of as a fourth- or fifth-century development that came with the establishment of an early church in Ireland. Rather, he believes that on linguistic grounds it is possible to backdate the script as early as the second century AD, before any churches are known to have existed in Ireland, but at a time when Roman influence from the neighbouring island is already attested by material finds.

Roman script arguably came into use in Ireland at a somewhat later date than ogam. It has been argued by the doyen of palaeography, the late Bernhard Bischoff, that it was the likes of missionaries such as Patrick and Palladius who were the first to apply script, presumably of a Roman variety, to other types of writing media besides inscriptions on stones. In Bischoff's view, the movement of script cannot be separated from the movement of literate individuals. But despite general agreement that the script used in Ireland is derived from Roman uncial (but not cursive), the precise way in which insular script developed continues to be debated among palaeographers. The oldest surviving examples of uncial (more precisely Insular half uncial) to survive from Ireland date from the sixth and seventh centuries and are therefore later than the period that concerns us. These are the Springmount Bog wax tablets (containing extracts from the Psalms), the Usserianus Primus (a Gospel book), and the Cathach (a psalter). As Dáibhí Ó Cróinín pointed out, these texts appear to be consistent with Continental practice and therefore testify to an active connection with literate culture in Continental Europe.

Contacts between Roman Britain and Ireland of the kind that have been surveyed here so far are of the utmost importance for understanding the cultural changes that Ireland was undergoing at the time of Patrick's arrival. And indeed, Patrick himself was an agent of change in a region that has recently been styled by Johnston a 'frontier zone' of the empire. As a frontier zone, Ireland attracted attention from classical authors who had no firsthand experience of it. Their accounts tend to be brief and not always reliable descriptions of the geography,

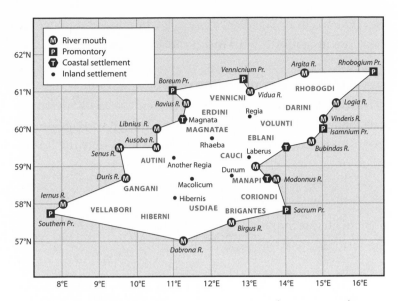

FIGURE 5. Reconstruction of Ptolemy's map of Ireland (2nd century AD), after R. Darcy and W. Flynn, *Irish Geography* 41 (2008): 51. Copyright Bob Darcy

flora, and fauna of the island, although Ptolemy (fl. 2nd century AD) does list names of places and sixteen population groups, six of which can be identified by reference to later analogues, and others arguably had a contemporary presence beyond the island, like the Brigantes, who are said to have straddled Ireland and Britain (see Figure 1).[8] The earliest datable reference to Ireland in antiquity, however, is by Julius Caesar (d. 44 BC), who invaded Britain in 55 BC and 54 BC but did not establish a settlement. In his Gallic War (*De Bello Gallico*) 5.13, he gives a brief geographical account in the context of a wider discussion of the island of Britain. The name he used for Ireland, Hibernia, was to become its common Latin appellation throughout late antiquity and the Middle Ages, although the prevalent Latin name for its people would remain Scotti. Caesar himself never set foot in Ireland, nor is he likely to have even gauged it with his own eyes, for so far as we know he did not reach the west coast of Britain. His information on Ireland is, therefore, derivative and is dependent mostly on the works of classical geographers.

Another early geographical overview of Ireland, by Strabo, contains the earliest ethnographic remarks on the inhabitants of Ireland, who are depicted in rather unflattering terms:

> Besides some small islands round about Britain, there is also a large island, *Hierne*, which stretches parallel to Britain on the north, its breadth being greater than its length. Concerning this island I have nothing certain to tell, except that its inhabitants are more savage than the Britons, since they are man-eaters as well as heavy eaters, and since, further, they count it an honourable thing, when their fathers die, to devour them, and openly to have intercourse, not only with the other women, but also with their mothers and sisters; but I am saying this only with the understanding that I have no trustworthy witnesses for it; and yet, as for the matter of man-eating, that is said to be a custom of the Scythians also, and, in cases of necessity forced by sieges, the Celts, the Iberians, and several other peoples are said to have practised it.[9]

The denigration of peoples on the fringes of Greek and Roman civilization was not uncommon among antique and late antique authors, from Herodotus (d. ca. 425 BC) to Ammianus Marcellinus (d. ca. AD 400). The character of such peoples was contrasted with the trappings of a civilised society in such respects as their appearance, dietary habits, sexual behaviour, morality, and practice of religion or lack thereof. These contrasts were topoi, or recurring clichés that audiences came to expect when hearing tales about remote cultures. Strabo's ethnographic caricature is a good example of comparisons that were often drawn with the 'Scythians', which became a catchall name for the quintessential antique and late antique 'Other'. As for the Irish specifically, some of the forms of behaviour that Strabo attributed to them went on to become stereotypes that continued to haunt them for centuries. Thus, one finds the charge of cannibalism repeated in Jerome's *Adversus Jovinianum* 2.7, where the Irish are further denounced for sexual impropriety on account of an alleged custom of sharing women among men, in the spirit of Plato's Republic. And in Jerome's Letter 69 to Oceanus, we find the Irish (Scotti) mentioned alongside the Attacotti in adhering to Plato's Republic by (again) sharing wives, but also raising children in common, which brings to mind the widespread Irish practice of fosterage (on which see chapter 6). Allegations of sexual misconduct, especially incest, and gluttony, usually in the form of excessive drinking, pursued the Irish both at home and abroad throughout the Middle Ages, from Saint Boniface in the eighth century to Gerald of Wales in the twelfth. Neither of these alleged faults seems to be grounded in any evidence, as Strabo himself admits. Rather, in the medieval period they were rolled out ad hoc to serve as rhetorical battering rams in local disputes, usually over church politics.

The next author to offer an account of Ireland that goes beyond a brief note on its size and proximity to Britain is Tacitus (d. ca. AD 118), whom we already met at the opening of this chapter. His knowledge of the region is more direct and comes from his father-in-law, the general Agricola, who served as governor of Britain between AD 77 and AD 84. His comments on Ireland are to be found in his biography of Agricola, within an episode concerning successful military campaigning in Britain:

> In the fifth year of campaigning he crossed in the leading ship and in repeated and successful battles reduced tribes up to that time unknown. He also manned with troops that part of the

British coast which faces Hibernia, in hope of future action rather than out of fear. For Hibernia, I believe, which lies between Britain and Hispania, and also commands the Gallic Sea, would unite, to their mutual advantage, the most effective portions of the Empire. The island compared with Britain is of smaller dimensions, but it is larger than the Mediterranean islands. In regard to soil, climate, and the character and ways of its inhabitants, it is not markedly different from Britain: thanks to commercial contacts we know most of its harbours and approaches. Agricola had given shelter to one of the petty kings whom faction had driven from home, and under the cloak of friendship [amicitia] held him in reserve to be used as opportunity offered. I have often heard my father-in-law say that with one legion and a fair contingent of auxiliaries Hibernia could be overpowered and held, and that the occupation would be useful with regard to Britain also, for so Roman troops would be everywhere and liberty would sink, so to speak, below the horizon.[10]

This quotation is especially interesting for the evidence it furnishes for direct contact between the Roman garrison in Britain and at least one Irish petty king. The king, as we have seen, is likely to have been the head of a *túath* who appears to have fallen out irredeemably with one or more of his domestic rivals. The term *amicitia*, which Tacitus uses to describe the relationship between the king and Agricola, is significant because of the technical sense it had in Roman political life, where it designated a relationship of dependency between an eminent man and his equals or subordinates (though usually the latter). It suggests that a formal relationship of client-patron existed between the general and the king. A client-patron relationship would have rendered the client a lesser member of the patron's extended family (*gens*) and entailed mutual obligations, such as protection, hospitality, and the vouching for each other in legal cases. Tacitus seems to imply that the two did not exercise *amicitia* between them in the full sense of the word but rather had a quasi-*amicitia*, perhaps because the Irish king was not a Roman citizen. This relationship is indicative of the international alliances and treatises that would have enabled political agreements to be reached with certain leaders in Ireland, like the agreement that Ammianus—writing in the late fifth century—reports was broken in 367 and resulted in the 'barbarian conspiracy' that brought about a concentrated attack on Britain by the Irish and Picts (see chapter 1, on Patrick's Britain).

From these secondhand reports, we return to our only contemporary eyewitness account of Ireland, Patrick's, and follow the sequence of events in the narrative of his sojourns there. The first mention of Ireland in the *Confessio* is in relation to Patrick's captivity. After being taken captive from Britain, he says, he was made to serve a master, probably near the Wood of Voclut (in present-day County Mayo), for six years: 'But after I reached Ireland, well, I pastured the flocks every day and I used to pray many times a day. . . . I would even stay in the forests and on the mountain and would wake to pray before dawn in all weathers. . . . I ran away and abandoned the man with whom I had been for six years'.[11]

Here Patrick appears to be describing the cycle of shepherding livestock, presumably cattle or sheep, in both winter and summer. Grazing during the summer would have taken place on hills, because they were wetter and because it was necessary to allow the grazing fields, which were sometimes fenced, nearer the home of the owner to recover in preparation for the winter months. It also allowed for the cultivated lands to be freed from livestock until crops were harvested. Grazing in the uplands, at least in early medieval times, took place by mutual consent between all those who made use of them, underscoring the contemporary importance of cooperation and reciprocity in farming communities.

Apart from acquiring shepherding experience, during his stay in Ireland, Patrick would undoubtedly have learned to speak the Irish language, a skill that would serve him well when he returned to Ireland later in life to preach the Christian faith. In Patrick's day the language spoken in Ireland was Q-Celtic, to use the linguistic jargon. To put it crudely, this was character-ised by the absence of the consonant *p*, which, in the case of words borrowed from other languages, could be omitted alto-gether or substituted by *q*. The consonant *p* only became inte-grated into the pronunciation of the Irish language by the sixth century. But before circa 500, one could identify significant phonetic changes to Latin loanwords. Among the more famous are the transformations of Latin *presbyter* into Old Irish *crui-mther* (via British Latin *premiter*), Latin *pascha* into Old Irish *cásc*, and Latin *planta* into Old Irish *clann*, which, after going through various iterations, came to be used in the now-familiar sense of 'clan'. During the Q-Celtic phase, Patrick's own name would have been pronounced 'Cothriche' or 'Cothairche'. The apparent alliteration with the name of the British captor of Pat-rick's newly converted, Coroticus, is intriguing, but it is unlikely to be more than a coincidence.

Whether or not Patrick was in fact taken captive and enslaved near the Wood of Voclut, as he himself says (for doubts, see chapter 3), there is no reason to doubt that Ireland did have slaves.[12] Slavery is further mentioned in his description of the harsh fate reserved to newly converted women who were in bonds.[13] Slave raids were also taking place on Irish soil, with captives being taken overseas, as the Letter attests. The outrage that Patrick expressed at seeing his newly converted abducted led him to excommunicate their captor, Coroticus, who was himself a Christian. Nevertheless, Patrick's membership in the church did not conflict with the prospect of owning slaves, nor does he appear to have objected to slave trafficking in principle (see chapter 1, on the Romano-British background).

Next in his narrative we are told that after six years, during which he served his master and grew more steadfast in the faith, Patrick returned to Britain, where he remained for a number of years. He then went to Ireland again, for what was to be the core period of his mission. It is from Patrick's description of this period that we gain most of our information about society, politics, and religion in contemporary Ireland. Let us take a closer look.

On his return to Ireland, Patrick immediately applied himself to missionary work, baptising thousands and ordaining clerics, but also enduring insults from unbelievers (*increduli*) while he was preaching.[14] He also suffered persecution and imprisonment, but these are mentioned almost in passing without further detail.[15] Apart from the unremitting hardships that befell him, Patrick also had to contend with what he perceived to be a challenge that threatened his reputation for meekness— namely, gifts that were being offered to him, which he says he turned down. These were lavished on him by people he met on his travels, as well as by female followers who left jewellery for him on the altar.[16] Moreover, he insists that he never received payment in exchange for baptism, which may be a response to rumours that he had.[17]

Quite apart from being offered gifts, Patrick says that he himself gave gifts to others. There were kings to whom he occasionally gave gifts, and he also rewarded their sons who travelled with him for protection: 'From time to time I gave presents to the kings, quite apart from the payments I made to their sons who travel with me'.[18] In a discussion of gifts in the *Confessio*, Thomas Charles-Edwards remarks that 'in part Patrick emphasised his attitude to gifts because of the accusation that he had gone to Ireland in the hope of enriching himself', but he regards this as only half the story, for he goes on to consider gift giving in light of later evidence from early medieval Ireland. When viewed from this (later) early medieval perspective, the gift giving that Patrick describes can be interpreted in a culturally specific context. Charles-Edwards draws attention to descriptions of eighth- and ninth-century overkings who are said to have behaved in the same way: they would give gifts but, as Patrick testifies regarding himself, they would refuse to accept gifts. By giving more than they received, they were asserting their wealth, status, and power. This practice is not without its parallels in other contemporary societies in Europe and beyond. The giving of gifts could be a way to negotiate relationships of power and friendship, especially during antiquity and the Middle Ages, when gift exchanges were enacted in formalised public performances. For example, by publicly bestowing gifts on Emperor Charlemagne on special occasions (especially an annual assembly in May), nobles would try to outdo each other's generosity and consequently be in a position to gain bigger favours in return. And the same might have been true of Patrick: to give a gift was also *to be seen* to give a gift; it was a way of exhibiting his lofty status and advertising to others that he could claim (or was due) privileges and entitlements.

We ought also to remember that on a more mundane level (as already noted), the gifts he gave ensured that, as a foreigner in his adoptive land with no kin to vouch for him, Patrick could engage native dignitaries on his side to secure his protection while he travelled. The exact nature and level of Patrick's status as foreigner have invited a fair bit of speculation from scholars.

In developing an argument first put forward by Charles-Edwards, Clare Stancliffe highlighted the potential for contradictory interpretations of Patrick's position when viewed through the (admittedly retrospectively) prism of early medieval Irish law. On the one hand, he might have been perceived as being of equal status to a king or chief poet (*ollam*) since he was seen riding with a princely retinue, but on the other hand, the reason he needed that retinue in the first place was that he did not really possess high status or even status at all. Rather, he might have been considered a *cú glas* (grey dog or wolf)—that is, an alien with no independent legal status whose survival and wellbeing depended on the goodwill of kings. The ambiguity of Patrick's situation is illustrated by the revelation that on one occasion his aristocratic minders threatened to kill him and his companions and snatched from them everything that they had. As he put it, 'They arrested me and my companions and that day were extremely eager to kill me, but my time had not yet come; they seized everything that they found on us and put me in irons'.[19]

The ordeal concludes with their being freed after fourteen days and having their possessions restored to them. Frustratingly, nothing more is said of this incident or its significance. Instead, Patrick's narrative continues with payments he had to make to various judges, to whom he gave the 'price of fifteen men', though it is not made clear what exactly he hoped to receive in return: 'But you know from experience how much I have paid to those who administered justice in all the regions, whom I was in the habit of visiting. I reckon that I must have dispensed to them the price of fifteen men at least, so that you may enjoy me and I always enjoy you in God. I have no regrets. Indeed, I am not satisfied with that. I still spend and will spend more'.[20]

The 'price of fifteen men' may be a reference to actual slaves, or a price equal to the value of fifteen slaves, or perhaps the price of redeeming fifteen men from captivity. Alternatively, Patrick may be alluding to what is known from early medieval Irish sources as *lóg n-enech* (honour price, literally 'price of a face'). This was the Irish equivalent of the Frankish *wergeld*, the Anglo-Saxon *leodgeld*, and the Welsh *wynebwerth*. Other Old Irish words used for honour price were *díre* and *eneclann*. All persons of independent legal status were assigned a *lóg n-enech* based on their wealth, political status, or ecclesiastical rank. The honour price was a measure of legal status, and as a consequence, it determined one's capacity to make and guarantee contracts, to testify, and to judge. It also determined the level and type of compensation for which one was entitled for offences committed against one's own person, property, kin, or clientele. Whatever exactly Patrick meant by this expression, it clearly signifies that he commanded considerable wealth.

If Patrick could make payments, the question therefore arises as to what kind of wealth Patrick could have brought with him from Britain to Ireland that would allow him to reward kings and judges. One might guess silver, which—as we have seen earlier—is also known to have been used to make payments to and by members of the elite, but our earliest evidence for this practice is from the early Middle Ages.

Another form of wealth of which Patrick could have been in possession in Ireland is slaves. His family in Britain owned slaves, and the ones who were not 'harried' by the raiders who are said to have taken him captive may have been restored to him upon his return to Britain. Alternatively, if we doubt that Patrick was taken captive (see chapters 1 and 3), then perhaps he himself had taken the family slaves from Britain at the time of his initial departure. Slaves were in fact a convenient form of movable property for wealthy travellers like Patrick. Not only could they have been ferried across the Irish Sea, but, as we have seen in the mention of converted slave women, there certainly was a market for them in Ireland, whose nonmonetary economy would also have rendered them a means of accumulating wealth. Their importance as a commodity is attested by the use of the Old Irish term *cumal* (slave woman) to denote a unit of value, roughly the worth of three milch cows. And as we already know, Patrick's ecclesiastical status would not have debarred him from owning slaves, just as his father and grandfather—both clerics—owned slaves.

In participating in gift exchange (albeit one-sided, if we take his word), Patrick was going through the motions of a social give-and-take that brought him deeper into the fold of his host society. But another activity in which he engaged, missionary work, for which he is most famous, could have led in the opposite direction. It ran the risk of alienating his hosts because religious conversion posed a threat to long-held religious beliefs and could also be perceived to undermine various conceptions of sacral kingship that protected the status of kings. His mention of conversion among sons and daughters of kings but not the kings themselves suggests that the fathers clung to their ancestral beliefs, the reasons for which are discussed in chapter 5, on Patrick's mission. Also, Patrick's depiction of daughters becoming nuns despite their parents' wishes shows clearly that his mission sometimes met with disapproval.[21] Possibly, the fathers objected because unmarried daughters could not contribute to expanding and reinforcing the family's ties with other families. Marriage, like gift giving, was a crucial form of maintaining the integrity of the social fabric in a society in which ties of kinship represented the strongest bonds of loyalty and formed the building blocks of identity. But the fathers may have had other reasons to object that were more mundane: the making of a nun would sometimes have required the kin to hand over an endowment to the church for her upkeep. Sadly, for the late antique period we have no evidence for attitudes in Ireland towards handing over family members or property to the church. However, by the early Middle Ages we are able to gauge certain ecclesiastical attitudes towards these issues. One of the best sources on these matters is the late seventh- or early eighth-century *Hibernensis*, a text that is usually classified as canon law. In it one finds examples of different circumstances in which individuals, both men and women, could join the monastic life. There are, for example, poor children, who are handed over to the church because their parents lack the means to raise them. These are said to become the slaves (*servi*) of the church, unless their relatives can afford to redeem them: 'A child who has been brought to the church is its slave, unless he is redeemed through payment'.[22] And we also find mention of wealthier children or young adults who are given over with an endowment to a church (the distinction between church and monastery in Ireland at this time is rather fuzzy). These, who are often called oblates in medieval times, could enjoy special status, sometimes corresponding to the rate of the endowment that their kin offered. Indeed, receiving child oblates was one of the church's main forms of income at a time when the distribution of land usually happened within a single kin group. The system that ensured that land was divided exclusively among members of the kin placed the church at a disadvantage because, strictly speaking, the church was not a member of any kin and could therefore not be the beneficiary of land allocations. A thesis by the anthropologist Jack Goody, which was made famous in his *Development of the Family and Marriage in Europe* (1983), argued that the medieval church's rule of allowing marriage only between those separated by more than six degrees (that is, beyond second cousins) was meant to force kin groups to alienate land.

As the 'Goody thesis' goes, the church was keen to curb the tendency of families to encourage marriage between first or second cousins for the purpose of preserving property within the kin. In Ireland, for example, before the eighth century, the Irish kin group consisted of all the descendants from a great-grandfather. Such a kin group was known in Irish as *derbfine*. Hence, second cousins would count as members of one's own kin group. But after the eighth century, Irish sources reveal a shift in the conception of kinship, such that more importance was given to the kin group consisting of three generations, the *gelfine*, which extended only as far as first cousins. Therefore, for the purpose of retaining property within the kin, it was necessary to marry one's first cousin. The second cousin would already count as a member of a different kin, with the consequence that property brought into a marriage between second cousins would be considered to be alienated outside the kin. Kin groups were reluctant to accept this disadvantageous scenario, but the church encouraged it and began to oppose marriages between first and second cousins. By the year 585 the forbidden degrees of separation received the sanction of canon law, when a church council at Auxerre declared marriages to second cousins incestuous.[23] When interpreted in the context of the Goody thesis, legislation such as this can be understood to facilitate the alienation of the kin's property and eventually set in motion a wider socioeconomic process that would break the kin's monopoly over land. In this way the church—and not just kin members—could become a beneficiary for receiving land. The Goody thesis has a lot to recommend it, but it also has its weaknesses, which have led it to be refined over the years in light of progress in medieval studies. In particular, it has been pointed out that church and kin were not always starkly set apart, and to regard them as separate entities is somewhat of a false dichotomy. As an alternative to the Goody thesis, a model that historians often use to explain how church and kin could coexist and reconcile their ostensible competition over landed properties is the 'proprietary church'. This model describes a system that enabled land to be alienated to the church while at the same time allowing the founding kin to retain a stake in it—for example, by reserving the right to appoint the head of the church. This was a convenient way to eat the cake and have it too: the church got something, so did the kin, and the two could appear to maintain a certain degree of separateness but at the same time exercise a form of 'subtle symbiosis'. Family churches were common throughout Europe, but in Ireland, families' control over churches (broadly defined) has been argued by the most recent authoritative study of proprietary churches, by Susan Wood, to have been more direct: 'The outcome was hereditary abbacies or coarbships [headships of churches] more tenacious than anywhere else in the West. . . . These were "family monasteries" in the sense that the abbacy belonged to one or more linked lineages; not in the sense that any outside lord or lay family controlled the office and through it the monastery's resources of revenue and influence'. To what extent the germ of this model of family churches was planted as early as Patrick's time is impossible to say with certainty, although Patrick's comment about the reluctance of parents to allow their daughters to become nuns may imply some degree of anxiety about the loss of kin property and its transference to the church. Consequently, kindreds might have sought ways to overcome the risk of property loss, and one such way was the establishment of family churches, which, indeed, proliferated in early medieval Ireland.

Whatever innovations Patrick's new religion might have introduced or inspired in strategies of landholding, his direct influence on Irish social mores could only last for so long. His activities eventually came to an end with his death at an unknown age. Ireland, so far as we can tell, was where he died. The two conflicting obits for Patrick in the Irish annals, 457 and 493, have already been mentioned in the previous chapter. The two dates, on the first of which the annals refer to Patrick as 'Patrick Senior' (Sen-Phátraic/Senex Patricius), may reflect an early tradition according to which there were two Patricks. The earliest written witness to this tradition is to be found in Patrick's seventh-century hagiography, which identified one Patrick with the protagonist of the *Confessio* and the other with Palladius, the Roman deacon who, in 431, was dispatched to a Christian community in Ireland by Pope Celestine. In the Book of Armagh we read the following paraphrase of an early fifth-century chronicle entry (by Prosper of Aquitaine) concerning Pope Celestine's consecration of Palladius as first bishop of the Irish: 'In the thirteenth year of the emperor Theodosius bishop Patricius is sent by bishop Celestine, the pope of Rome, for the teaching of the Scots. This Celestine was the forty-fifth bishop, beginning from Peter the apostle, in the city of Rome. Bishop Palladius is sent first, who was named Patricius with another name, who suffered martyrdom at the hands of the Scots, as is the tradition of the holy men of old. Then Patricius is sent as second bishop by the angel Victor and by Pope Celestine: he was believed by all Ireland, and baptised almost all of it'.[24]

This suggestion, that one of the two Patricks was in fact a byname for Palladius, might have been, as David Dumville holds, a way of opposing a tradition concerning 'two Patricks' by maintaining, instead, that it resulted in a conflation of Palladius with Patrick. It was therefore not the Book of Armagh that sparked this tradition.

Palladius, on whom more in chapter 5, on the mission, has always been an inconvenience for the followers and promoters of Patrick's cult because, unlike Patrick, he was sent to Ireland with Rome's blessing and was consecrated bishop by the highest canonical authority. Patrick's consecration, on the other hand, cannot even be verified. The 'two Patricks' tradition reflected in the Book of Armagh was a way of attempting to reconcile—albeit rather awkwardly—what were seen as conflicting accounts of the conversion of Ireland—through Palladius's mission and through Patrick's mission—the discrepancies of which threatened to diminish Patrick's role as the primary instigator of Christianity in Ireland. The curious possibility that there were indeed two Patricks was debated vigorously in the 1940s and 1950s, culminating in what one of Patrick's more accomplished translators, Allan B. E. Hood, described as a 'mass of rubbish that has been piled about the memory of Patrick'. The most cogent case for two Patricks has been made by Thomas O'Rahilly, but he regarded the two only as folkloric or literary creations. His paper *The Two Patricks: A Lecture on the History of Christianity in Fifth-Century Ireland* (1942) argued that hagiographical texts in the Book of Armagh conflated Palladius, who might have been known as Patricius Palladius, with Patrick, such that the two missionaries became one. This came under sustained criticism by some historians who misunderstood the nuances of his argument and others who were reluctant to acknowledge the fanciful nature of certain medieval accounts that they cherished. But more sceptical historians, like Daniel Binchy, were prepared to continence O'Rahilly's hypothesis and came out strongly against credulity and the tendency to artificially impose consistency despite obvious contradictions across texts. In 1962 he wrote that 'if the theory of the two Patricks is a heresy, it is at least a very ancient heresy.... O'Rahilly was merely the latest of a long line of scholars to have held this view'. The different scholars who formed this 'long line' had different things in mind when they proposed that there were two Patricks, and Binchy rightly drew a distinction between theories based on hagiography (and on an epithet from the Martyrology of Óengus interpolated in Patrick's annalistic obit in 457), which he believed to have occasionally combined two figures, and theories based on contemporary historical evidence, which shows Patrick and Palladius to have been separate personalities. In 'Patrick and his biographers: Ancient and modern', Binchy aimed to redress speculative theories, but also to reassess the evidence and question the motivations of certain scholars, some of whom were said to have been actuated by nothing other than animosity towards one another. Although that paper did not bring the speculative debates to a definitive end—and, indeed, this very book offers a measure of speculative arguments that are flagged as such—it concluded with an edifying observation: 'No historian, however, will be prepared to accept a theory merely because it solves problems that have hitherto baffled other scholars; indeed, he must closely examine the possibility that the theory has been invented precisely in order to solve the problems. Hence, while I think O'Rahilly's solution of the Patrician question is more coherent and more credible than anything that has hitherto emanated from the orthodox school, I am not prepared to go farther than [Osborn] Bergin in taking it to be the "least improbable" of the theories which at present hold the field'. These compelling words resonate as strongly today, and the present study, it is hoped, is just as successful in attaining the coveted status of 'least improbable'.

To conclude, our knowledge of the political and social circumstances of Ireland in Patrick's time is rather sketchy and depends almost exclusively on his own testimony, which cannot be corroborated. Archaeology provides some reprieve, but—as we have seen—its interpretation, especially in light of Continental comparanda, can be quite controversial. Patrick's description of his own interaction with the Irish elite and with ordinary people suggests that he kept company primarily with those of higher social standing, who were on a par with his. And he gives a fascinating glimpse into some of the customs and etiquette of Ireland's nobles. Difficulties remain in establishing exactly what his source of wealth was and how he was able to maintain it when he crossed over to Ireland. Slaves were suggested as a likely possibility. The rumours that (as Charles-Edwards put it) 'he had gone to Ireland in the hope of enriching himself' continually haunted him, and they raise important questions for us as historians, especially in regard to the matter of his purported captivity and the overall aims of his operations in Ireland.

Notes

1. Tacitus, *Agricola* § 24, trans. M. Hutton (Cambridge, MA, 1914).

2. *Confessio* § 41.

3. Caesar, *De Bello Gallico* 6.13, in *Caesar: The Gallic War*, trans. H. J. Edwards (London, 1917), 336.

4. Tacitus, *Annales* 14.30, trans. John Jackson (Cambridge, MA, 1937).

5. Tacitus, *Agricola* § 24, trans. Hutton; I modified the translation slightly.

6. *Confessio* § 42.

7. *Confessio* §§ 37, 49, 52.

8. Pliny, *Geographia* 2.1, 2.2, ed. Alfred Stückelberger and Gerd Graßhoff, *Klaudios Ptolemaios, Handbuch der Geographie: griechisch–deutsch; Einleitung, Text und Übersetzung, Index* (Basel, 2006), 138–46.

9. Strabo, *Geography* 4.5.4, in *Strabo: Geography*, 8 vols., trans. H. L. Jones (Cambridge, MA, 1917–32), 2:258–62.

10. Tacitus, *Agricola* § 24, trans. Hutton; I modified the translation slightly.

11. *Confessio* §§ 16, 17, and see § 23 for the inference that Voclut was his alleged place of captivity.

12. *Confessio* §§ 10, 23.

13. *Confessio* § 42.

14. *Confessio* §§ 38, 50.

15. *Confessio* §§ 37, 38, 51.

16. *Confessio* §§ 37, 49.

17. *Confessio* § 50.

18. *Confessio* § 52.

19. *Confessio* § 52.

20. *Confessio* § 53.

21. *Confessio* § 42.

22. *Hibernensis* 42.24, ed. Wasserschleben, 168–69.

23. *Sinodus Autisioderensis* § 31, ed. C. de Clerq, CCSL 148 (Turnhout, 1963), 265–72, at 269.

24. Notes supplementary to Tírechán's *Collectanea*, 56.1–3, in *Patrician Texts in the Book of Armagh*, ed. and trans. L. Bieler (Dublin, 1979), 164–67.

3

Captivity

PATRICK'S CAPTIVITY IN IRELAND is probably the most familiar episode of his biography. Captured in Britain by raiders while still a youth, then labouring as a slave for six years in Ireland until finally escaping in the seventh, Patrick employs the motif of captivity as the main driver of the narrative of the *Confessio*, which reaches its climax with his conversion from a fledgling Christian to a committed believer. Apart from what he wants his readers to believe was his own personal experience with being servile, an experience that he frames in terms of a rite of passage, captivity as endured by others is a recurring theme in both the *Confessio* and the Letter to the Soldiers of Coroticus. In fact, in the Letter, which tells of the tragedy that befell Patrick's newly converted who were abducted by Coroticus, captivity is not only the central theme but also the reason for which the letter was written in the first place: the Letter is at once a response to the abduction, a public condemnation of Coroticus, and a call for the captives' release.

Incidents of captivity and enslavement would have been all too familiar to Patrick and his contemporaries. Slavery was ubiquitous in the Roman world, and more so from the end of the Republic and into the era of imperial government. From the mid- to late Republican period onwards, accelerated political expansion significantly increased the proportion of slaves in Roman society who poured into Roman cities and villas from the rural settlements and other civilian centres of vanquished foes. Often described as a slave economy, the Roman Empire relied heavily on slaves for its ongoing building projects, both grand and ordinary; for the maintenance of its ever-expanding cities; for agricultural work on the vast landed estates (sometimes called *latifundia*) of its wealthiest citizens, as well as the more modest estates of ordinary landowners; for domestic labour and craft production; and for specialised services offered by educated slaves—for example, teaching or bookkeeping. The Romans were in no way unusual in relying heavily on slaves, who were a significant part of the workforce of every society in the ancient world. Nevertheless, proper records of slave management as well as laws governing slavery are known only from literate societies, like the Israelite society of the Old Testament, whose legislation on slavery (Hebrew *avdut*) describes a range of ways in which one could become a slave: from being captured in war to willingly enslaving oneself to cover a debt. On the other hand, societies that were predominantly illiterate, of the kind that Patrick encountered in Ireland, left no record of the circumstances in which people could be enslaved, the only exception in the present case being Patrick's own works. These works, we ought to remember, are the only surviving texts to contain a purported eyewitness account of contemporary Ireland, and their subjective testimony can therefore not be corroborated.

We are nevertheless fortunate to possess a good deal of documentation from Ireland concerning servitude and social status, but the earliest of these documents date from around the seventh century, two centuries or so after Patrick's time. Most prominent among them are normative sources consisting of laws and jurisprudence, some of which are assumed to reflect traditions that go back centuries. But how faithfully they depict earlier traditions and to what extent the traditions themselves preserve practices from as early as Patrick's own time, we simply don't know. Unlike other societies from this period, which were in the process of extricating themselves from the Roman Empire or being ejected from it, Ireland had never been affected by Roman conceptions of servitude or by Roman laws governing servitude. Historians would therefore place it outside the grand narrative of what Marc Bloch famously saw as the transition from a Roman economy fuelled by slaves to what may be labelled simply an economy with slaves in the Middle Ages. The culmination of this transition is usually portrayed in the historiography as the emergence of the rent-paying tenant, or serf, who inhabited a status limbo between being free and servile. In Ireland certain normative texts describe people who held status of this kind—for example, the *fuidir*—but their existence owes nothing to changes that took place in former Roman territories. In the absence of Roman towns, lavish public spaces and buildings, roads, and luxurious villas, the economic and lifestyle differences between the haves and have-nots in Ireland would have been much less conspicuous to begin with. Social differentiation was flatter, closer to what Chris Wickham believes was a peasant-mode economy—that is, an economy in which the rates of exploitation of those at the bottom of the social ladder by those at the top were minimal, and so was the accumulation of wealth.

Patrick can be said to have floated between two worlds: he would have had experience of both the Roman (or early post-Roman) and the Irish forms of slavery, which constituted an expression of what recent scholarship tends to designate by the catchall term 'unfreedom'. Once more, we see him as a connecting agent between the *romanitas* of Britain and the very different conditions of late Iron Age Ireland. Let us now turn to Patrick's biographical account to explore the way in which captivity—both his own and that of others—is depicted, before examining the theme of captivity more generally in Patrick's thought world.

Patrick introduces the story of his captivity in Ireland in the very first chapter of his *Confessio*. He was taken, he says, with thousands of others from his hometown of Bannavem Taburniae when he was just sixteen and 'ignorant of the true God' (*Deum verum ignorabam*). The slavers, as he says in Letter § 10, 'harried the slaves of my father's house, male and female'. Being the son of a deacon and grandson of a priest, Patrick's admission of being ignorant of God is unlikely to mean that he was brought up a pagan; rather, it should be read in the context of the next passage, in which he attributes the slavers' attack to divine punishment for failing to observe God's commandments and for 'withdrawing from God' (*Deo recessimus*). This may, perhaps, be an allusion to apostasy that was spreading through his native region, and that might also have gripped him.

His years in captivity were spent drudgingly labouring as a shepherd, his only respite being unceasing prayer, through which he gradually discovered God and was at last deemed worthy of receiving His grace: 'And I was not worthy nor such that the Lord should grant His humble servant this, should, after such trials and hardships, after captivity and a long period of years, give me such grace in regard to that people [*in gentem illam tantam gratiam*]—something which I never hoped for nor imagined in the days of my youth. But after I reached Ireland, well, I pastured the flocks every day and I used to pray many times a day; more and more did my love of God and my fear of Him increase'.[1]

The expression *in gentem illam tantam gratiam* is ambiguous, perhaps deliberately so, because in this context *gratia*, the noun that one would be inclined to translate literally as 'grace', can also mean 'power' or 'influence'. The analogy between the power that Patrick was given over 'that people'—namely, the Irish—and the description of the pasturing of livestock may allow the reader to interpret this act of pasturing allegorically, as anticipating his eventual ascendency to the episcopate, with its oversight of the spiritual needs of the flock of believers. But before that moment could arrive, the youth Patrick had to continue serving his master until, one night, a mysterious voice revealed to him that a ship was being made ready to take him home to Britain.[2] Moved by this vision, he fled the master whom he had served for six years, travelling what he believes was a distance of two hundred Roman miles (*ducenta milia passus*) until he reached the ship. The ship was manned entirely by pagans (*gentes*), and the captain refused to allow him on board.[3] Disappointed, he was about to withdraw back to a hut in which he had been waiting but was suddenly called back by one of the sailors, who announced that the crew agreed to take him, after all. At this point the text continues with a curious passage: Patrick, we are told, being afraid of God (*propter timorem Dei*), refused to 'suck the breasts' (*reppuli sugere mamellas eorum*) of the pagan sailors. The somewhat unusual expectation that Patrick should have sucked the breasts of men offering him passage to Britain has attracted much interest from scholarship, which has tended to interpret it as a uniquely Irish ritual performed in deference to men of higher status, especially kings. Most recently, following the discovery in 2003 of two uncannily well-preserved Iron Age bodies in bogland in Counties Meath and Offaly, attention has been drawn to the fact that both men had their nipples removed. The two men—now known affectionately as Clonycavan Man and Oldcroghan Man—seem to have been aristocrats, as suggested by such diagnostic markers as manicured fingernails, smooth hands that show no signs of having performed manual labour, and a hair lotion containing imported resin. Nevertheless, both died by execution. Eamonn Kelly, of the National Museum of Ireland, where both bodies are displayed, speculates that the two were deposed kings and that the removal of their nipples, perhaps while they were still alive, rendered them ineligible for the kingship. However, there are no textual references to support this hypothesis, and the only written accounts of men suckling others occur in three episodes of medieval Irish hagiography, where we find holy men suckling infants. As tempting as it is to imagine Patrick resisting an idiosyncratic Irish pagan custom, it is more likely that he was not reporting an actual incident but alluding to a biblical verse, Isaiah 60:16: 'And you shall suck the milk of the gentiles, and you shall be nursed with the breasts of kings: and you shall know that I am the Lord your saviour, and your redeemer, the mighty one of Jacob' (*Et suges lac gentium, et mamilla regum lactaberis; et scies quia ego Dominus salvans te, et redemptor tuus, fortis Iacob*). The close correspondences in the Latin vocabulary corroborate the allusion to this verse, which—in its original context—anticipates a prophecy on the expansion of the nation of the Israelites. Given that prophecy, Patrick's invocation of the Isaian verse at this very point makes perfect sense because boarding the ship marks the beginning of a long voyage that will, eventually, lead him back to Ireland, where he will increase the flock of Christians. But in a more immediate context, Patrick's rejection of the 'nourishment' of their breasts and also of wild honey that they found, is to be contrasted with his offering them pigs, which miraculously materialised as he was urging them to convert (on which more anon).[4] This contrast, therefore, occasions a metaphor of conversion as spiritual nourishment. Such multiple layers of interpretation, as we have just encountered in the case of the allusion to the passage from Isaiah and, earlier, of the ambiguous meaning of *gratia*, are a reminder of what has been said in the introduction to the present book about the possibility that Patrick intended some parts of his *Confessio* to be understood literally, allegorically, or in both senses at once. In the case of the last quotation that we analysed, it is to be assumed that Patrick expected at least some of his readers—certainly the more learned among them—to be able to recognise the biblical allusion and appreciate his competence as an author who was capable of subtly weaving biblical references into his text.

As we rejoin Patrick and the sailors, we find them arriving in Britain after an uneventful three-day journey.[5] But their travails had only just begun. For twenty-eight days they were to wander through what Patrick describes as a wilderness (*desertum*) until they ran out of food, and, reaching the point of exhaustion, the sailors mocked Patrick for his unwavering faith in the Christian God despite their predicament. In a clear allusion to the taunting of Jonas by the ship's captain on the way to Tarshish (Jonas 1:6), the crew exclaimed, 'You say your god is great and all-powerful. Well, then, why can you not pray for us?' But unlike Jonas's invocation of God, Patrick's was requited at once and, miraculously, a herd of pigs materialised to sate the men, followed by a discovery of wild honey, a portion of which the men proceeded to sacrifice in thanksgiving to their gods. Despite his hunger, Patrick, ever the faithful Christian, held fast to the Apostles' injunction against eating sacrificed foodstuffs (Acts 15:29) and rejected the honey offered by the sailors, who clearly did not heed his call to convert. Avoiding the forbidden foods and remaining undaunted by the prospect of upsetting his companions, Patrick continued marching with the pagans for ten days.[6] Altogether, Patrick says, he spent sixty days with the sailors, a period that he describes as a second captivity.[7] It is difficult to see how Patrick reached the figure sixty, because three days' sailing plus twenty-eight days in the 'wilderness' plus the final ten days of journeying do not add up to sixty. It is possible, of course, that the figures are meant to be etiological rather than taken at face value, but if so, it is unclear what exactly Patrick wanted them to symbolise. If they *are* meant to be understood literally, then we must accept that—holy man though he was—Patrick was simply not very good at maths.

We are not told how he came to extricate himself from this 'second captivity' of his, save that his freedom was obtained through the grace of God. Once freed, he was able to reach his family, which welcomed him warmly. He must have stayed with his kin for quite some time, because when we next find him in dire straits, he is already a bishop, and by his own account aged forty-five.[8] At this point we find a hapless Patrick contending with an accusation that some of his elders brought against him, the details of which remain unknown and are only hinted at in rather opaque terms.[9] By his account, the accusation goes back to a sin he had committed as a boy of fifteen and later revealed in confidence to a friend, who betrayed his trust.[10] The consequences of this betrayal, as you will remember from the introduction and from chapter 1, were to set in motion a chain of events that led to his decision to return to Ireland, culminating in his greatest achievement: the fulfilment of his calling as missionary. These events do not need to be reiterated here, but I shall dip into them occasionally insofar as they contextualise the story of Patrick's captivity and his release from it. It is captivity in a more general sense that I wish to address now.

The captivity narrative raises a number of questions, all of them factual, and as Patrick himself says, his version was not believed by all:

But what is the point of excuses, however truthful, especially when linked with my audacity in aspiring now, in my old age, to what I did not acquire in my youth? For my sins prevented me from consolidating what I had previously read through. But who believes me even if I repeat what I have said before? As a youth, indeed almost a boy without any beard, I was taken captive, before I knew what to desire and what I ought to avoid. And so, then, today I am ashamed and terrified to expose my awkwardness, because, being inarticulate, I am unable to explain briefly what I mean, as my mind and spirit long and the inclination of my heart indicates.[11]

Being the linchpin for the entire biographical narrative, the captivity theme and the questions it raises for us—and undeniably raised for his contemporaries—deserve to be considered at length. But in order to address them properly, we must allow ourselves to be—of necessity—critical of Patrick's version of events and somewhat irreverent towards it, even challenging his integrity and his motives. However, given the doubts expressed by his own contemporaries, we will not be the first to do so. It is now our turn as readers to assume the role of the sceptic and ask whether we can take Patrick at his word when he says that he was taken captive, freed from captivity after six years, and subsequently restored to his former status in Britain. There are indeed reasons to doubt this account. The main reason is that a runaway slave was fair game for malefactors when travelling alone and is unlikely to have made it safely from the westernmost to the easternmost shores of Ireland without being discovered, captured, or killed. We have no cause to assume that captives in Ireland at that time fared any better than the chattel slaves of the Roman Empire or the oppressed base captives of the Irish law tracts of the early Middle Ages. A captive, being without family in a kin-based society such as Ireland, would have had no legal status of any kind unless someone could be found who could vouch on his behalf. A wandering captive of this kind would, essentially, be left to the mercy of strangers. Early medieval Irish law would have regarded Patrick as *cimbid* (captive or prisoner), with no legal rights and no recourse to legal protection against being recaptured or killed. It cannot be assumed that Patrick's master willingly freed him, in the first place because Patrick does not hint at this and second because early medieval Irish law on slavery (if we believe it had late antique roots) strongly discouraged masters from freeing slaves.

Patrick would not have enjoyed more protection under Roman law, which prevailed in Britain at least up to the time of his father's tenure as decurion, if not later. Roman law is known to have been harsh towards a Roman citizen who fell into the hands of enemies or hostile non-Romans, deeming him without legal rights and, to add insult to injury, revoking his Roman citizenship. There was no guarantee that such a person could be readmitted into Roman society or have his property restored to him. However, his chances of being rehabilitated would be significantly improved should he be able to demonstrate that he was taken away honourably—that he was not, for example, captured because of cowardly defection from battle or any other undignified behaviour. In order to be restored to his former position, he would also have had to prove that he returned to his homestead in the first possible instance that became available. Should all these conditions be fulfilled, he might achieve restitution to his (former) status and civic community through *postliminium*, a technical legal term roughly meaning 'restoration': 'All his rights are restored to him just as if he had not been captured. . . . If we have neither friendship nor *hospitium* with a particular people, nor a treaty made for the purpose of friendship, they are not precisely enemies, but that which passes from us into their hands becomes their property, and a free man of ours who is captured by them becomes their slave, and similarly if anything of theirs passes into our hands. In this case also [that is, not just in war-time] *postliminium* is granted'.[12]

In the late Roman Empire, as Kyle Harper has recently shown, *postliminium* was among the most common causes in disputes involving slaves—for example, in determining whether one should be given free status. The two-stage procedure that I have just outlined—of proving that there was no cowardice and that there was no unnecessary delay in returning home—is the best legal tactic of which Patrick could have availed himself on his return to Britain, assuming that he had recourse to Roman law or that he believed he should have. Otherwise, without *postliminium*, his long absence could have resulted in his remaining legally servile and his property being declared *res nullius* (no one's property), to which anyone could lay claim.

Patrick's *Confessio*, of course, says nothing of technical legal difficulties, but as modern historians we are free to infer them from reading his work in the context of contemporary Roman law and of early medieval Irish law (bearing in mind the caveats about the application of either law in Patrick's time). We may also remind ourselves of the eighth-century attempt, quoted in the introduction, to interpret the legalities of Patrick's release from captivity through the lens of another kind of law altogether: biblical law. In reading the *Confessio* with Mosaic law in mind, the glossator of the eighth-century verse text known as Fiacc's Hymn noted in Old Irish that Patrick's release after six years in captivity was 'after the manner of the little jubilee of the Hebrews' (*fo intamail na hiubile Ebreorum*), a reference to Exodus 21:2 (repeated in Jeremiah 34:14): 'If you buy a Hebrew servant, six years shall he serve you, but in the seventh he shall go free without owing anything'.[13] Can we push the glossator's line of thought further and argue that Patrick was trying to legitimise his escape by suggesting that it complied with the biblical law of the jubilee? This is not such a farfetched proposition, because Irish canon law of the early eighth century upheld a modified version of the Old Testament jubilee laws, which may already have been practiced in Ireland from an earlier date, perhaps introduced by Patrick himself.[14] If Patrick was seeking to rehabilitate his status and ingratiate himself with both the Irish and the Britons, then he seems to have left no legal stone unturned.

In sum, we have here a series of events that were doubted by some of Patrick's contemporaries, events that can be interpreted in more than one sense (the biblical allusion is a giveaway) and that invite a very particular kind of interpretation when they are read in conjunction with Roman law and Irish law (though we must make allowance for the caveat of anachronism). Ought we conclude from this that Patrick was offering a titivated account of the truth in an attempt to cover up for an unsavoury occurrence? Let us explore this question further.

The place to begin is by reiterating the undisputed fact that he was accused of a certain misdeed, as he himself admits. But what we have not considered in detail yet are the allegations, which he hints at, that he left Ireland for financial gain. Crucial to understanding his response to these claims is his declaration that he rejected gifts 'to safeguard myself carefully in everything so that they would not catch me out or the ministry of my service under some pretext of my dishonesty'.[15] As Thomas Charles-Edwards observes, 'In part Patrick emphasised his attitude to gifts because of the accusation that he had gone to Ireland in the hope of enriching himself'. In order to further deflect any criticism of misconduct, Patrick adds that he never asked for anything in return for the thousands of baptisms that he performed, nor for the ordinations of clergy, which did not earn him so much as 'the price of my shoe' (*pretium calciamenti mei*).[16] Rather, as we have already seen in chapter 2, he spent his own movable wealth to gain admittance into Irish society and to be allowed to baptise and ordain in different places.[17] We may also recall his disclosure, which has repeatedly surfaced in our discussion, that he paid the sons of kings to secure safe passage, and that he paid judges 'the price of fifteen men at least' (*non minimum quam pretium quindecim hominum*).[18] At last, this generosity, which he portrayed as the hallmark of his missionary activity, left him destitute, such that every day, by his own account, he expected to be killed or enslaved.[19]

These professions of selflessness will gain the sympathy of some readers, while others will put emotion aside and make allowance for the scepticism of Patrick's detractors. The sceptical reader may recall the discussion in chapter 1 concerning the possibility that Patrick, like his father, would have been loath to serve as a decurion and to carry out the more onerous obligations that this office demanded in the decades leading up to or immediately following 400, a period characterised by social, economic, and political unrest in Britain. At such times, certain curial obligations, like collecting and underwriting taxes, would have been difficult and even dangerous to discharge. Patrick might then have decided, perhaps with his father's consent and encouragement, that the best escape route open to him would be to establish himself in Ireland and, by so doing, ensure that the family wealth would not be depleted through the underwriting of taxes or malicious lawsuits. Patrick, who by his own admission was a wealthy man when he returned to Ireland as an adult, must have been able to take some movable wealth, although presumably much of the family's landed wealth could not have been liquidated and would have had to be left behind in Britain.

When contemplating this scenario in light of the stipulations of Roman law concerning *postliminium*, an alternative narrative—albeit speculative—presents itself. Arguably, by claiming to have been abducted around the age of sixteen in circumstances that were not dishonourable, Patrick could seek redress under the principle of *postliminium* upon his return to Britain, thereby enjoying the restoration of both his former free status and his landed property. This admittedly speculative interpretation can give us an idea of the manner in which Patrick's detractors framed their accusations against him. They could, perhaps, have said something along the following lines: Patrick left Ireland rather conveniently before his coming of age and being appointed decurion. By leaving, he would have eschewed all curial responsibilities, lived as a wealthy man in Ireland, and increased his wealth abroad until finally, by feigning righteousness, he was able to return to Britain and seek to regain his property under the protection of the law.

This, roughly, could have been the thrust of the argument of Patrick's antagonists. Patrick, of course, gives no details, save for noting the fact that his career was hounded by rumours of wrongdoing. He admits that there were rival narratives for his first, and perhaps second, departure to Ireland—his detractors' and his own—but he cannot be expected to have reiterated the case against him in detail. After all, he was caught up in a controversy and needed to defend his own position as effectively and righteously as possible, suppressing some of his opponents' arguments and dismissing others. Nevertheless, that Patrick did not entirely omit the controversy in which he was implicated suggests that it was widely known and could not have been passed over in silence. Whatever the actual facts were, it is impossible for the modern historian to recover them entirely, nor should she or he sit in judgement of a late antique personality. The most we can strive for is to insinuate a rival narrative by pointing out the gaps in his account, gaps that we may occasionally try to fill by drawing on the clues that he himself scatters throughout. This is indeed what we have done in our investigation so far, and we continue in this vein as we turn our attention to Patrick's depiction of the captivity of others.

When Patrick tells of the captivity of others rather than his own, then we appear to be on less ambiguous ground. The capture of a group of newly converted Irish men and women prompted him to write to Coroticus, their captor, demanding their release. The background to the Letter and aspects of its rhetorical ingenuity have already been considered in the introduction. Here I shall focus exclusively on the manner in which captivity is conceptualised and portrayed in the Letter in comparison with the *Confessio*.

The survival of the Letter and *Confessio* affords us the opportunity to examine the theme of captivity across different texts with different objectives: one is a public condemnation, while the other is an apologetic discourse with autobiographical undertones. Both mention Patrick's own captivity, but strangely the abduction of Patrick's converts is absent from the *Confessio*. There are, however, similarities. The first similarity is in the vocabulary that is used not for captivity but for freedom. Freedom was the state of which both he and his newly converted were said to have been robbed. In drawing an analogy between himself and his followers who were taken captive, Patrick makes it explicit that both he and they were born free:

I was freeborn [*ingenuus*] according to the flesh; my father was a decurion. I sold my nobility [*nobilitas*] in the interest of others, not that I am ashamed or regret it. . . .

. . . The church mourns and weeps for its sons and daughters who so far have not been put to the sword, but have been carried far off and transported to distant lands, where sin is rife, openly, grievously and shamelessly; and there free-born men [*ingenui*] have been sold, Christians reduced to slavery.[20]

Patrick was, therefore, 'freeborn' at the time in which he says that he was captured, and so were his converts. The Latin expression he chooses for asserting his and their freedom, *ingenuus* (plural *ingenui*), is a technical term taken from Roman law that would have been familiar to anyone with an experience of imperial legal culture, including Coroticus and his men, being, as they were, self-professed Roman citizens. Most importantly to the Roman mind, a freeborn Roman could not be enslaved, except in very unusual circumstances, none of which applied in this case (these consisted mainly of the selling of infants into slavery and various forms of punitive enslavement).

In both the Letter and the *Confessio*, captivity and conversion go hand in hand. In the Letter it is the converts who are abducted, and in the *Confessio* Patrick converts to a stricter form of religious observance while in captivity. But in the Letter, of course, the conversion is not simply a personal inner journey of reigniting a weak faith but rather a conversion from paganism to Christianity undertaken through a formal, ritualised process of being admitted into the communion of the church. The Letter describes how the converts, some murdered and some taken by the raiders, had just completed the process of conversion. Their foreheads are said to have still been marked with the chrism, a ritual oily mixture made from olive oil and balsam that was used as a complement for baptism in the admission of new members into the Christian community: 'On the day after the neophytes, clothed in white, had received the chrism—its fragrance was on their brows as they were butchered and put to the sword by those I have mentioned—I sent a letter. . . . The letter requested that they should return to us some of the spoils and baptised prisoners'.[21]

As the text says, the neophytes (that is, the newly converted) were still wearing white, the distinctive colour of the garments of catechumens—those who were in the process of being inducted into the new faith. The details here are significant and invite close attention. What they suggest is that the abduction took place during Easter, when catechumens were traditionally admitted as full members of the church. In either of Patrick's writings, this is the only time that Easter is implied, though as we shall see later when reading from the seventh-century hagiography from Armagh, Easter will eventually occupy centre stage in the cult of Saint Patrick.

Easter was a festival that brought together a peaceful crowd of worshippers who would be caught off guard if attacked. Such would have been the occasion on which Patrick's catechumens completed their process of induction, and on which they were assailed by their captors. From a narrative perspective, however, there is something almost too convenient in the juxtaposition of the abduction and murder to the date of Easter. Easter, after all, is the Christian feast that commemorates the ultimate act of sacrifice, Christ's crucifixion. Yet the coincidence in this case is unlikely to be a narrative invention, for there are certain comparanda that would support the proposition that Coroticus deliberately timed his attack to Easter, taking advantage of the prospect of easy prey. Slavers' attacks on Christian festivals are a nefarious tactic made famous by the quintessential slavers of later centuries, the Vikings, who had a penchant for raiding on holy days, such as saints' feast days or Easter. For example, the community of Kildare and the city of Nantes were both attacked on the Feast of Saint John (24 June, in 833 and 843, respectively), and Paris was attacked during Easter in 845. The attacks of the

Vikings and of Coroticus were nevertheless distinguished by one crucial difference: the Vikings were heathen, whereas Coroticus and his men were Christian. Instead of celebrating the chief festival of their own religion, they were desecrating it with the greatest irreverence. This irony was not lost on Patrick, who, in his condemnation of them, makes much out of Coroticus's disregard for fellow Christians. As Patrick saw it, Coroticus was prepared to sell the captives to Pictish pagan masters without batting an eyelid, while depriving the slain the glory of being crowned with a martyr's crown, which they would have received had they been put to the sword by heathens. Though not heathens themselves, Coroticus and his soldiers are depicted as the embodiment of evil, as demons in all but appearance: 'With my own hand I have written and composed these words to be given, delivered and sent to the soldiers of Coroticus. I do not say to my fellow citizens nor to fellow citizens of the holy Romans [*sancti Romani*], but to fellow citizens of demons, because of their evil actions. Like the enemy they live in death, as allies of Irish and of Picts and apostates. These blood-thirsty men are bloody with blood of innocent Christians.'[22]

It has been suggested by David Dumville and Richard Hanson on separate occasions that the epithet 'citizens of the holy Romans' can be understood metaphorically to mean something like 'devotees of the Roman saints', and therefore 'Christians'. By this interpretation, Patrick can be understood to be contesting the very Christian identity of the soldiers, and he continued to do so by comparing them with Irish (pagans) and Picts. For Patrick, the attack was a senseless, unprovoked act of aggression on a soft and arbitrary target—not the sort of behaviour that Patrick would expect of a good Christian. Coroticus was indifferent to the religion of the crowd he assaulted and showed no mercy towards the innocent. Those who survived the attack had nothing positive to look forward to as they were dragged into a life of slavery. Patrick was especially concerned about the baptised female captives. In numbering them among the 'free-born', Patrick might have intended to remind Coroticus that Roman law discouraged men from taking freeborn women as concubines.[23] It is doubtful, however, that Coroticus's soldiers, despite being self-professed Roman citizens, would have been deterred by indignation at an unlawful act. Nevertheless, for Patrick the implications of illegality would have been another tool in his rhetorical arsenal for asserting the women's rights. These vulnerable captive women, Patrick says, are the most ter-rorised among the captives, and they are being given away like prizes (*qui mulierculas baptizatas praemia distribuunt*).[24] What Patrick is likely to have been alluding to is the unenviable fate of women as chattel slaves who could also be sexually ex-ploited by their male masters, including for the purpose of bear-ing children. Early medieval Irish hagiography offers examples of such exploitation, and among the most vivid is an episode from Cogitosus's seventh-century Life of Saint Brigit in which a noble-man gives a brooch to a woman he fancies to keep as a deposit, but then steals it from her and throws it into the sea 'so that because she would not be able to return it she would become his slave-woman and thereafter he would use her in any way he wishes'.[25] In fact, Brigit herself is said to have been a child born to a master and his slave woman.[26] The additional 'utility' of slave women would have increased their value in relation to ordi-nary unskilled male slaves such that, as we have already seen in the previous chapter, the importance of slave women as a com-modity would eventually lead to the use of the Old Irish term *cumal* (slave woman) as an expression for denoting a unit of value and exchange.

While Patrick was personally outraged by the enslavement of his recently converted catechumens, he does not appear to have had any moral objections to the use of slaves or to the trading of slaves. His family, as we have seen, owned a substantial number of slaves, and he may have transported slaves with him to Ireland. What he did disapprove of was Coroticus's intention to sell innocent Christians to non-Christian Pictish masters: 'There freeborn men have been sold, Christians reduced to slavery—and what is more, as slaves of the utterly iniquitous, evil and apostate Picts'.[27]

The question of Christians serving non-Christian masters was one that vexed Christian authorities at the highest level in late antiquity. The Theodosian Code, the collection of legislation issued since AD 312 under Christian Roman emperors, is unequivocal in forbidding the ownership of Christian slaves by non-Christians. But the early medieval papacy can be seen to have taken a more pragmatic approach to this form of ownership, an example of which is the permission that Gregory the Great gave to Jewish merchants to traffic Christian slaves if they did so on behalf of Christian masters or sold them within forty days.

The Easter Day captives of the Letter were not to enjoy any papal protection, and it was entirely up to Patrick to seek their release, which he attempted to do by means of the two letters he sent to Coroticus and his men (only the second survives). In doing so, he was among the earliest Insular clerics to assume the role of redeemer of captives. Later in Irish history, in 686, another holy man was to lead a famous initiative to secure the release of captives taken from the territory of Brega, in the east of central Ireland. Adomnán, the ninth abbot of Iona, set out to Northumbria on a diplomatic mission to King Aldfrith to arrange for the release of the captives who were abducted two years previously by Aldfrith's late brother and predecessor, Ecgfrith.[28] Unlike Patrick, Adomnán appears to have been successful in obtaining the captives' release. Such diplomatic endeavours—in both Patrick's and Adomnán's time—were often the province of high-ranking churchmen who would find themselves tidying up after violent kings.

Being well aware of the role that clerics would be expected to play in the release of captives, Patrick drew the attention of the intransigent Coroticus to the protocol for freeing captives in Gaul, a protocol that guaranteed that clerics would be given what they came for once they paid the appropriate ransom: 'Here is the custom of the Roman Christians in Gaul; they send suitable holy men to the Franks and other peoples with so many thousand *solidi* to ransom baptised captives; whereas you kill them or sell them to a foreign people which does not know God; you commit the members of Christ as though to a brothel'.[29]

Here, once more, we see a specific concern for Christian captives rather than captives who may or may not be Christian. Patrick also draws a clear distinction between the foreign aggressors, the Franks, who had of late arrived in Gaul and gradually consolidated themselves as the new ruling elite, and the long-established Gallo-Roman population, which had formed a central pillar of imperial politics and culture ever since Emperor Claudius admitted the Gallic elite into the Senate in AD 48. Both groups were also distinguished by their religion because the Gallo-Romans had long been Christians, whereas the Franks, who were relative newcomers to the west and south of Europe, are conventionally believed to have started to become Christian only after King Clovis's conversion, traditionally dated to 496. Like other such newcomers, often styled 'barbarians', the Franks are also known to have habitually raided Roman territories and former Roman territories (the Western Empire fell in 476, and the last Roman military leader in Gaul was defeated in 486). Roman citizens taken captive from bordering regions were redeemed by their relatives or by the church, such that bishops were even allowed to sell liturgical utensils to raise the ransom, as observed by A.H.M. Jones.

The fact that Coroticus and his soldiers were Christian enabled Patrick to place on them the worst sanction that he could, which was excommunication:

> Therefore let every man who fears God acknowledge that they are estranged from me and from Christ my God, for whom I am an ambassador. . . .
>
> . . . And therefore I make this earnest appeal to all of you men of piety and humble heart; it is not right to curry favour with such as these nor to take food and drink with them, nor ought one to accept their alms, until they make amends to God by gruelling penance, with shedding of tears, and free God's servants and the baptised handmaidens of Christ, for whom He died and was crucified.[30]

Although taking different forms in different places throughout the Christian centuries, excommunication broadly implied that a Christian was excluded in whole or in part from interacting with members of the Christian community, from attending church services, and from receiving the sacraments, which at that time consisted at the very least of baptism, the Eucharist, and unction (anointing with oil), as well as the extreme unction that one would receive before death. The excommunicated were also excluded from commensality with Christians, as indeed Patrick's text makes clear. In the tense confrontation between Patrick and Coroticus, we can see how the rivals mutually wield the weapon of exclusion: Coroticus is physically excluding Patrick's converts from their own society (or even from the world of the living), and Patrick is excluding the soldiers from partaking in the rites of Christian worship and from keeping company with Christians. The mutual exchange of measures of exclusion has a particular resonance when viewed from the perspective of modern social-scientific discourse. For theorists like Orlando Patterson and Alain Testart, exclusion from the most essential forms of social participation is the primary means for turning a free person into an unfree person. The tug-of-war between Patrick and Coroticus seems to have been acted out on a similar premise. In retaliation for the exclusion that Coroticus inflicts on the converts, Patrick retorts with the most significant form of exclusion that he knows and that is in his power in a last-ditch quid pro quo.

As is made evident from the wording of Patrick's pronouncement of excommunication, the excommunication imposed on the soldiers could be undone through the performance of penance. However, Patrick seems to anticipate that excommunication will not deter the evildoers, and so he goes on to threaten them with eternal damnation. This damnation they will not be able to escape because the slain captives, taking their place in the afterlife alongside the prophets and saints, will be the ones judging the soldiers on judgement day:

> It was as baptised believers that you departed from this world to go to Paradise. . . .
> And so you will reign with the apostles and prophets and martyrs. . . .
> So then, what of Coroticus and his villains, these rebels against Christ, where will they see themselves, they who allot poor baptised women as prizes, for the sake of a miserable temporal kingdom which will in any case pass away in a moment? Like clouds of smoke which is soon scattered by the

wind, so deceitful sinners shall perish from before the Lord's face; but the righteous shall feast in full assurance with Christ; they shall judge the nations and hold sway over wicked kings for ever and ever, Amen.[31]

In making the point that Christian captives will sit in judgement alongside Christ, Patrick is doing his level best to restore some sense to a situation that seems to defy the natural and moral order of things: the slavers, instead of being pagan, were Christian, and the future masters of the Christian slaves, instead of being Christian themselves, were pagan. This was a world turned upside down, in which Christians were inflicting harm on fellow Christians and Christian slaves were denied their faith under pagan masters. How far apart the mentalities of pagans and Christians were is one of the questions that we are about to explore in the next chapter, as we turn to examine religion in Patrick's time.

Notes

1. *Confessio* §§ 15–16.
2. *Confessio* § 17.
3. *Confessio* § 18.
4. *Confessio* §§ 18, 19.
5. *Confessio* § 19.
6. *Confessio* § 22.
7. *Confessio* § 21.
8. *Confessio* §§ 26, 27.
9. *Confessio* § 26.
10. *Confessio* §§ 27, 32.
11. *Confessio* § 10.
12. *Digesta* 49.15.5.1–2; cf. *Codex Iustinianus* 8.50.
13. An edition and translation of Fiacc's Hymn is W. Stokes and J. Strachan, *Thesaurus Palaeohibernicus*, 2 vols. (Dublin, 1901–3), 2:307–21. The gloss is on p. 309, lines 13–14.
14. *Hibernensis* 36, ed. Wasserschleben, 128–31.

118 SAINT PATRICK RETOLD

15. *Confessio* §§ 37, 49.

16. *Confessio* § 50.

17. *Confessio* § 51.

18. *Confessio* §§ 52, 53 (quote).

19. *Confessio* § 55.

20. Letter §§ 10, 15.

21. Letter § 3.

22. Letter § 2.

23. Letter §§ 19, 21; Marcian, *Institututiones*, bk. 12 (*Digesta* 25.7.3).

24. Letter §§ 42, 19 (quote).

25. Cogitosus, Life of Brigit § 28, ed. K. Hochegger, in 'Untersuchungen zu den Ältesten *Vitae Sanctae Brigidae*' (MPhil diss., University of Vienna, 2009), 18–58, at 42. An English translation is by S. Connolly and J.-M. Picard, in 'Cogitosus's "Life of Brigit": Content and value', *Journal of the Royal Society of Antiquaries of Ireland* 117 (1987): 5–27, at 21 (§ 25).

26. *Vita I* §§ 1–3, trans. S. Connolly, in '*Vita Prima Sanctae Brigitae*: Background and historical value', *Journal of the Royal Society of Antiquaries of Ireland* 119 (1989): 5–49.

27. Letter § 15.

28. Bede, *HE* 4.26, ed. and trans. Colgrave and Mynors, 426–31; Adomnán, Life of Columba 2.46, in *Adomnán of Iona: Life of St Columba*, trans. R. Sharpe (Harmondsworth, 1995), 203–4.

29. Letter § 14.

30. Letter §§ 5, 7.

31. Letter §§ 17, 18, 19.

4

Religion in Britain and Ireland

PATRICK'S LEGACY IS PRESERVED for posterity exactly how he wanted it to be: he is remembered as a bishop and missionary who successfully converted, if not all, at least a significant portion of the Irish. Religious conversion anywhere, at any time in history, invites two fundamental questions: What religion (or religions) did people convert from, and what new religion did they convert to? The latter question is easy enough to answer with reference to Patrick's time: they converted to Christianity. But identifying what they converted from can be a little trickier, and the answer is often reduced to the catchall expression 'paganism'. There is, of course, more to it than that. In this chapter I wish to put an extended gloss on this elusive expression and on the impact of Christianity by considering the religions with which Patrick and his contemporaries in both Britain and Ireland would have had direct experience.

Christianity never succeeded in eradicating entirely the religions that it purported to supersede, and in the west of Europe, Christianity was not without competition throughout the early medieval period. True, Christianity made a serious dent in the practice of rival religious cults after the Roman Empire embraced it in the early fourth century, and later missionary enterprises

among the empire's European successor states were also successful in spreading Christianity, especially to aristocracies that had
not practiced it before. However, a good number of early medieval
sources portray the Christianisation process as incomplete as late
as the ninth century (and in Scandinavia even later). They describe rival cults contending with Christianity, like the cults of the
Saxons, who were violently being brought under Frankish rule,
and they also describe practices that coexisted peacefully with
Christianity or were even incorporated into Christian rites. Such
practices range widely from what might have been genuine pre-
Christian survivals to practices that historians sometimes refer to
as harmless 'folk magic' or simply folklore. There are also cases in
which it can be shown that Christian authors simply made up or
exaggerated certain rituals in compliance with contemporary literary conventions that determined how pagans ought to be portrayed. Most challenging for the present-day historian is the fact
that paganism could be strictly in the eye of the beholder: certain
customs could be perceived by some as inoffensive but would be
condemned by others, who advocated an uncompromisingly
strict observance of Christianity, as non-Christian abominations.
The purists themselves were often prominent preachers incensed
by the slightest hint of what they regarded as religious deviance,
which rivalled approved ecclesiastical ritual. In one of the more
extreme examples, the early ninth-century abbot of Tours, Alcuin, who was also a leading adviser to Emperor Charlemagne,
even objected to the telling of heroic folk stories about legendary figures. 'What has Ingeld to do with Christ?' he famously
asked in a letter to Bishop Higbald of Lindisfarne, with reference to one of the chief heroes of Anglo-Saxon myth.

On a conceptual level we must distinguish between two different phases of paganism: paganism before Christianity and paganism within the Christian era. In the absence of a contrast

with Christianity, the former can simply be called 'religion'. Nevertheless, even in pre-Christian times, the Romans distinguished between what they deemed acceptable and unacceptable forms of religion, the former of which they called *religio* and the latter *superstitio*. The concept of *religio* was identified with Roman state religion, whereas *superstitio* was a blanket term for a plurality of cults that were not sanctioned by the state. These, according to Roman law, were not necessarily bad but were idiosyncratic (*propria superstitio*)—for example, because they were private or local.[1] Nevertheless, some authors, like Cicero and Seneca, regarded them as the converse of the worship of what was true and good. Probably the main criterion for denouncing a cult as *superstitio* was that it was perceived—in one way or another—to rival the authority of the state or (by Seneca's time) undermine the emperor's dignity.

As the Roman Empire underwent the process of embracing Christianity in the fourth century, the binary *religio/superstitio* was appropriated by the new religion for framing the growing gap between the domains of Christian and non-Christian, such that it became interchangeable with *Christianitas/paganitas*. For example, a law of 392 determined that 'if any person should venerate, by placing incense before them, images made by the work of mortals . . . such person, as one guilty of the violation of religion, shall be punished by the forfeiture of that house or landholding in which it is proved that he served a pagan superstition'.[2] In this quotation, paganism and superstition are interchangeable.

As for the noun *paganus* itself, it is also a borrowing from pre-Christian times. Hitherto, the noun *paganus* in its classical sense meant 'rustic' and 'uncultivated', as opposed to 'urban' and 'civilised'. Early in the Christian era, it had taken a metaphorical twist and came to denote not only those who were removed from an actual city but also those from the *civitas Dei* (city of God). The late antique Christian scholar Orosius (d. 420) articulates this sentiment exactly when he glosses *paganus* as 'those who are strangers from the city of God and are called pagans [*pagani*], taking their name from crossroads and fields in the countryside.'[3] Nevertheless, Jews, who would also have been considered by Christians to be 'strangers to the city of God', are almost never described as *pagani*. It would appear, therefore, that the epithet *pagani* was not a blanket expression for all non-Christians.[4] The etymological background of *paganus* and *paganitas* has generated a good deal of academic debate over the years. Among its main protagonists were Robin Lane Fox, Pierre Chuvin, and most recently Christopher Jones. In Jones's opinion, 'Latin-speaking Christians first applied the term "villagers" (*pagani*) to peasants among whom the old beliefs and practices lingered on, and eventually extended the term to all "pagans"'.

Patrick himself prefers the noun *gentes* to *pagani*. This is consistent with the preponderance of the noun *gentes* that we find in Ireland later, in early medieval times, when the use of the noun *paganus* and variants is rare. A survey of Latin texts that were unequivocally written in Ireland between the fifth and ninth centuries shows that in cases in which the non-Christian Other was designated by a single word, the preferred word was *gentilis* (Old Irish *gentlide*) rather than *paganus* (Old Irish *págán*, *págánach*). The use of either is quite uncommon, but the gap is tantalising: eighty-five occurrences of the former in comparison with only four of the latter. For some authors, like the seventh-century Cogitosus, *gentilis* and *paganus* were interchangeable, as one can infer from his Life of Brigit, where a man is described as *quidam paganus et gentilis*.[5] It seems, therefore, that for the purpose of describing the non-Christian Other, Irish authors preferred a biblical word for 'Otherness', *gentilis,* instead of an expression drawn from Roman idiom. Another word for denoting 'pagan' in Ireland was *laicus* (and, later, Old Irish *láech*), but its semantic range is rather broad, and therefore the sense in which it was used could sometimes be ambiguous.

The changing usage of terminology over time in both Ireland and the empire broadly corresponds to actual changes in practice. The fourth century saw a major transformation in the religious orientation of the Roman Empire: from what were to be the final state-orchestrated persecutions of Christians under Emperor Diocletian between 303 and 311, to the wholesale outlawing of paganism under Theodosius by the end of that century. The defining period of change, the reign of Emperor Constantine (from 306, but as sole Augustus between 324 and 337), saw the cessation of persecution, the restoration of property to individual Christians and churches. It also inaugurated the imposition of imperially sanctioned orthodoxy in opposition to rival yet widespread forms of Christian observance that were denounced as heresies, and the reconfiguration of the empire as a Christian political and physical entity with a new Christian capital founded in Constantinople (the capital of the Western Empire had by this stage been relocated to Milan), glittering with lavishly conspicuous building projects that proclaimed the majesty of the newly adopted religion. Of no less importance (though often neglected in textbook accounts) is the temporary pagan resurgence under Emperor Julian (a.k.a. 'the apostate'), who reigned as sole emperor with the title of Augustus between 360 and 363. Throughout the fourth century, therefore, the changing fortunes of Christianity correlated with the contingencies of imperial politics.

In the fourth and fifth centuries, as Christianity assimilated itself—not without setbacks—into imperial society, the empire's pagan legacy remained a constant force to be reckoned with. In pre-Constantinian times, the Roman state religion was centred largely on the persona of the emperor, who could be venerated as a god himself—just as Caesar was when he assumed the epithet 'divine' (*divus*)—or otherwise have sacrifices made for his well-being. The festivities at which sacrifices were made were associated with public displays of loyalty to the state, and they often occasioned resentment or even hostility towards Christians, who could not participate because their religion forbade them to make sacrifices. By the early years of Constantine's reign, the public worship was directed especially at one specific deity, Sol Invictus, which translates literally as the 'Undefeated Sun'. From 310 Constantine invoked Sol—who was first promoted to chief imperial deity by Aurelian (270–75)—as a means for legitimising his rule, and the special spiritual affinity that he asserted with the deity can be seen, for example, in the stamping of his own profile on coins alongside the image of Sol, with his distinctive rays radiating from his forehead. Coins of this type were minted well into the second decade of the fourth century, when Constantine became, nominally at least, a follower of Christianity. Such ostensibly irreconcilable combinations of religious beliefs are sometimes referred to by scholars as 'syncretic', which will be defined here as the fusion of two contradictory beliefs without attempting to rationally reconcile them. Another apparent syncretism can be seen in the fourth-century cult of Christ, which was in correspondence with the cult of Sol. The most staggering example of this syncretism is the earliest attestation of the date of Christ's birth, 25 December, which is celebrated on Sol's feast day according to a calendar from the mid-350s.[6] The predilection for sun veneration in its different guises throughout the ancient world did not spare the Insular world, and later we shall scrutinise a hypothesis concerning a form of worship involving the sun that may have been the target of Patrick's preaching.

Sun worship was also central to the pagan revival under Julian, who venerated a solar divinity under its Greek name, Helios. Around the same time as he restored blood sacrifices in 360, he also embarked on a campaign to extricate Christianity from the state by forbidding clergy to hold public office, withdrawing the privileges given to churches, and fomenting factionalism between rival Christian groups. Symptomatic of his attitude was a sharp sarcasm towards Christians and their faith. In his so-called fragments, he mocks Christians for what he saw as the futility of their beliefs. Here are two of the more irreverent examples:

> Moses after fasting forty days received the law, and Elijah, after fasting for the same period, was granted to see God face to face. But what did Jesus receive, after a fast of the same length?[7]
>
> Listen to a fine statesmanlike piece of advice: 'Sell your possessions and give to the poor; provide purses for yourselves that will not wear out' [Luke 12:33]. Can anyone quote a more statesmanlike ordinance than this? For if all men were to obey you, who would there be left to buy? . . . If everything in the city were being sold at once, there would be no one left to trade.[8]

Despite Julian's failure to suppress Christianity and promote a Roman state religion centred on Helios, it would be a teleology to describe the period after Constantine as a time of linear upward motion towards an ever 'purer' Christian worship, free of the taint of paganism. Christianity was indeed prevalent, but its hold was far from secure, and the winds of change could have blown either way at any time. In the late fourth century and even as late as the early fifth century, we find examples of the imperial cult still being practised. Christian emperors could still be seen to be eulogised by pagan notables, with explicit mention of the worship of the figure of the emperor. In a panegyric delivered to Emperor Valentinian I and his son Gratian, the pagan senator Symmachus said, 'How much less expensive is the worship of Your Divinity [Valentinian] than that of the gods'.[9] Christopher Jones draws attention to Christian emperors' continuing to cultivate the idea that they were surrounded by the aura of divinity known as *numen*, even though they were not formally recognised as gods. He quotes a passage from the Theodosian Code to this effect: 'In the games also, our images when displayed should only show that our *numen* and our praises flourish in the thoughts of the competitors and in the recesses of their minds'.[10]

My final example of ostensible syncretism—in the sense of a fusion of Christian and pre-Christian notions of the imperial role—comes from the fifth-century historian Priscus of Panium, who offers an account of a diplomatic mission from the court of Emperor Theodosius II to Attila the Hun, in which one of the officials from the imperial embassy exclaimed in an exchange with Hunnic delegates that 'it was not right to juxtapose a god and a man, meaning by "man" Attila and by "god" Theodosius'.[11] Paradoxically, at the same time, Theodosius himself was reenacting legislation against pagan cults, although perhaps it was not so much the non-Christian nature of those cults that troubled him, so much as the fact that they were not focused on the veneration of the emperor. He was also the emperor who commissioned the Theodosian Code, a division in which is devoted to abominable practices and is titled 'Concerning pagans, sacrifices and temples' (*De paganis, sacrificiis et templis*).[12] Emperors continued to issue legislation against pagan cult practices until as late as 472, suggesting that the process of Christianisation was still very much ongoing as late as four years before the (conventional date for the) collapse of the empire in the west.

In Britain itself, it is unclear how widespread conversion to Christianity was under imperial occupation. There is, nevertheless, solid evidence of episcopal church organisation along the Continental European pattern with a clear hierarchy. Famously, and as already mentioned in chapter 1, the church council convoked by Constantine at Arles in 314 was attended by three bishops from Britain: Restitutus of London, Eborius of York, and Adelphius of Lincoln. They were accompanied by a presbyter and deacon. Their presence at the council, alongside forty other bishops from different Christian provinces, suggests a degree of involvement in high-level ecclesiastical diplomacy and legislation on an international scale.

Identifying ordinary believers (as distinct from clergy) in the sources or in archaeology is more challenging. We rely primarily on chance finds such as inscribed objects or Christian symbols, and although each has an individual story to tell, the accumulative evidence is so disappointingly meagre that it cannot tell a broader story. Some such revealing objects are listed by David Mattingly: a silver dish with a dedicatory inscription to a church, lead fragments with the names of clerics, lead (perhaps baptismal) tanks with Christian symbols, and silver and gold vessels inscribed with the names of those who gave them as offerings. The women and men who made the offerings—among them certain named individuals: Innocentia, Viventia, and Publianus—must have been relatively wealthy. In contrast, followers of Christianity from the lower rungs of Christian society simply did not leave their mark. There is also a dearth of clearcut examples of churches in the archaeological record. The haphazard nature of chance finds is partly to blame, but this dearth is also due to the unremarkable morphology of contemporary churches, which were often indistinguishable from Roman temples and public buildings—namely, *basilicae*. The *basilicae* of old could have been reused as churches without incurring any significant or observable forms of structural adaptations, but some nevertheless acquired a distinct architectural morphology as churches in the post-Roman era (for example, Saint Paul in the Bail, in Lincoln). Indeed, as mentioned in chapter 1, house churches might have been the most common venue for Christian worship, but these are rarely distinguishable, with the possible exception of a villa in Lullingstone in Kent that contains Chi-Rho symbols (the first two Greek letters of Christ's name), one of which is combined with an alpha and omega, echoing Christ's saying, 'I am alpha and omega, the beginning and the end' (Revelations 21:6, 22:13; also in 1:8, first part only).

The complex nature of Roman Christianity—exhibiting, as it did, a combination of non-Roman and Roman cultural influences—might have been taken for granted by British Christians of Patrick's generation, who inhabited the westernmost fringes of the empire. Those among them who would have been lucky (or rich) enough to be invited to a party in a luxury villa like Hinton St Mary's (Dorset) would have feasted their eyes on lavish mosaics with syncretic artistic expressions: on the one hand depicting Christ with a Chi-Rho and on the other depicting a mythological scene of the Bellerophon slaying the Chimera. The juxtaposition of mosaics with Christian and mythological elements is another manifestation of the fusion of Christian beliefs with beliefs that conflicted with Christianity, just like the idea we encountered earlier that Theodosius could be held as a god despite the Christian character of his rule. Insofar as ordinary Christian believers or wealthy villa owners were interested in a rationale for justifying this fusion, they could find it in a principle dating from pre-Christian times: the principle of *inter-pretatio Romana* enabled Romans to accommodate the deities of other peoples within their own religious system. It interpreted non-Roman deities by analogy to Roman religion, an interpretation that was entirely valid within the Roman pluralistic religious mind-set. Some material expressions of *interpretatio Romana*, such as inscriptions and sculptures, would still have been visible in Patrick's day, even though they dated from an earlier time. For example, an inscription on an altar from Corbridge, on Hadrian's Wall, exalts the deity of the Brigantes, Brigantia, by the epithet 'heavenly' (*caelestis*) and pairs her with Jupiter. In the Roman fort at Birrens in Dumfriesshire, we find Brigantia sculpted in the form of the Roman Minerva, above an inscription dedicating the sculpture to Brigantia. Farther south, in Colchester (Essex), a bronze plaque pairs the Roman god of war, Mars, with a local god, Medocius, who is not known from any other source. And a silver plaque from Barkway (Herefordshire) pairs Mars with Toutatis, whose cult is also attested in Gaul, where it is mentioned, for example, by the first-century poet Lucan (who also names two other Celtic deities: Hesus and Taranis).[13] He will also be familiar to readers of René Goscinny's Astérix comic books for the made-up Gallic colloquial exclamation 'Par Toutatis!' (By Toutatis!).

It is also thanks to various ethnographic accounts of classical authors who applied the principle of *interpretatio Romana* that we possess early descriptions (albeit not wholly reliable) of cultic practice among the Gauls, whose religion is often taken as the benchmark for what generations of scholars have styled 'Celtic' religion. Among the best-known examples is Caesar's depiction of Gallic religion in his Gallic War, which superimposes the names of Roman deities on Gallic deities that corresponded to them in their special qualities: 'Among the gods, they [the

Gauls] most worship Mercury. . . . After him they set Apollo, Mars, Jupiter and Minerva. Of these deities they have the same idea as all other nations: Apollo drives away diseases, Minerva supplies the first principles of arts and crafts, Jupiter holds the empire of heaven, Mars controls wars'. Caesar continues, 'The Gauls affirm that they are all descended from a common father, Dis, and say that this is the tradition of the druids'.[14]

Here, Caesar portrays a universal pantheon in which ultimately the same deities—albeit with different names—were venerated by different peoples. In his depiction of this all-encompassing pantheon, he was echoing a mentality that was prevalent throughout the pre-Christian Roman era, in both Republican and imperial times, when Rome was extending its political influence over many peoples, each with its own deities. It was not uncommon for Romans to venerate deities that originated from the religions of other peoples. For example, the cults of Egyptian and Persian gods, like Isis, Osiris, or Mithras, became widespread among Romans, with the last being especially popular among the soldiers and officers of the Roman armies. A site that allows for an awesome visual illustration of the plurality of deities is the city of Ostia, which served as Rome's port. The archaeological remains on this well-preserved (and in some cases reconstructed) site contain a spectacularly large number of temples and shrines dedicated to different deities venerated by the multitude of sailors, merchants, and passengers who would have made their way through the port. Certain cults were nevertheless excluded as the Romans attempted to exert some degree of regulation from above and bar unsavoury *superstitiones*, especially ones that were believed to foment political dissent. The ambiguous status of Judaism in this context—after the revolt of AD 63–73 and the destruction of the Jewish Temple in Jerusalem—is also evident in Ostia, which has the remains of the earliest synagogue in Europe, but it is located immediately outside the city walls and not within them.

The notion that, despite the plurality of cults and deities, different nations arguably venerated different manifestations of *the same* deities (as Caesar believed) resonated with early Christians and facilitated the process by which Christianity spread. A poignant example is Saint Paul's famous address to the Athenians at the Areopagus, as it is described in the Acts of the Apostles 17:16–23:

> While Paul was waiting for them in Athens, he was greatly distressed to see that the city was full of idols. So he reasoned in the synagogue with both Jews and God-fearing Greeks, as well as in the marketplace day by day with those who happened to be there. A group of Epicurean and Stoic philosophers began to debate with him. Some of them asked, 'What is this babbler trying to say?' Others remarked, 'He seems to be advocating foreign gods'. They said this because Paul was preaching the good news about Jesus and the resurrection. Then they took him and brought him to a meeting of the Areopagus, where they said to him, 'May we know what this new teaching is that you are presenting? You are bringing some strange ideas to our ears, and we would like to know what they mean'. All the Athenians and the foreigners who lived there spent their time doing nothing but talking about and listening to the latest ideas. Paul then stood up in the meeting of the Areopagus and said: 'People of Athens, I see that in every way you are very religious. For as I walked around and looked carefully at your objects of worship, I even found an altar with this inscription: to an unknown god. So you are ignorant of the very thing you worship—and this is what I am going to proclaim to you'.[15]

In other words, what Paul was preaching to the Athenians was that they had been venerating Christ all along even though they were not aware of this. Not only is this passage from Acts central for understanding some of the philosophical and theological underpinnings of the dynamics of the relationship between Christianity and paganism, but—more importantly for the context of Patrick and his mission—it also presents us with a concept of conversion to Christianity that is not about radical transformation but about 'sobering up' or awakening to the true nature of one's already-existing religious practices. This of course is redolent of the principle of prefiguration (discussed in the introduction), which enabled the righteous figures of the Old Testament who did not consciously profess the Christian faith (because they lived before Christ) to be venerated on the proviso that their deeds nevertheless prefigured Christ.

From the observance of religions in the late empire, we now turn to the religious practices of the indigenous British and Irish, practices that are often given the epithet 'Celtic', like the Gallic cults mentioned earlier. Any discussion of 'Celtic' religion is hindered by two related problems. The first is the problem of uniformity across the 'Celtic' world, and the second is the problem of continuity from Continental Celtic cults, primarily located by scholarship in Gaul, to the cults of the Insular Celtic-speaking peoples who inhabited Ireland and Britain (and, from the early Middle Ages, mostly associated with the territories broadly coterminous with present-day Cornwall, Wales, and Scotland). The question of uniformity in Celtic religious practice is a corollary of a broader issue, which is Celtic identity itself. Although the word 'Celtic' has for a long time been acknowledged to be an imprecise generic designation for a variety of different and often unrelated phenomena, it continues to be widely used, even by those who contest its validity. For example, a recent major exhibition at the British Museum (24 September 2015–31 January 2016), held under the title 'The Celts', saw the curators themselves dismissing the notion of 'Celtic' as a meaningless designator: 'There never was a single pan-European ancient people called the Celts; there was no single culture; there was no single language. There were relations and connections, but the certainties of a Celtic Europe rapidly unravel under the sharp scrutiny of critical scholarship. It is a more complicated story than the history of a single people and a more fascinating one because of it'. The sceptical tone that the curators apply to what is meant to be the subject of their own exhibition may strike readers as somewhat self-defeating. But it is not without precedent. By the middle of the twentieth century, the study of Celtic history and culture had already taken a turn from a relatively self-assured endeavour, often feeding into the grand narratives of nationhood of certain modern European nations, to a more questioning and self-reflexive exercise, which began to challenge its own premises, especially the notions of a biologically determined ethnicity, but also the notion of a discrete religion observable in texts or material culture. As early as 1948, Joseph Vendryes noted the plurality of cults among the Gauls and proclaimed that 'it is a nomenclature of local deities' in which 'one cannot find even traces of great deities which had been common to all Celtic peoples'. Others have since drawn attention to the diversity of epigraphic evidence from Gaul that suggests a good deal of regional variation, with specific groups venerating their own eponymous deity—for instance, the *dea Brigantia* for the Brigantes of Scotland and the *dea Tricoria* for the Tricorii of the Narbonne region of Gaul (and we may wish to recall that, according to Ptolemy, some Brigantes also lived in Ireland; see Figure 5). The types of evidence in which such deities are mentioned vary from inscriptions of the kind that we have seen earlier, through classical ethnographic writings like Caesar's, to mythologies written centuries later but purporting to preserve the vestiges of Iron Age cults. These three forms of evidence do not always agree with one another, such that when contradictions do occur—for example, between epigraphic evidence and classical ethnography—'we are faced with what appears to be a tangle of heterogeneous elements bearing little or no resemblance to Caesar's neat classification', as remarked by Proinsias Mac Cana already in 1968 with reference to Caesar's description of the Gallic religion. Most historians nowadays would side with the view (also espoused by Mac Cana) that Caesar exaggerated the coherence of a pantheon among the Gauls by imposing an *interpretatio Romana* on the identity of individual deities as well as on Gallic religion as a whole, which he conceptualised as structurally identical to Roman religion. Whatever the Gauls worshipped, they did not all worship the same thing or things.

In the absence of any uncontroversial markers of uniformity across cultures that are considered Celtic, language remains the central attribute that comes close to defining a Celtic identity. But an identity based on language is a broadly defined identity, which often comes close to equating a family of languages with an ethnicity. Whether or not speakers of Continental and Insular Celtic (like Gaulish, Old Irish, or Old Welsh) believed they belonged to a single (albeit broad) cultural sphere and whether it is possible for us to identify retrospectively any commonalities beyond language continue to be hotly debated issues. The debate remains open as to whether language can be seen to inform a common identity that straddles the European Continent and the islands of Britain and Ireland.

The question of language and identity brings us to the second problem that I mentioned in relation to defining Celtic religion or religions, which is the problem of continuity across space and time. Even if one accepts that certain similarities are in evidence across the religions of Celtic-speaking peoples (a contested issue, as we have seen), is it then possible to argue for a direct transmission of attributes of Celtic culture, including religion, from the Continent to the isles or vice versa? And is it possible to argue for continuity from the prehistory of Britain and Ireland (or their Iron Age) into the historical era of these isles in the early centuries AD? In other words, can we observe any all-European continuities whatsoever in so-called Celtic religion? Very influential in addressing these questions, but now largely discarded as outmoded, have been the theories of Georges Dumézil, and especially his model of the 'three functions' for social organisation among Indo-European cultures (Celtic culture being classified as one of its branches), functions corresponding to a tripartite division in both mythology and social organisation. Dumézil's three 'functions of religion'—namely, sacred sovereignty, force, and fertility—were said to be mirrored in three social orders: the order of priests, warriors, and peasants. This division, or in his parlance 'ideology', he believed to have been established since before the Indo-European peoples began to spread and to form subgroups like the 'Celts', a group that he regarded as self-evidently historical.

Continuity of different kinds has been posited by others after Dumézil, mostly on anecdotal evidence. For example, while a Celtic scholar like Barry Raftery could acknowledge that the veneration in different places of a god bearing the same name should not necessarily be interpreted as attesting a single cult, he nevertheless believed that these are, as he called them, 'the local veneration of specific aspects of common pan-Celtic deities'. More recently, Patrick Sims-Williams argued cogently against the case for cultural continuity between 'the ancient Celts and the medieval Celtic-speaking inhabitants of Britain, Brittany, and Ireland'. Yet the case for continuity has not been entirely lost, with scholars such as Matthias Egeler rigorously scrutinising methodological legacies and refining the historiographical approach to cultural continuity by examining the extent to which it can be detected (at least) in relation to specific traditions (for example, concerning female demonic figures) that inform religion in Scandinavia, Ireland, Roman Britain, and areas regarded as Celtic in Continental Europe.

The debate concerning continuity and uniformity across space and time is one that embeds within it important questions about the origins and movement of peoples that transmit culture from one place to another. Participants in the debate hold polarised views. For example, in a recent provocative and controversial contribution, *Celtic from the West*, one can find voices arguing that searching for the origin of the Celts is 'perfectly meaningless' but also a radically new hypothesis accounting for that very same origin. According to Barry Cunliffe and John T. Koch, who argue largely on linguistic grounds against the prevalent notion that Celtic (broadly defined) spread from central Europe to the west, 'Celtic probably evolved in the Atlantic Zone during the Bronze Age', by which the authors mean the period between the third millennium BC and circa 750 BC. They hold that the means by which 'Celtic' spread were diverse and do not necessitate a hypothesis of mass migration. Indeed, the notion of mass migration has found more subtle alternatives in discussions about the formation of European peoples. Two such hypotheses are, for example, 'wave of advance', which posits a takeover by a superior technological culture, and 'elite transfer', which posits an aggressive external force replacing the existing ruling elite without uprooting a settled population. Such views obviate the need for identifying culture with a single race, a notion that could be and has been misappropriated to support racial ideologies.

Such modern ideas about the complexities of cultural exchange would not, of course, have been debated in Caesar's time. According to him, the direction of cross-cultural religious influence was clear: it was the Gauls who came under the influence of British Celts and their cultic practices. Among the most important manifestations of these cults was the priestly caste of druids, which the Gauls are said to have inherited.[16] Like his contemporaries Cicero and Dio Chrysostom, Caesar depicts druids not only as religious figures officiating over rituals but also as wise elders who performed a range of social functions. Not only in Caesar's time but also in modern historiography, druids can be seen to hold a central place in discussions of the cross-cultural remit of 'Celtic' religion. For early descriptions of druids in Britain, we may recall Tacitus's telling of the destruction of a sacred site at Anglesey in northwest Wales in AD 61 (see chapter 2).[17] Tacitus, however, writing in commemoration of the deeds of his father-in-law, the general Agricola, was not an eyewitness, nor are his druids given the same attributes as Caesar's, Cicero's, or Chrysostom's. We must not, therefore, infer similarities in religious practice across cultures on the strength of the recurrence of a single word. It cannot be ruled out that Tacitus may simply have been using 'druid' in the sense of 'a practitioner of a religion that is not ours'.

Whereas Britain did not leave us with any reliable early accounts of druids, Ireland has left us no early accounts of druids at all. A single possible exception is the word DRVVIDES in an inscription from County Kildare, which, according to Damian McManus, may date from the early fifth century.[18] Sadly, there is no context for interpreting this word, and the only contemporary author from Ireland, Patrick, does not mention a priestly figure of any kind who is not Christian. As for later sources, their testimony is anachronistic and their terminology can be ambiguous: for example, as Catherine McKenna has shown, the noun *magi* in Irish hagiography can variably invoke the idea of the New Testament magi or of pre-Christian Irish druids. The silence of our contemporary sources both in and outside Ireland regarding druids and pre-Christian religion (some later vernacular sources do mention them) is no proof that there were no druids or that there were no connections in the religious domain between Ireland and Britain. Such connections, when they are revealed by other forms of evidence, are a window for inferring, by analogy, what religion was practiced in Ireland. A case in point is the finding of Irish artefacts in an Iron Age hoard of metalwork at Llyn Cerrig, on Anglesey, which were already discussed in chapter 2. Dating between 150 BC and AD 60, these artefacts are commonly believed to have been votive offerings that Irish pilgrims brought to a sacred lake.

Archaeology remains our single most important route into cult practices, and it is an indispensable complement to Patrick's own writings and to later Insular mythologies, on which more toward the end of this chapter. Nevertheless, Patrick's time is not as well served by archaeology in comparison with the prehistoric period in both Ireland and Britain, or with the Anglo-Saxon period in Britain. Prehistoric Britain is dotted with monumental man-made landscape features whose function and meaning continue to be debated. The most conspicuous are the hillforts, mounds constructed from earth that has been dug out of ditched enclosures around them. A famous example is Maiden Castle (Dorset), consisting of multiple ramparts, most of which date from the first century BC. Covering an area of approximately twenty hectares, it was built on the site of a Neolithic enclosure (ca. 3500 BC) and reused by the Romans for the erection of a temple. In the Iron Age it was used for habitation, still evidenced today by postholes that sustained storage structures and by finds suggesting industrial activity, such as metalworking. Unlike Maiden Castle (see Figure 6), the majority of

FIGURE 6. Maiden Castle hillfort (Dorset). Available from Geograph.
© Copyright David Robinson and licensed for reuse (CC BY-SA 2.0)

Britain's other hillforts are rather modest. Altogether, an extraordinary 3,840 Iron Age hillforts have been recorded in Britain, some of which have been argued to have served as places of ritual activity—for example, at Carrock Fell (Cumbria)—on the evidence of features that have been interpreted as funerary monuments, in addition to graves.

Other types of cult sites have also been conjectured. According to a tally by Ronald Hutton, by 2009 there were eighteen such sites in fifteen different places. They consist of rectangular wooden buildings, some of which survive only in outline. They show a certain uniformity in size and layout, with doors on either side and a capacity to hold up to a dozen people. In 2000 an exceptional find by amateur archaeologists led the Archaeological Unit at the University of Leicester to excavate what appears to be a site of ritual deposit at Hallaton in Leicestershire. The site contained a hoard, which was deliberately buried, consisting of over five thousand locally minted coins dating between the mid-first century BC and the mid-first century AD. The minting of coins in the decades preceding and following the year nought is believed to have taken place under the impetus of Caesar's abortive visit to Britain and was not simply a means of generating currency for the exchange of goods but rather a means of asserting identity by tribes and their leaders, whose names are stamped on the coins. The site also contained approximately 350 Roman coins and a Roman cavalry helmet. The finding of animal bones that show no signs of having been butchered suggests that they were buried as sacrificial offerings, an interpretation that has been extended to the coins.

As we turn to Ireland, we find a more pronounced presence of unequivocal ritual sites from the first millennium BC, some on an extraordinarily grand scale. Since there are no contemporary written sources from Ireland before Patrick's time, we find ourselves more dependent than we would wish to be on the archaeology, consisting of both landscape evidence and material finds, the interpretation of which can take many forms. There has for a long time been a tendency to complement the archaeological evidence with texts from the early and later Middle Ages that purport to preserve echoes of earlier myths. This approach, more common among previous generations of scholars, is not without its limitations. I shall take these three forms of evidence in turn: Patrick's writings, archaeology, and medieval literary mythology.

There is a limited amount of detail in Patrick's texts that can be used to infer something about religion in Ireland in his time and before his time. We have already encountered the description of sailors offering wild honey to certain unnamed gods (see chapter 3, on captivity), as well as Patrick's use of the word *gentiles* to denote pagans. These anecdotes tell us nothing of real value apart from confirming that polytheism existed. However, another passage that drew the attention of scholars searching for clues on religious practice in Patrick's time is *Confessio* § 60, which has been interpreted by some as evidencing a sun cult: 'For this sun [*sol*] which we see rises for us every day by his command, but it will never reign nor its splendour endure; no, all who worship it shall be doomed to dreadful punishment. But we believe in and worship the true sun, Christ [*credimus et adoramus solem verum Christum*], who will never perish.'[19]

As we have seen earlier in the present chapter, the fourth century witnessed a revival of the cult of Helios under Julian, a cult that would not have seemed incongruous to anyone who had even a dim familiarity with the adoration of Sol Invictus at the time of Constantine and earlier. The imperial predilection for sun adoration is therefore one context in which this passage from the *Confessio* may be read. But over the years other interpretations have been offered that attempted to tie this description with a putative form of sun worship among the Continental Celts. In an imaginative analysis dating from 1946, Thomas O'Rahilly argued that the Irish worshipped a sun god who is to be identified with the Irish deity the Dagda (attested only in later medieval Irish literary mythology), whom he believed to have been the local manifestation of a sun god inherited from a pan-Celtic culture. Mac Cana, however, writing two decades later, rejected this interpretation, arguing that the passage in the *Confessio* 'is more likely to be one of the theological commonplaces acquired by Patrick through his religious reading and training'. In other words, this is a metaphor that we should not read into too much. The debate was reignited in 2014 when John Waddell restated the case for a solar cult 'of some description', albeit not necessarily a cult that was widespread. Much of his argument hinges on an image on a Bronze Age Petrie Crown discovered in County Cork and bronze discs from Monasterevin (County Kildare) and from County Armagh. Waddell interprets the image—for which he finds parallels on the Iron Age Battersea shield recovered from the Thames—as a 'solar boat', representing the sun's journey across the sky. He then attempts to place this cult in a line of continuity from pre-Celtic times by invoking the Neolithic passage tomb at Newgrange in the Boyne Valley, which offers clear evidence of an interest in solar motion (on which more shortly). We see here, therefore, two attempts to adduce a solar cult in Ireland: one based on the written testimony of Patrick and the other on different types of archaeological evidence. Both, however, are speculative and they draw on rather impressionistic interpretations of textual and material evidence that, in and of itself, remains inherently ambiguous.

Staying on the topic of sun veneration, but moving the focus more firmly to archaeology, we continue with some of the better-known and most monumental cultic sites in Ireland: the Neolithic passage tombs of the valley of the Boyne river. These sites, Newgrange, Knowth, and Dowth, dating from circa 3300 BC, have parallels, but on a less impressive scale, along the western and northern European seaboards—for example, in the Orkney Islands and Anglesey. Morphologically, the Boyne sites exhibit prominent man-made mounds built over long passages formed from large rocks, at the end of which there is a chamber. The passage would be aligned with the sun in such a manner that, for example, on the winter solstice (21 December) at Newgrange, one can observe how a ray of sunlight penetrates through it and illuminates the chamber within (see Figure 7). However, although the mechanics of what appears to have been a form of sun adoration are still visible, the religious notions

FIGURE 7. Neolithic passage tomb at Newgrange (County Meath).
Available from Geograph. © Copyright Graham Hogg and
licensed for reuse (CC BY-SA 2.0)

behind them are inaccessible to us, and they would also have
been to Iron Age dwellers. Nevertheless, what is of importance
is the continual reuse of the site by subsequent generations of
worshippers of various kinds, each likely attaching a different
significance to the site. As an alternative to this pattern of continuous reinterpretation, some scholars, like John Carey, believe that representations of Newgrange in medieval Irish saga
of the Christian era may reflect astonishingly resilient traditions
that spanned millennia, such that 'the Boyne legends were still
relevant, and important, in the Christian period'.

Reuse of cult sites was not uncommon, and we have already
encountered it in Britain, at Maiden Castle, where the Romans
had built a temple. An early phase of reuse at Newgrange is attested by gold Roman coins and Roman jewellery, dating between the third and fifth centuries AD. The coins, some of

which depict the Christian convert Emperor Constantine and his Christian son Constantius, appear to have been adapted to be used as pendants and are suggestive of familiarity with Christianity (albeit perhaps localised and on a small scale) in Ireland from a relatively early stage in the empire's promotion of Christianity to the status of privileged religion. However, despite being evocative of Christianity, the coins and other Roman objects from the site are commonly regarded as reflecting votive offerings either by Romans or by locals influenced by the Roman practice of making offerings at shrines and other sacred places. We may therefore be witnessing a curious combination of evidence, whereby artefacts from a Christian source, which might even have been brought by Christians, were deposited in what may be interpreted as a ritualistic fashion evocative of pre-Christian Roman custom. In any case, we have here clear evidence of a certain familiarity with Christianity before the arrival of Patrick.

There is ample evidence for votive offerings at sacred sites, including places in which natural landscape features themselves appear to have been venerated. Edel Bhreathnach interprets the combination of certain finds from the Rath of the Synods at Tara as votive offerings. Tara, itself in the valley of the Boyne in the vicinity of the grandiose passage tombs, is a monumentally sculpted landscape from the first millennium BC, which was used continually into Christian times, when it assumed associations with Saint Patrick, which are discussed in chapter 6, on hagiography. The finds include high-status goods like second-century British and Gallic pottery and Roman glass, but also more ordinary objects like copper-alloy pins, rings, a grinding stone, and pebbles.

Votive offerings are also in evidence in natural features, especially lakes and rivers—for example, in the river Bann, in which were found ornate bronze scabbard plates, spear ferrules, bridle bits, and spun-bronze bowls. Probably the most famous is the decorated bronze 'Bann disc' found on the bank of the river near Loughan Island (County Derry). Likewise, votive finds were recovered from the Shannon river, including swords, spear ferrules, and brooches. A bowl with a handle in the shape of a bird's head, now known as the Keshcarrigan bowl, likely of British production from the first century AD, was found in a river flowing into the Shannon's Lough Scur (County Leitrim). More votive offerings were found on the river Roe at Broighter (County Derry; including a gold model ship), Lough Beg (County Antrim), Lough Inchiquin (County Clare), Lough Gur (County Limerick), and Lake Loughnashade (County Armagh), where— among other artefacts—a first-century BC horn was recovered beside a collection of skulls.

As we continue our search for archaeological evidence of cults in Ireland, we return again to Tara, but this time in conjunction with three other sites that were continually reused from the Iron Age: Crúachain (County Roscommon), Dún Ailinne (County Kildare), and Emain Macha (Navan Fort, County Armagh). In the historical Christian period, all three became known as former sites of pagan royal activity of one kind or another—for example, as places of royal inauguration or ceremonial political centres. The best-known mention of ritual at these places is probably the account by the eighth-century author Óengus the Culdee, who eulogises the transformation of the old landscape under Christianity and in the course of his eulogy reveals that he and his contemporaries regarded sites such as Tara as having strong pagan associations. In a triumphalist verse prologue to the text known as the Martyrology of Óengus (767 × 825), the author frames the demise of paganism in Ireland as the final episode in a preordained litany of collapsing pagan powers, beginning with Herod and Pilate, and culminating with the eradication of later royal powers. We hear of the adoration of the kings of old being replaced by the veneration of saints—as Patrick supersedes Lóegaire and as Brigit overcomes Aillenn—and of the places of royal authority and cult being supplanted by Christian foundations either at the original sites or close by:

> Herod and Pilate under whom our Lord had suffered their powers have been ended, their pains abide forever
>
> Though fair and many were the sons of wrathful Decius whom we love not, neither known nor very great is the name of any of them on earth
>
> Tara's mighty fortress perished at the death of her princes: with a multitude of venerable champions the great Height of Macha (Armagh) abides
>
> Right valiant Lóegaire's pride has been quenched—great the anguish; Patrick's name, splendid, famous, this is on the increase
>
> The faith has grown: it will abide till Doomesday: guilty pagans who are carried off, their raths are not dwelt in
>
> The fort of Crúachain, it has vanished with Ailill, offspring of victory: fair the sovereignty over princes that there is in the monastery of Clonmacnoise
>
> Aillenn's proud fortress has perished with its warlike host: great is victorious Brigit: fair is her multitudinous cemetery.[20]

There is little doubt that Tara, Crúachain, Dún Ailinne, and Emain Macha were primarily sites of ritual activity because they lack obvious defensive features that would have marked a high-status place of habitation. Royal inaugurations with pagan undertones are known to have taken place at the Feis Temro (Feast of Tara), the last of which, according to the Annals of Tigernach, was celebrated by King Díarmait mac Cerbaill in 558 or 560.[21] At

Emain Macha we may even witness the vestiges of what some archaeologists believe was a temple. A large oak post, the remains of which were uncovered on-site, has been argued to have sustained the structure, although there is no certainty that it was covered by a roof. The precise dating of wood by dendrochronology suggests that the oak was felled in 95 or 94 BC. However, given that temples (as distinct from shrines) in pre-Christian Europe are known almost exclusively from the Roman world, the likelihood that Emain Macha had a temple is low. Apart from presumed temples, the archaeological evidence for continual use of the sites as centres of ritual activity tends to be more banal and is composed mainly of graves. For example, the so-called Mount of the Hostages at Tara was originally a passage tomb dating from the late Neolithic period (ca. 2000 BC), but it continued to be used for burial throughout the Bronze Age. Burial at the Rath of the Synods, which we have already encountered in the context of votive offerings, continued into the early centuries AD. Crúachain and Emain Macha, which are known as ceremonial royal sites from the heroic legend of the Ulster Cycle, both show evidence of continual burial activity.

Tara and Crúachain are two of the many cultic sites that have been reused repeatedly for burial. Again, we have here examples of the reuse of prehistoric sites, but in this case for burial. Reuse of places that had man-made burial mounds (*tumuli*) was common. The Middle Bronze Age barrow at Carrowbeg North (County Galway) had Iron Age burials inserted into it. At Kiltierney (County Fermanagh), nineteen Iron Age barrows were erected around a Neolithic tumulus, and the tumulus itself has Iron Age cremation burials inserted into it. Complexes of tumuli of various kinds are known from other places that were inhabited since prehistoric times in Britain, Ireland, and the adjacent isles. Sutton Hoo in Suffolk is the most famous example (although it had no preexisting tumuli). Established on a site occupied since Neolithic times, it consisted of around twenty barrows dating from the late sixth or early seventh century that contained luxury grave goods, a ship, and even a horse buried beside a warrior.

The reuse of a cemetery site made it possible to assert the antiquity and continuity of community identity across generations, but also to stake claims to ancestral land. This often involved the veneration of an ancestor or of ancestors, which is among the reasons why, in Ireland, ordinary family cemeteries, *ferta*, were disapproved of by certain churchmen, who advocated burial in a church instead.[22] In terms of its physical appearance, a *fert* would be characterised by a round ditch, the earth from which was piled to form a burial mound. They rarely exceeded fifteen metres in diameter. Initially they consisted of cremations, but when reused in the Iron Age, they also had inhumation burials inserted into them. From the fact that relatively few skeletons are found (although there are exceptions, like Collierstown in County Meath or Holdenstown in County Kilkenny), it may be assumed that only prominent members of the kin were buried in these ancestral cemeteries. Reuse was rife. Take, for example, Ballymacaward (County Donegal), a cemetery established on a boundary and later reused as a Christian cemetery, excavated by Elizabeth O'Brien. It was located on the northern bank of the river Erne, which marked the boundary between the Connachta and the Ulaid, and is a clear testimony of its political importance. The marcher land on which it lay was often contested between dynasties that ruled these peoples. The site at Ballymacaward had been reused for burial at least four times. It was initially used during the Bronze Age (two graves date ca. 2000 BC–ca. 1500 BC), then approximately a thousand years later in the Iron Age (two graves from the second or first century BC), and by the third century AD it was the site of a cremation cemetery. Between the fifth and seventh centuries, two further phases can be distinguished, both exclusively of women, with the latter consisting of nine extended inhumations oriented west–east, six of which are shrouded. Although arguably recalling the shroud in which Christ's body was wrapped according to the Hebrew custom (Matt. 27:59; Luke 23:53), the identification of these burials as Christian is not conclusive. The pattern of reuse that is evident at Ballymacaward is not unique to this site but rather can be observed throughout *ferta* sites exhibiting late Iron Age burials (AD 400–700), mainly of women, inserted into ancestral *ferta* of prehistoric times.

Archaeology, as we keep seeing, is often interpreted in light of the testimonies of early medieval written sources—all invariably written by Christian authors—such as chronicles, prose tales (saga), and verse texts. The association of ritual places in the landscape with heroic tales from the Ulster Cycle has been noted already and continues to attract attention from scholars. There is a debate on the extent to which heroic tales of this kind, which form the foundation of what we have come to regard as Irish mythology, really allow us to gauge aspects of Iron Age cult—for example, the worship of deities. As described in chapter 2, it is commonplace to divide Irish mythological tales into four cycles: a Mythological Cycle, the Ulster Cycle, the Finn Cycle, and the Cycle of Kings. Despite recurring events and personalities across these cycles, none attests a coherent pantheon or the practice of cults devoted to specific deities. It is the Finn Cycle, however, that consciously offers a more explicit statement about the relationship between Christianity and what went before, as one of its principal texts, the *Acallam na Senórach*, places the narrative structure within a dialogue between Saint Patrick and two extraordinarily long-lived heroes from the pagan past,

Cáilte and Oisín. In an earlier chapter (chapter 2), we have already seen the risks of attempting to infer the realities of the Iron Age from later myths that purport to depict it. The most that we can say about these later myths is that they echo earlier medieval sources. This is what literary scholars call 'intertextuality': one text influencing another or older motifs appearing in more recent texts. Such echoes across texts from different periods consist primarily of place-names and personal names, like Ethne and Fedelm, the two of whom are mentioned both in the Ulster Cycle and in a seventh-century hagiography written at Armagh, their identities fluctuating between divine (or spiritually elevated) figures and princesses. We shall become more familiar with them in chapter 6, on hagiography. It is, of course, impossible to say whether such figures were interpreted in exactly the same way by readers of the early and the later medieval accounts, the latter of which appear to have modified them to suit more coherent, yet artificially constructed, pantheons. Another example of potentially different interpretations at different times comes from a manuscript gloss written in the ninth century by John Scottus Eriugena. He chose to gloss Latin *lamia*, sometimes translated as 'witch' or 'vampire' in modern dictionaries, with the Old Irish noun *morrigain*.[23] We do not know, however, whether he intended Morrígan in the sense of the goddess of war mentioned in the Ulster Cycle or simply as another word for a monstrous being.

The transmission of concepts with potential religious connotations throughout the ages, and the difficulties in interpreting them, vexed Eriugena in the ninth century as much as it vexes us in the modern era. The preceding discussion of religion in this chapter, which covered a number of categories of evidence, was at times a rewarding exercise, but at times also frustrating because of the inconclusiveness or the unavailability of evidence. Nevertheless, we appear to have gained a number of insights into Patrick's biography and the background to his activities. In particular, we have seen how familiarity with Christianity is attested in the archaeological record in Ireland before the arrival of Patrick. This may be used to corroborate the evidence for the existence of a Christian community, which is implied in Prosper of Aquitaine's account of the dispatching of Palladius to serve Christians in Ireland in 431.

Other aspects of material culture, like syncretism, hint at the way in which Christianity was assimilated into an existing system of ritual and symbols, sometimes through mutual fusion rather than through the replacement of one by the other. Burial sites and their reuse are another area in which it is possible to see interaction between the old and the new, with later graves continuing to be inserted into existing burial sites, some dating from the first millennium BC or earlier. This reuse would have allowed for a certain continuity in ritual observance, instead of a complete break with the past on the occasion of the adoption of Christianity; although the more flagrant aspects of pre-Christian worship would undoubtedly have had to cease. But the places at which the commemoration of ancestors has always taken place could continue to serve as focal points for community identity and memory.

The association of ritual sites with ceremonial political centres in Ireland suggests how far-reaching the impact of religious conversion could have been and how careful Patrick had to be in his engagement with kings so as not to compromise their authority when introducing Christianity into a culture in which religion and politics were intertwined. Although no details can be recovered from the archaeology about the spiritual role that kings had in society, later texts do depict kings as having sacral status, and the landscape evidence seems consistent with this. This too should make us appreciate Patrick's tactfulness in his dealings with royalty without antagonising kings and undermining his mission.

But the greatest challenge for the historian remains the near impossibility of saying much that is meaningful about the pre-Christian religion that Patrick encountered in Ireland. Nevertheless, the mere identification of cult sites and the reuse of many of them speaks volumes about the correspondence between the new and old religions and the delicate and prolonged negotiations—over generations—that made Christianity a permanent fixture of both the actual and the mental landscapes of Ireland, just as permanent as the monumental prehistoric sites continue to be.

Notes

1. Ulpian, citing Antoninus Pius: *Digesta* 12.2.5.1.

2. *Codex Theodosianus* 16.10.12.

3. 'Qui alieni a civitate Dei ex locorum agrestium compitis et pagis pagani uocantur': Orosius, Histories, 1 prol. 9, in *Seven Books of History against the Pagans*, trans. A. T. Fear (Liverpool, 2010), 32.

4. See *Thesaurus Linguae Latinae*, ed. E. Von Wölfflin et al. (Leipzig, 1900–), s.v. 'paganus' (I.A.3.a).

5. Cogitosus, Life of Brigit § 35, ed. K. Hochegger, in 'Untersuchungen zu den Ältesten *Vitae Sanctae Brigidae*' (MPhil diss., University of Vienna, 2009), 18–58, at 52. An English translation is by S. Connolly and J.-M. Picard, in 'Cogitosus's "Life of Brigit": Content and value', *Journal of the Royal Society of Antiquaries of Ireland* 117 (1987): 5–27, at 25 (§ 31).

6. The Calendar of Filocalus from 354. The original calendar does not survive, but a seventeenth-century volume (Vatican Barb. Lat. 2154) reproduces the calendar from a lost eighth-century Carolingian manuscript copy.

7. Fragment § 2, in *The Works of Emperor Julian*, 3 vols., trans. C. Wright (London, 1930–53), 3:428–33 at 428.

8. Fragment § 5, trans. Wright, 430.

9. Oration 2.32, in *Symmaque: Lettres*, 4 vols., ed. and trans. Jean-Pierre Callu (Paris, 1972–2002).

10. *Codex Theodosianus* 15.4.1.1.

11. Priscus, Fragment 8.5, in *The Fragmentary History of Priscus*, trans. John Given (Merchantville, NJ, 2014), 48. A forthcoming edition of the fragments, all preserved in later texts, is Pia Carolla, *Excerpta historica quae Constantini VII Porphyrogeniti dicuntur*, vol. 1, *De legationibus Romanorum ad gentes*, Bibliotheca scriptorum Graecorum et Romanorum Teubneriana (Berlin, forthcoming).

12. *Codex Theodosianus* 16.10.

13. Marcus Annaeus Lucanus, *Pharsalia*, bk. 1, lines 445–46, in *M. Annaei Lucani: De Bello Civilis Libri X*, ed. D. R. Shackleton Baily (Stuttgart, 1988), 16. An English translation is J. D. Duff, trans., *Lucan: The Civil War* (London, 1928).

14. Caesar, *De Bello Gallico* 6.17, in *Caesar: The Gallic War*, trans. H. J. Edwards (London, 1917), 341–43.

15. Translation from the New International Version of the Bible.

16. Caesar, *De Bello Gallico* 6.13, trans. Edwards, 336.

17. Tacitus, *Annales* 14.30, trans. John Jackson (Cambridge, MA, 1937).

18. This is 'CIIC 19. Colbinstown I', now at the National Museum of Ireland, Dublin.

19. 'Nam sol ipse quem videmus <ipso> iubente propter nos cotidie oritur, sed numquam regnabit neque permanebit splendor eius, sed et omnes qui adorant eum in poenam miseri male devenient; nos autem, qui credimus et adoramus solem verum Christum, qui numquam interibit'. I have omitted the relative pronoun 'qui' before 'credimus' in the translation in order to ease the reading.

20. *Félire Óengusso*, Prologue §§ 85, 133, 165, 169, 173, 177, 189, in *The Martyrology of Oengus the Culdee*, ed. and trans. W. Stokes (London, 1905), 20–27.

21. Chronicle of Ireland 558.2, 560.1.

22. *Hibernensis* 18.3, ed. Wasserschleben, 56. But, in a fashion typical of the *Hibernensis*, other churchmen are said to have endorsed burial in the family cemetery, for which see *Hibernensis* 18.2, ed. Wasserschleben, 56.

23. Eriugena, *Glossae Divinae* § 298, in *Glossae divinae historiae: The Biblical Glosses of John Scottus Eriugena*, ed. J. J. Contreni and P. Ó Néill (Florence, 1997), 146: 'Lamia, monstrum in feminae figura, id est morrigain'.

5

The Missionary Life

THE MISSION TO CONVERT the Irish to Christianity is the pinnacle of Patrick's career. For Patrick, conversion was not simply a means by which to win over more souls to the Christian faith but rather a prophetic calling. In his *Confessio* he describes the mission as both the fulfilment of a biblical prophecy and a response to Christ's call to teach all peoples (*omnes gentes*), as in Matthew 24:14.[1] His eagerness to convert is inextricably bound with an eschatological anticipation for the end of time, which he believed was imminent, a feeling that was probably shared by many of his Romano-British contemporaries, who were witnessing the unravelling of their familiar world. The eschatological sentiment is repeated a number of times in Patrick's writings, for example in *Confessio* § 34:

> You appear to me in such divine power, so that today among the heathen I might steadfastly exalt and magnify Your name wherever I find myself. . . . I shall give thanks to God . . . who helped me so that I, for all my ignorance, should in the last days venture to undertake such devout and wonderful work, so that I should follow to some extent the example of those who the Lord long ago foretold would proclaim His gospel

as a testimony to all the nations before the end of the world. And so we have seen, and so it has been fulfilled. Look, we are witnesses that the gospel has been preached to the point beyond which there is no one.

As we hear of God appearing to Patrick as he appeared to the biblical prophets, the apocalyptic anticipation is reinforced, culminating in the calling to preach 'before the end of the world'. The theme continues in *Confessio* §§ 38, 39, where we find further biblical verses incorporated into the text, from Jeremiah, the Gospels, and Acts. Patrick's text echoes the biblical motif of the proselytiser as fisherman (Jer. 16:16; Matt. 4:19) and Christ's command to preach to all peoples while 'I am with you every single day right to the end of the world' (Matt. 28:19–20). The rhetorical climax arrives with the proclamation that 'the gospel of the kingdom shall be preached throughout the whole world as a testimony to all nations, and then the end shall come' (Matt. 24:14). It would appear, therefore, that the conversion project is one that does not merely follow a divine command and look forward to the end of times but actually ushers in the Second Coming. And where would the efficacy of conversion be better proclaimed than on the westernmost island of Europe, regarded by many an ancient author as the edge of the world—or, in Patrick's own words, 'the point beyond which there is no one'? It was there that the physical end and temporal end converged.

The spiritual excitement, or even ecstasy, that is conveyed in the passages quoted in the previous paragraph allows us to appreciate the power of religious zeal that motivated Patrick. It also tells us something about an awareness of the inevitability of his mission: he was driven by a sense of prophetic determinism that moved him, at God's behest, to make a contribution to the salvation of humankind in preparation for the imminent dawning of the Second Coming. What we are shown here in the clearest manner is the way in which he conveys to his readers the ideological motivation for his missionary activity. But what about the practicalities?

For a saint whose fame stems from his missionary work, Patrick is rather frugal on the nuts and bolts of his evangelising campaign and its objectives. For example, we are not told whether he set out to convert all or only some of the inhabitants of Ireland, by what means he hoped to win over souls for the new faith, and whether there were already Christians present on the island, as we are told by other contemporary sources and as the archaeology suggests (see chapter 4, on religion). The tricks of the trade are also largely kept hidden from view. Nevertheless, certain practical aspects of the mission do occasionally surface, especially its travails. For example, we hear of the need to pay kings for protection, of being robbed, of being detained, and of daughters assuming holy orders against their parents' wishes. But otherwise the account is rather unspecific and perfunctory, creating the (probably false) impression that certain communities and individuals were drawn to the new religion almost instinctively, needing neither persuasion nor coercion. And there is surprisingly little and sparsely detailed mention of systematic preaching, but more on this later in the chapter.

Patrick might have been one of a number of missionaries who operated in Ireland in the late fourth or fifth century. Linguistic evidence consisting of Latin loanwords in Irish has for a long time been invoked by historians to show that church-related vocabulary entered the Irish language after it had already been phonologically affected by the British language. Some have interpreted this as clear evidence for early British missionary work among the Irish and have argued, mainly on the place-name evidence, for early British foundations in Ireland, among them

Gailinne na mBretan (Gallen, County Mayo), Tuilén (Dulane, County Meath), Dermag Britonum (in Brega, County Meath), Tech Bretan (County Dublin), Lann Léri (Dunleer, County Dublin), and Tech na mBretan at Kells (County Meath). Apart from Patrick, no British missionary or church founder is known by name. But we do have the name of a Roman missionary who was active in contemporary Ireland. This is Palladius, whom we have already met in chapter 2, on Ireland in Patrick's time.

Palladius, the Roman deacon-turned-bishop, was either a precursor to Patrick or a contemporary of his, depending on how we choose to date Patrick's career. Unlike our contemporary evidence for Patrick, that for Palladius does not depend solely on the writings of a single author, nor on texts written by the protagonist himself. But the biggest difference is that we are able to fix Palladius on the historical timeline with a precision that we wish we had for Patrick. Palladius and his activities are recorded directly and indirectly in a number of contemporary sources, first and foremost among them the Chronicle of Prosper of Aquitaine. A laconic entry for the year 431 describes Palladius's main claim to fame: 'Palladius, having been ordained by pope Celestine, is sent as the first bishop to the Irish who believe in Christ'.[2] Succinct though this entry is, it nevertheless reveals a couple of crucial details. First, Palladius was sent by a pope. And second, he was dispatched to an existing Christian community in Ireland. This would therefore appear not to have been a mission in the conventional sense, but more of an exercise in preaching to the converted. The mention of Irish Christians is as good a proof as one can have of contacts between Ireland and Rome in this period. Otherwise, such contacts only appear in the historical record from early medieval times—for example, in the record of an Irish expedition that arrived in Rome in 630 to learn about the Roman manner of observing Easter (discussed further in chapter 6, on hagiography). There are also hagiographical traditions, whose reliability is uncertain, that would have us believe that several Irish saints had visited Rome in the sixth and seventh centuries.[3]

It has been suggested by Thomas Charles-Edwards that Prosper's insistence that Palladius would be received by a Christian community was in keeping with Celestine's fourth letter, in which the pope established the rule that no bishop should be sent to a community unwilling to receive him.[4] In issuing this ruling, the pope might have been following the second canon of the Council of Constantinople (381), which forbade a bishop from ministering in another diocese unless he was invited.[5] This would have enabled Palladius to exercise authority even if he entered the jurisdiction of another bishop, without risking a violation of ecclesiastical legislation, which normally regarded such intrusions as grave offences.[6] Though, as we shall see later, Celestine (according to Prosper) believed that the mission to Ireland eventually reached non-Christians as well as Christians.

What should we make of the fact that the pope deemed it necessary to send Palladius to preach to the converted? The idea of religious conversion, which would have been entirely alien to Romans of the pre-Christian era, was absolutely central to the church and the Roman state from the early days of imperial Christian legalisation, legislation that also covered the topic of Christian worship. Increasingly, the legislation enacted by emperors sought to extend the appeal of Christianity by privileging its followers over pagans, and churches embarked on conversion enterprises aimed not only at non-Christians but also at heretics—namely, those who were believed to hold a perverse Christian doctrine. Some heresies even espoused doctrines that undermined the idea of mission itself, thereby challenging one of the central tenets of Christian Orthodoxy, which saw the

expansion of Christianity as the sine qua non for the very survival of the Christian church and religion. One such heresy was
Pelagianism, which flourished in the time of Patrick and also
appears to have reached Britain. We owe much of our understanding of what Pelagianism was to its detractors, who—as
detractors often do—maligned it and misrepresented it. But we
also have a number of surviving writings by adherents of the Pelagian doctrine, and even twenty by the eponymous 'founder'
of the heresy, the British-born Pelagius. Among these are a commentary on the Catholic Epistles, a commentary on Job, eight
letters, and a tract on free will. The concept of free will was central
to the debate between Pelagius and his opponents, the most celebrated among them being the giant of Christian theology of late
antiquity, Saint Augustine. Pelagius appears to have attributed
to humanity a greater degree of free will than Augustine and his
followers were willing to countenance. They, on the contrary, believed that human will was directed by divine grace (*gratia*),
without which no human could do good. The Pelagian position
(insofar as it was consistent among the doctrine's followers and
as we are able to reconstruct it) stemmed from the belief that the
Fall brought about a wholesale corruption of humanity but that
original sin could nevertheless be washed away by baptism. As
against this, the Augustinian view held that original sin persisted
regardless of baptism and that divine grace was the means by
which humans could be deemed righteous despite it. In other
words, one camp believed that grace enabled free will, while the
other saw grace as a divine force working within the human soul
and over which the individual had no control. However, Pelagius's own view was often conflated with the position of his disciple and associate Caelestius, who seems to have denied the
need for infant baptism altogether. By adhering to this form of
Pelagianism and holding that humans could exercise free will

without having their sins remitted through baptism, the role of the church as mediator of divine grace and expunger of sin would be severely diminished. Consequently, the need for a Christian mission was reduced. For why bother with the church if you can do it yourself?

The controversy that arose around the doctrines of Pelagius and Caelestius engulfed some of the most prominent theologians and church leaders of the time, including the aforementioned Augustine, but also his contemporary esteemed church father Jerome, the historian and theologian Orosius, and Pope Innocent I and his successor Pope Zosimus. The debates took place at church councils, the most famous being that in Carthage in 418. Occasionally Pelagius enjoyed some successes in fending off accusations of heresy—at one time proving that Caelestius's views were wrongly imputed to him—but it was the Western emperor Honorius who struck the fatal blow, decreeing on 30 April 418 that Pelagius and Caelestius, along with their followers, must leave the empire.

Britain, which by 418 was irredeemably outside the empire after the withdrawal of the legions in 410, became a refuge (perhaps the main refuge) for Pelagian exiles. It is in this context that our old friend the Roman deacon Palladius made his first appearance on the historical stage. In 429, according to Prosper's Chronicle again, he advised Pope Celestine to appoint Germanus of Auxerre (later Saint Germanus) as his emissary to Britain, where he was to confront the 'enemies of grace' who had settled there and free the Christians of Britain from the taint of heresy. In another of his works, concerning free will, Prosper draws a connection between Germanus's mission to Britain and Palladius's to Ireland when he says of Pope Celestine that 'as he strives to make the Roman island Catholic, he has also made the barbarian island Christian'.[7] The 'Roman island' is, of course, a reference to Britain, and the 'barbarian island' to Ireland. The description of the 'barbarian island' turning Christian suggests that Palladius's mission was perceived as being aimed not only at the Christians who invited him but also at those who were not yet Christian. Prosper's words clearly show that he judged the mission a success, and that Ireland—to his knowledge—was converted. This narrative was reinforced in 441 by a close friend of Prosper's: Pope Leo the Great. In a sermon preached on Saint Peter and Saint Paul's Feast Day (29 June) that exalted the successes of the Christian missionary enterprise, the pope contrasted the geographical extent of imperial Rome with the wider extent of the Christian dominion subject to papal government: 'You [Rome] govern more widely by divine religion than by worldly domination. For although you have been increased by many victories and extended the power of your empire over land and sea, what the toils of war submitted to you is less than that which a Christian peace subjected [to you]'.[8] The additional territory that, according to Leo, Christian Rome brought under its sway has been interpreted by Charles-Edwards as the island of Ireland, which was never within the political borders of the Roman Empire. For Leo and his friend Prosper, therefore, Ireland was a missionary success story driven by Rome, a success that vindicates Rome's eternal glory.

It has recently been suggested by Colmán Etchingham that Germanus's mission could perhaps have been conceived with the intention of preempting Pelagians from establishing themselves in Ireland, an island that lay even more securely out of reach of imperial authority than Britain. This is an attractive speculation, although it cannot be confirmed or disproved on the available evidence. The oldest recorded attempt to argue for a connection between the Irish and not simply Pelagianism but Pelagius himself was made by Saint Jerome in a fifth-century acerbic condemnation in which he claimed that Pelagius was Irish. This is unlikely to have been intended as a statement of fact but rather was meant as an insult for diverging from established dogma.[9] We have already encountered Jerome's derogatory remarks about the Irish in chapter 2, where we saw instances of his rhetorical use of the Irish as a prototype of a semisavage 'Other'.

Apart from Leo's and Prosper's oblique references to the conversion of Ireland, nothing else is known of the activities of Palladius, whose legacy has been all but muted in Ireland. Unlike Patrick, Palladius never enjoyed his own cult, and in fact he may have been deliberately written out of history by the earliest hagiographers of Patrick, the seventh-century Armagh propagandists Muirchú and Tírechán, who sought to give their protagonist sole credit for the conversion of Ireland. Contrary to the testimonies of Prosper and Leo, Muirchú even went as far as to portray Palladius's mission as a failure that ended in tragedy when he died in Britain on his way back to Rome.[10] Whereas Muirchú can be argued to have deliberately played down Palladius's achievements, Prosper and Celestine might be said to have trumped them up. Prosper's congratulatory praise of Celestine as the instigator of Palladius's successful mission and Leo's triumphalist assertion that Christian Rome had extended its reach farther than the Roman imperial state may have overstated the achievement somewhat. As we know from both medieval and modern examples of missions that are better attested than Palladius's, 'blitz missions' are rarely a success, and in fact they often end in failure. Such failure would be known by the more technical name 'apostasy', which is the process of lapsing back into paganism, such as is said to have happened after the death of Æthelberht, king of Kent, when his son Eadbald and his subjects reverted to pagan worship in 616.[11] But more on this later.

Patrick was therefore not alone on the scene, although his own writings make no mention of other missionaries and do not even hint at Palladius's or another foreigner's presence. Nevertheless, it is possible, of course, that, given the uncertainty about Patrick's dates, as discussed in chapter 2, the two never coincided. Since it was not Patrick's intent to offer a running commentary on the activities of other clerics in Ireland, be they British or of other extractions, he can be forgiven for omitting any mention of their presence. Although, had any of them encountered him, one can imagine an ironic moment of the kind that took place when, in 1871 on the shore of Lake Tanganyika, Henry Morton Stanley finally found the missionary David Livingstone, the only other white-skinned man in the area, and uttered the now famous greeting, 'Dr Livingstone, I presume'. The analogy with Livingstone, the Victorian adventurer-cum-missionary, is also a reminder to the modern reader of Patrick's works that he or she must be mindful of potential rhetorical overstatements of Patrick's travails and achievements. Recent biographers of Livingstone have noted that the colourful autobiographical accounts of their protagonist's operations in Africa were more often than not embellished portrayals of a rather ordinary sojourn in a foreign land, with largely unsuccessful attempts to convert locals. But such were the contemporary conventions of the genre of nineteenth-century travel tales (both written and delivered orally) that one ought not apply a value judgement to the choices that the missionary made as a storyteller. And the same goes for our appreciation of Patrick as a storyteller.

What, then, does Patrick say about his mission? When he raises the topic for the first time in the *Confessio*, he gives his readers a sense of scale when he says, echoing the trope of remoteness, that he baptised thousands from 'the ends of the earth' (*ab extremis terrae*). This was for him the crowning accomplishment of his career and the pinnacle of his legacy.[12] On a more personal level, Patrick draws a connection between his mission to bring salvation to others and the religious transformation that he himself underwent, from a lax Christian to a fully committed one.[13] But the initiative to embark on a mission, Patrick says, was not his. Rather, like Palladius, he too was called to service. Patrick describes a vision that he had had while in Britain after his return from his alleged captivity, in which a certain Victoricus, arriving from Ireland and carrying many letters, presented him with a letter that opened with the phrase 'the voice of the Irish' (*vox Hiberionacum*). As Patrick read the opening lines, he imagined the voice of those living beside the forest of Voclut, 'near the western sea', beckoning him to return.[14] There has been some debate among scholars regarding the identity of this Victoricus, but no consensus was ever reached. Allan B. E. Hood attempted to identify him with Victricius, a fourth-century missionary bishop of Rouen and a disciple of Saint Martin of Tours, himself remembered for his extensive missionary work among the rustics of Gaul. Hood seems to have accepted at face value Muirchú's seventh-century account that Patrick himself visited Gaul (see chapter 6), believing that it was there that Patrick met Victoricus/Victricius. More recent suggestions, that he was an old friend or fellow Briton and former slave, are pure speculation. Frustratingly, the identity of this personality remains shrouded in obscurity.

We read more of the mission's success when Patrick describes how he ordained clergy.[15] The scale of ordinations, however, is likely to have been moderated by the absence (so far as we know) of other bishops in Ireland, such that Patrick would only have been able to ordain clerics below the rank of bishop. This is because early ecclesiastical legislation required at least three bishops to be present at the consecration of another (early Irish hagiography will indeed invent suffragan bishops to assist Patrick).[16] Consequently, Patrick could not have established a church with a robust episcopal hierarchy of the kind that existed in, say, Gaul or Britain. However, one can argue that the number of believers in his time would not have required more than one bishop and that the ordination of subordinate clergy would have been enough. As a further sign of success, Patrick notes that the sons and daughters of petty kings (*reguli*) became 'monks and nuns of Christ' (*monachi et virgines Christi*).[17] An Irish *regulus*, as we have seen in chapter 2, is likely to be a reference to a *rí túaithe*. These are the same kings and sons of kings who are said to have received presents from Patrick and in return to have ridden with him on his travels, presumably for protection but also as a way of lending their authority to his missionary endeavour.[18] It would appear, therefore, that the *Confessio* describes a top-down conversion process, whereby the conversion at the top levels of society cascaded down the social ladder. Patrick's mission is the earliest known example of a process of this kind, which is otherwise only attested from the early Middle Ages, beginning with the Gregorian mission to the court of Æthelberht of Kent in 597.

But the top-down mission that Patrick describes seems to have been directed at sons and daughters of kings, bypassing their fathers. The princes and princesses were the ones turning to the new religion, sometimes pursuing such a high degree of commitment that they submitted to the monastic life. There seem to be no comparable contemporary examples of this disparity between the royal fathers' response to a mission and the response of their offspring, but there are a number of later parallels. For example, King Penda (d. 655) of Mercia never converted himself, but he had his son Peada baptised.[19] The princely conversion described in Patrick's *Confessio* and in the Mercian example are of a piece with a wider phenomenon of princely conversions, which were styled a 'double insurance policy' by Henry Mayr-Harting in a study of the conversion of the Carinthians of southeast Bavaria in the mid-eighth century. He drew attention to a pattern whereby a ruler would have his sons baptised (or acquiesce in their conversion) but not convert himself so as not to sever the connection with the old deities and risk offending either them or his subjects. If this is indeed what the converted royal families in Ireland were doing, then the *Confessio* is the earliest attestation of this practice too.

Patrick, as already noted, says not simply that the sons and daughters of kings converted to Christianity but rather that they became monks and nuns. He also mentions a noblewoman who was baptised and willingly submitted to him as a nun, as well as widows and daughters becoming nuns despite their parents' wishes, consequently enduring persecution by their kin.[20] Ostensibly, therefore, Patrick shows sympathy or even admiration for those converts, especially women, who committed themselves to a monastic and celibate lifestyle. To regard virginity or perpetual widowhood as a great virtue was a staple of early Christian thinking in both East and West. As Peter Brown observes in relation to Jerome, 'Jerome made constant propaganda for widowhood and virginity as immobile, consecrated states. By idealizing perpetual virginity and by praising perpetual widowhood, Jerome did nothing less than threaten to freeze two vital moving parts in the structure of Roman aristocracy'. Patrick appears to have been engaged in a similar kind of praise propaganda, and the persecution that he says women had to endure would have issued from the same sort of anxieties experienced by male Roman aristocrats—namely, that women who remained virgins would prevent their families from forging social bonds through marriage, and widows who did not remarry (usually a member of the extended kin) exposed their portion of the family wealth to the risk of alienation.

It is not quite clear what exactly a monastic life would have entailed in Ireland at this time. The monastic ideal of a secluded lifestyle in celibate communities was formalised in a set of regulations for monastic living known generically as 'rules'. But these rules would only become prevalent in the west of Europe a few centuries later. And even as late as the ninth century, at the height of Carolingian monastic activity, many monasteries would remain far off the mark of ideal monastic practice, which was by then based on the late sixth-century Benedictine Rule. But in Patrick's time, Benedict had yet to be born, and monasticism in the West was in its infancy. Monasticism is first attested in the West from the mid-fourth century, and its most famous exponents—Jerome, Rufinus, Melania the Elder, and Melania the Younger—in fact left Europe for the more established monastic centres of North Africa and Palestine. The earliest monastery to have been established in the West, Martin's near Tours, was probably more like a hermitage, although in time it drew followers who appear to have called themselves monks. On his return from pilgrimage in Palestine and Egypt in 415, John Cassian, often regarded as the father of Western monasticism, founded in Marseilles a monastery for men and another for women. He is also credited with the introduction of monastic rules from the East, which served as the basis for modified rules for Western monks. Patrick, therefore, has a good claim for being among the earliest monastic founders in the west of Europe. Sadly, we know nothing about the sort of monasticism that he championed: there is no hint of a monastic rule, nor is there a suggestion that this early version of Irish monasticism was meant—at least in ideal, if not in practice—to offer an alternative or a complement to an episcopal hierarchy (as, for example, parallel monastic and episcopal hierarchies emerge in Gaul from the late sixth century).

Patrick's emphasis on girls' taking the veil against the will of their kin and suffering 'persecution and unfair reproaches' (*perescutionis patiuntur et impropria falsa*) suggests that monasticism, rather than conversion to Christianity itself, was upsetting certain family members. Assuming that the monks and nuns lived apart from their families in their own communities, the families that they would have left behind could be affected in at least two adverse ways. First, they would lose control over a family member who instead committed himself or herself to a community of purpose that (in theory, at least) was beyond kin loyalties. And second, the monastic community would need to set itself up on land, which would (once more, in theory) be granted by a kin group. Patrick says nothing about monks or nuns relinquishing portions of the land of their kin for the sake of their communities, but he does remark on their attempts to give him gifts of other kinds. This is what he says in an important passage that we have already examined in other contexts, which I quote here in full:

> I have done my best to safeguard myself, even in my dealings with Christian brethren and virgins of Christ and with pious women, who would give me unsolicited gifts and throw some of their jewellery on the altar, and I would return it to them, and they would take offence at my doing so; but I did so for the hope of eternity, to safeguard myself carefully in everything so that they would not catch me out or the ministry of my service under some pretext of my dishonesty and so that I would not give unbelievers the slightest opportunity for denigration or disparagement. But perhaps when I baptised so many thousands I hoped for even half a scruple [*scriptula*]

from any of them? Tell me and I will give it back. Or when the Lord everywhere ordained clergy through someone as ordinary as me and I conferred on each of them his function free, if I asked any of them for even so much as the price of my shoe [*pretium calciamenti mei*], tell it against me, and I shall give it back to you.[21]

By saying that he did not receive as much as half a scruple (a scruple being a small measure of weight) for baptising, nor 'the price of [his] shoe' for ordaining clergy, Patrick is revealing that clerics could in fact expect to be compensated for their trouble, an expectation that may be justified by scripture—for example, Paul's First Epistle to the Corinthians 9:11, which reads, 'If we have sown spiritual things among you, is it too much if we reap material things from you?' However, when this passage is read contextually, a more complex picture emerges. In the following verses (12–15), Paul says, 'If others partake of this right from you, should we not share in it all the more? But we did not make use of this right. Instead, we put up with anything rather than hinder the gospel of Christ. Do you not know that those who work in the temple eat of its food, and those who serve at the altar partake of its offerings? In the same way, the Lord has prescribed that those who preach the gospel should receive their living from the gospel. But I have not used any of these rights'.

In other words, preachers of the gospel are entitled to be supported by the communities they serve, but they are free to forgo that entitlement, as Paul had done. Patrick, it seems, is echoing the greatest of Christian proselytisers and role model for later missionaries when he also declares that he renounces his right to claim recompense for his pastoral work.

As for the repeated attempts to give Patrick gifts, these can be interpreted as a refusal on his part to partake in the social custom of mutual gift exchange, which was discussed in chapter 2. But perhaps there is more that he is trying to tell us here, for it may be significant that he mentions the gifts immediately before saying that he never received money in exchange for performing baptisms or ordinations. Could Patrick be saying that he acted in good faith by rejecting gifts himself, while at the same time accepting gifts of land that were intended for monastic communities that he founded? This possibility takes us into the realm of speculation, which we can undertake by drawing on recorded practice from later centuries. In the Middle Ages there would have been nothing unusual in accepting gifts for monasteries. Such gifts were usually part and parcel of what is technically known as oblation (from the Latin *oblatio*, meaning 'gift'), a donation that would accompany youths entering a monastery. The physical setting in which Patrick describes the gift giving taking place, by the altar, is significant. We know from later texts that the granting of land to a church would be a public act that would take place in the most conspicuous place of a church building: in the chancel, by the altar. In the seventh century, we read of Fith Fio's grant to a monastery in Drumlease (County Sligo): 'This is Fith Fio's declaration and his testament, made between the chancel and the altar two years before his death to the community of Druim Lías and the nobles of Calrige.'[22]

In his description of people throwing gifts at the altar, Patrick mentions not only monks and nuns but also pious women. Why should these be women rather than men? Perhaps he intended to evoke the scriptural passage about the widow leaving a donation at the Temple (Mark 12:43–44; Luke 21:3–4): 'Truly I say to you, this poor widow has put in more than all those who are contributing to the treasury. For they all contributed of their abundance, but she out of her poverty'. Widows are explicitly mentioned in the *Confessio* as being among those who are welcome among Patrick's worshippers.[23] Women in general, and widows in particular, are often portrayed in late antique and medieval texts as potential alienators of wealth. The concern that they might alienate family wealth stemmed from the possibility that a married woman may transfer some of her family's wealth to her husband's kin, or that a widow would grant away (or, being vulnerable, would be made to grant away) property, especially if she had no male heirs. A widow could often control property as a dowager, a woman who had title to her husband's property, which would eventually revert to his kin on her death. Beginning in late antiquity, the church benefitted a great deal from the generosity of widows.

But gifting land to the church did not always have to end in a wholesale irrevocable loss of property to the kin. Some wealthy benefactors could avail themselves of an institution that allowed them to eat the cake and have it too. This was the 'proprietary church', which has been discussed in chapter 2. In a nutshell, this was a system that allowed kin groups to gift land to the church but to continue to retain a stake in the land in perpetuity. The donation of land made by the nobleman Fith Fio, whom we have just met, provides a classic example of the foundation of a proprietary church. A fuller version of the text cited earlier reads as follows: 'This is Fith Fio's declaration and his testament, made between the chancel and the altar two years before his death to the community of Druim Lías and the nobles of Calrige: that there is no family right of inheritance of Drum Lías for any except the people of Fith Fio'.[24] One can see here very clearly how Fith Fio's kin secures for itself a stake in the church that it founds, by ensuring that only its own kin members can inherit the headship of the church. Perhaps in rejecting the gifts of jewellery and other precious movables, Patrick was leaving the door open to donations of land made under conditions stipulated by the kin groups of the monks and nuns. But this suggestion, it must again be acknowledged, is speculative.

Whereas certain kin groups welcomed the conversion of some of their members, others did not. We have already encountered the retribution experienced by daughters who received baptism against their parents' wishes. But a worse fate, we are told, awaited convert women kept in slavery (*quae in servitio detinentur*), who were threatened and terrorised more than others.[25] No detail is given as to why they endured a worse fate than, say, male Christian slaves, nor are we told whether the masters of the slave women were Christians themselves or whether they remained pagan. Another crucial detail that is missing is the path by which slave women could convert: Did they need their masters' permission? How did they have access to preaching? Did they convert without any formal process? Unfortunately, the text gives no answer, and no hint of an answer, to these questions. Nevertheless, the possibility that an informal form of conversion did take place, which Patrick acknowledged as valid, is one worth considering, for it raises an important question: What would Patrick have crowned a successful conversion? Would he have expected his converts to attain a deep level of conviction in the new faith, or would he have settled for conversion as a formality, consisting only of a rudimentary understanding of central tenets of the faith? Under normal circumstances, the formal requisite of any Christian conversion was baptism, usually administered to the newly converted in a public ritual in which they were also expected to profess the Orthodox Nicene Creed, which affirms the belief in the one creator God and his only begotten son. Patrick certainly envisioned a ritual of this kind as a fundamental rite of passage in the conversion process. It is possible to infer the formula of the creed that Patrick used in baptisms from the words of his own profession of the faith, given early in the *Confessio*:

> For there is no other God, nor ever was before nor will be hereafter except for God the Father, unbegotten, without beginning, from whom is all beginning, possessing of all things ... and His son Jesus Christ, whom we declare to have existed always with the Father, before the beginning of the world spiritually with the Father, begotten ineffably before all beginning; and by Him were made things visible and invisible; having been made man He conquered death and was received up into heaven to the Father; and He gave him all power over every name of things in heaven and on earth and under the earth, that every tongue should confess to Him that Jesus Christ is Lord and God; in whom we believe, and we look to his imminent coming, as judge of the living and the dead, who will render to each one according to his deeds; and He poured on us abundantly His Holy Spirit, the gift and pledge of immortality, who makes those who believe and obey to be sons of god and heirs along with Christ; Him we confess and worship as one God in the Trinity of sacred name.[26]

With its promise of future judgement, this particular version of the creed goes beyond the Nicene template by introducing an eschatological hue, typical of Patrick. In fact, this text does not correspond to any known creed. Patrick appears to have compiled it by drawing on a melange of excerpts from biblical passages and late antique scholia. For example, the phrases 'in heaven and on earth and under the earth' and 'judge of the living and the dead' are taken, respectively, from Paul's Letter to the Philippians 2:10 and Acts 10:42. But the phrases 'before the beginning of the world spiritually with the Father', 'having been made man He conquered death and was received up into heaven to the Father', and 'will render to each one according to his deeds' only have parallels in the writings of the theologians Cyprian (d. 258) of Carthage and Victorinus (d. ca. 304) of Pettau.[27] This does not mean that Patrick had direct access to complete works by these authors, but he could have encountered them in collections of sayings (*florilegia*), which were a common medium for accessing texts that were not always available in complete form. Patrick's pastiche creed is therefore an original compilation of excerpts, but it nevertheless appears to adhere to an entirely orthodox programme.

As one would expect, on its own, a formal sacramental conversion that consists merely of baptism and the uttering of a creed may be too superficial to be a reliable guarantee for a durable conversion. Indeed, the English converts of the early seventh century who reportedly participated in mass public baptisms were the very same people who apostasied only a few years later when Eadbald ascended to the throne in Kent (mentioned earlier in this chapter). But it seems that apart from a sacramental conversion, Patrick demanded more, at least from those he converted himself. This we can infer from the way he describes his newly converted in the Letter to the Soldiers of Coroticus. There, the converts were catechumens. The process of the catechumenate, which culminated at Easter, was the prolonged induction that the newly converted underwent as they were preparing for baptism. The process varied in the early centuries of Christianity, but generally speaking it would have included a series of sessions in which those who were about to convert were gradually brought into the fold of the church over a period of weeks, sometimes (as in Alexandria) lasting up to forty days altogether and overlapping with the period of Lent before Easter. In its fullest form, the catechumenate consisted of receiving an introduction to Christian ideas about morality, doing a certain amount of fasting, undergoing exorcism, learning prayers, and submitting to various tests. There was never a uniform protocol for the catechumenate in late antiquity, and given Patrick's openness to combining traditions, it is impossible to know exactly what he followed. What can be said, however, is that he carried out the catechism during Lent (on the significance of the timing, see chapter 4) and that he followed a tradition—attested widely in Christendom—of requiring catechumens to wear distinctive dress, which, by the time that they approached their baptism, consisted of a white garment.[28]

Patrick does not say how locals were drawn to becoming catechumens in the first place. Some individuals, like the noblewoman he admitted as a nun, appear to have accepted Christianity of their own volition.[29] Others, one may assume, converted out of loyalty to their convert elders or leaders, who may even have coerced them to convert. Preaching, according to Patrick's account, was a routine part of his activity, but it did not always meet with success. Instead of winning over souls, he sometimes suffered insults and persecution.[30] His preaching, we may assume, would have been done by him rather than through an interpreter because his youth in Ireland (whether we believe he was a slave or an exiled aristocrat) would have rendered him fluent in the vernacular, a language known by the technical name Archaic Irish.

While the arguments or methods by which he tried to bring people to convert are not known, we may nevertheless speculate about them by analogy with other missionary enterprises or with the way in which those enterprises were described by Christian scholars writing to contemporaries and future generations. The most pertinent to our case is the missionary work of Patrick's contemporary or near contemporary Saint Martin of Tours (d. 397). His biography, by Sulpicius Severus, was completed around the time of his death and became one of the most popular works of hagiography, influencing numerous later hagiographies and exciting the imagination of a great many readers and listeners throughout the Middle Ages. It was, in fact, copied into the Book of Armagh alongside the Patrician dossier. Martin attained great renown in his lifetime, which is likely to have reached Patrick if the two were contemporaries or near contemporaries. There is no indication, however, that Patrick read Sulpicius's text, even if it had been completed during his lifetime. Therefore, one cannot expect Patrick to have attempted to cast himself in the hagiographical image of the great evangelist of Gaul. The central pillars of Sulpicius's construction of Martin's identity are his depictions as a relentless miracle worker and as an oppressor of demons. Neither of these is present in Patrick's works, which do not even hint at miracles of the kind that Martin was associated with, ranging from healing the sick to raising the dead. Admittedly, one would not expect such fanciful and blatantly boastful things to be told by a purportedly meek author writing his autobiography. But even the more plausible activities that Martin is said to have been involved in (albeit contested by modern scholars) find no echo in Patrick's account. Especially missing are the descriptions of a saint destroying pagan shrines and setting up Christian churches in their place. It can therefore be said that Patrick's texts offer an entirely different model for a mission from Martin's. The two great evangelisers of late antiquity, one from within the Roman ambit and the other operating outside it, are seen as independent and antithetic. Eventually, it would be Martin's mission (as told by Sulpicius) rather than Patrick's that would serve as the template for early medieval missionary hagiographies, including Irish ones.

The absence in Patrick's texts of any description of the destruction of pagan sites and their replacement with churches draws

attention to another curious fact: in neither the *Confessio* nor the
Letter is there mention of pagan cult sites or the erection of
churches. Priests are ordained, as we have seen, but no churches
are said to have been built. Indeed, the word 'church' (*ecclesia*)
is mentioned only once in the *Confessio* and once in the Letter,
neither mention referring to a specific church.[31] Rather, in both
cases it denotes the universal collective of Christian believers.
Oddly, in the world that Patrick describes, cults—be they pagan
or Christian—appear to take place in a physical vacuum, having
no geographical or architectural substance. There are no sacred
trees, no sacred water sources, no pagan shrines, and no churches.
Possibly, churches simply did not figure in Patrick's narrative
agenda and so he chose to omit them. However, it seems somewhat strange that Patrick would choose to gloss over physical
mementos to his missionary achievements. Could it be that Patrick did not mention churches simply because none were built
in his time? Is it possible that Patrick's idea of conversion did not
involve the use of buildings dedicated to the act of worship? Even
the mention of an altar, which we have encountered in the context of almsgiving, does not necessarily imply the existence of
a church. Portable altars from Patrick's time have been excavated
at Vindolanda, on Hadrian's Wall, and we know of portable altars being used in missionary expeditions—for example, in the
mission to Frisia in the late seventh century, where we find two
Anglo-Saxon priests carrying a *tabula altaris* for celebrating the
Eucharist.[32] Indeed, churches, for whatever reason, are oddly absent from Patrick's narrative, an absence that will be more than
compensated for by Patrick's seventh-century hagiographers,
whom we shall meet in the next chapter of this book.

Also missing are mentions of the cults of other saints and the
physical manifestations of those cults—namely, relics. Relics, in
the form of either remains from saints' bodies (for example,

bones or hair) or things associated with the saints (for example, garments they wore or manuscripts they wrote), were a staple of later missionary enterprises and were among the most conspicuous physical manifestations of the transition from pagan cult to Christian worship. One of the better-known examples of the role of relics in this transition is Pope Gregory the Great's command to his missionaries in England not to destroy pagan shrines but to purge them of effigies of idols and replace them with the relics of saints. By 609 the Pantheon in Rome, formerly a centre for polytheistic worship, was itself consecrated as a Christian church, following the precedent set by Gregory. But Patrick seems not to have employed any of this toolkit known from later missionary work. Once more, we see in Patrick's narrative an entirely different and independent strand of missionary account in comparison with the influential accounts of Sulpicius and (later) Gregory, in which the material and the tangible have a more prominent presence.

Nevertheless, despite the absence of any explicit mention of churches, Patrick says he ordained many clerics, of which he distinguishes two categories: *clerici* and *presbyteri*.[33] Another sacramental grade found in Patrick's writings, the bishop (*episcopus*), is only mentioned with reference to Patrick himself.[34] As we have already observed in connection with the absence of bishops in Ireland other than Patrick, it would appear that Patrick was describing a hierarchy at the top of which he presided as the sole bishop over *presbyteri* and *clerici*. The distinction that Patrick envisioned between the two subordinate grades is open to interpretation. In contemporary Roman imperial usage, *clericus* was—as in present-day English parlance—a generic name for all clerics.[35] The ecclesiastical hierarchy that Roman law recognised corresponded to the traditional seven sacramental grades, consisting of bishop, *presbyter*, deacon, subdeacon (and, occasionally, deaconess), exorcist, lector, and doorkeeper.[36] A *presbyter* was therefore second in line after the bishop, which is also the way in which Patrick seems to have understood the relationship between these two grades. Consequently, 'priest' is a reasonable translation. Deacons came third, and Patrick himself, like his father, was a deacon as he was ascending the ecclesiastical hierarchy towards becoming bishop.[37] Nevertheless, Patrick mentions no deacons in Ireland, and this impinges on our interpretation of *clericus*, which may simply have been Patrick's way of designating a catchall third tier below bishop and *presbyter*. Perhaps the nascent church in Ireland was as yet too small and institutionally unsophisticated to be able to accommodate an elaborate hierarchy consisting of all seven grades, resulting in all grades between deacon and doorkeeper being collapsed into one.

Patrick says he ordained *clerici* not in one place but rather in many places as he was travelling and preaching.[38] These clerics, we may assume, were tasked with dispensing pastoral care of one kind or another. At the very least, one would assume, this consisted of baptism, mass, and burial services. But some clerics performed other roles too, including participating in diplomatic expeditions. We find such clerics accompanying a *presbyter* on an ill-fated mission to secure the release of the newly converted who were captured by Coroticus.[39] On arriving at Coroticus's camp, they read a letter (which does not survive) by Patrick demanding both the release of the captives and the return of *aliquid de praeda* (some of the spoils) that the British raiders carried off with them. However, according to Patrick, his emissaries were laughed off, prompting Patrick to write his famous surviving letter of condemnation. The mention of spoils is a puzzle: What kind of spoils could be taken from a group of catechumens? Is this episode related at all to the accusation that Patrick received payment in return for baptism? Once more, we find ourselves challenging the narrative but unable to see behind the text and interpret it fully.

The terrible fate that a group of Patrick's converts suffered at the hands of Coroticus and his soldiers would have vindicated the eschatological urgency of his missionary work. For the captives, the end was indeed nigh. Patrick's penchant for apocalyptic rhetoric, a topic with which the present chapter opened, suggests something about the content of his preaching to those whom he sought to convert. The impending end was something to prepare for, and the new faith offered hope that another, happier chapter is about to follow.

Notes

1. *Confessio* §§ 34, 40.

2. Prosper, Chronicle 431, in *Chronica Minora saec. IV. V. VI. VII*, ed. Theodor Mommsen, Monumenta Germaniae Historica: Auctores Antiquissimi 9 (Berlin, 1892), 473.

3. On the expedition concerning Easter, see *Cummian's Letter 'De controversia pachali'*, ed. M. Walsh and D. Ó Cróinín (Toronto, 1988), 55–97. For saints' visits to Rome, see, among others, Life of Cainnech § 6 (Heist, 183), Life of Colmán Élo § 20 (Heist, 216), Life of Déclán § 9 (Plummer, 2:38), Life of Enda § 7 (Plummer, 2:63), Life of Ciarán of Saigir § 3 (Heist, 347), Life of Lugaid § 68 (Heist, 144), Life of Laisrén §§ 7–8 (Heist, 341–42), Life of Tigernach § 5 (Heist, 108), and Life of Bairre § 11 (Plummer, 1:70).

4. 'Nullus invitis detur episcopus. Cleri, plebis et ordinis, consensus ac desiderium requiratur': Celestine, *Ad episcopos per Viennensem et Narbonensem prouincias* 4.5, in *Epistolae Romanorum Pontificum ... ab anno Christi 67* A.D. *annum 440*, ed. P. Coustant (Paris, 1721), 1065–72.

5. A. Strewe, ed., *Die Canonessammlung des Dionysius Exiguus in der ersten Redaktion* (Berlin, 1931), 60–61.

6. See, for example, Apostolic Canons §§ 14, 35; Council of Nicaea (AD 325) § 15; Council of Antioch (AD 341) § 22; and Council of Constantinople (AD 381) § 2. For modern editions, see, respectively, Strewe, *Die Canonessammlung*, 1–10, 24–31, 44–52, 60–61.

7. Prosper of Aquitaine, *De gratia Dei et libero arbitrio contra Collatorem*, in *Sancti Prosperi Aquitani S. Augustini discipuli, S. Leonis Papæ primi notarii Opera omnia*, ed. Luc Urbain Mangeant (Paris, 1711), repr. PL 51:213–76, at 51:271C: 'Dum Romanam insulam studet servare catholicam, fecit etiam barbaram Christianam'.

8. 'Latius praesideres religione divina quam dominatione terrena. Quamvis enim multis aucta victoriis ius imperii tui terra marique distenderis, minus tamen est quod tibi bellicus labor subdidit quam quod pax Christiana subiecit': Leo, Sermon 82.1, in *Leo Magnus: Tractatus*, ed. A. Chavasse, CCSL 138–138A (Turnhout, 1973).

9. Jerome, Commentary on Jeremiah, ed. S. Reiter, CCSL 74 (Turnhout, 1960), prologue, lines 20–21.

10. Muirchú, Life of Patrick I.8, in Bieler, *Patrician Texts*, 72.

11. Bede, *HE* 2.5, ed. and trans. Colgrave and Mynors, 148–55.

12. *Confessio* §§ 14, 38, 50.

13. *Confessio* § 28.

14. *Confessio* § 23.

15. *Confessio* § 38.

16. As in canon 13 of the fourth-century *Statuta Ecclesiae Antiqua* (ed. C. Munier, CCSL 148 [Turnhout, 1963], 164–88), which requires at least three bishops for consecration.

17. *Confessio* § 41.

18. *Confessio* § 52.

19. Bede, *HE* 3.21, ed. and trans. Colgrave and Mynors, 278–81. Contrast with Sæberht of Essex (d. 616), who converted but his three sons never did.

20. *Confessio* § 42.

21. *Confessio* §§ 49, 50.

22. *Additamenta* § 9, in Bieler, *Patrician Texts*, 173. I changed the translation slightly.

23. *Confessio* § 42.

24. *Additamenta* §9, in Bieler, *Patrician Texts*, 173. I changed the translation slightly.

25. *Confessio* § 42.

26. *Confessio* § 4.

27. The phrases *ante originem saeculi spiritaliter apud patrem* and *hominem factum morte devicta in caelis ad patrem receptum* are from Victorinus's Commentary on the Apocalypse of John 11.1, ed. M. Dulaey, Sources Chrétiennes 423 (Paris, 1997); and the phrase *reddet unicuique secundum facta sua* is from 3.23, ed. R. Weber, CCSL 3 (Turnhout, 1972).

28. Letter § 3.

29. *Confessio* § 42.

30. *Confessio* § 37.

31. *Confessio* § 48; Letter § 15.

32. Bede, *HE* 5.10, ed. and trans. Colgrave and Mynors, 482, 483.

33. The noun *clericus* occurs in *Confessio* §§ 38, 40, 50, 51; and Letter § 3. The noun *presbyter* occurs in *Confessio* § 1, with reference to his grandfather, and in Letter § 3.

34. The noun *episcopus* occurs in *Confessio* §§ 26, 32; and Letter § 1.

35. *Codex Theodosianus* 5.3.1, 11.39.10, 12.1.49, 12.1.121, 12.1.163, 16.2.23, 16.2.24, 16.2.41, 16.5.5, 16.5.19, 16.5.54.1, 16.5.57, 16.8.2, 16.8.13, 16.8.14.

36. *Codex Theodosianus* 16.2.24. The bishop, though not explicitly mentioned there, is implied. We encounter female deacons in *Codex Theodosianus* 5.3.1, 16.2.27, 16.2.28.

37. *Confessio* §§ 1, 27.

38. *Confesio* §§ 37, 38.

39. Letter § 3.

6

Imagining Patrick in
the Middle Ages

THE EARLIEST REFERENCES to the veneration of Patrick in
Irish sources are found in the seventh-century literature emanating from what has come to be known in the historiography as
the Easter Controversy. This is often simplified in textbooks as
a clash between a 'Celtic' and 'Roman' Easter, because the most
conspicuous aspect of the controversy was the debate on the correct way of reckoning the date of Easter, a subject that divided
opinion among Christian theologians since the first ecumenical
council in Nicaea in 325. Arguably, Easter was a mere symptom
of a deeper issue—namely, the submission to Rome as the authority for enforcing unity and uniformity of custom in the universal church. By accepting the Roman Easter reckoning, one
accepted, in the words of Richard Sharpe, 'the assertion of a belief in the oneness of Latin Christendom, with its hierarchy
culminating in the papal primacy of the Bishop of Rome'.

The Easter Controversy in Ireland, spanning the seventh and
early eighth centuries, has come to define much of the way in
which early Irish church history of the period is framed. It was
apparently sparked by a letter by Pope Honorius from 628/9,

which called on the Irish church to reform its method of the dating of Easter and align it with the method used in Rome. The end of the controversy is usually dated to 716, the year in which Iona, the last stronghold of the old Easter reckoning in the Gaelic-speaking world, converted to a new calendar. Honorius's appeal, preserved in Bede's Ecclesiastical History (completed in 731), triggered a number of church synods in the south of Ireland at which the dating of Easter was debated.[1] A delegation of southern Irish clerics was then dispatched to Rome, returning in 632 with a recommendation to reform the practice of Easter, a recommendation that appears to have been adopted at once by the churches of the South. The reasoning for the delegation's recommendation has been preserved in a letter by a cleric of unknown rank, Cumméne (possibly to be identified with Cumméne Fota, bishop of Clonfert, who died ca. 662), addressed to Abbot Ségéne of Iona. The letter, commonly known as Cumméne's Paschal letter, urges Iona to forsake the old Easter reckoning, which was based on an eighty-four-year cycle, and adopt instead a nineteen-year cycle sanctioned by Rome (Rome was then transitioning from the Victorian to the Alexandrian cycle, sometimes called Dionysiac in the Latin West).[2] It is in this letter that we find the earliest reference to the veneration of Patrick in Ireland. Cumméne describes Patrick as introducing the first Easter reckoning into Ireland, a reckoning that allowed Easter to be observed between the fourteenth day and the twenty-first day of the first lunar month of the year (the Jewish spring month of Nissan). According to Cumméne, 'The first [cycle] is that which holy Patrick, our bishop [*papa noster*], brought and followed, in which the moon is regularly observed from the fourteenth to the twenty-first, and the equinox from March twenty-first'.[3] In this passing reference, Patrick is given the epithet *papa noster*, which can be translated as both 'our bishop' and 'our father', indicative of his status among the Irish at this time, or at least among the Irish of the south of Ireland. The Easter table that he is said to have introduced can be identified with the eighty-four-year 'Celtic' table.

Two other texts of the seventh century testify to Patrick's veneration in contemporary Ireland, both dating close to the end of that century, and both associated with the church of Armagh, whose claims of supremacy they were promoting by edifying Patrick as its patron saint. Their authors were writing at a time when the Easter Controversy subsided in much of the Gaelic-speaking world (with the exception of Iona), but Easter nevertheless figures in them as a narrative device. As authors of hagiographical texts, Muirchú and Tírechán (both likely to have been writing in the 690s, although Tírechán's work is sometimes perceived to have preceded Muirchú's) were primarily concerned with Patrick's saintly image and the manner in which it could buttress the contemporary interests of the church of Armagh and its patrons in the Uí Néill dynasty, rather than with Patrick as an actual historical personality. Their commitment to furthering the interests of Armagh (especially Muirchú) and the southern Uí Néill (especially Tírechán) has led to them being occasionally portrayed in the historiography as 'propagandists'. They were not unlike other authors of hagiography of the seventh century, Cogitosus (designated by Muirchú as his spiritual father) and Adomnán, who were furthering the cults of their saints, Brigit and Columba, in the service of the expansionary ambitions of their churches, Kildare and Iona, respectively. Indeed, their project was of a piece with the work of fellow hagiographers throughout the Christian world who wrote *vitae*, or saints' Lives, of protagonists whose pious lives and miraculous deeds etiologically reinforced the present-day claims of the hagiographers' own religious establishments. Muirchú and

Tírechán drew the material for their accounts partly from Patrick's own writings, partly from other written traditions, partly from local oral traditions, and partly from applying their own imagination to constructing more or less coherent narratives that could tap into contemporary concerns. Both texts were copied into the Book of Armagh (completed in 807) by the scribe Ferdomnach, who included additional material related to Patrick and the church of Armagh, material that is known by its modern title *Additamenta*. He also copied another text asserting Armagh's claims for supremacy, which is titled in the manuscript *Liber Angeli* (The Book of the Angel).

Despite the fact that Muirchú's and Tírechán's texts are both hagiographical and emanate from broadly the same milieu, these biographies nevertheless differ from one another in significant ways. Writing at the behest of Bishop Áed of Sleaty (Old Irish Sléibte) in present-day County Laois, Muirchú maccu Machtheni (himself venerated by later generations) composed what can be seen as a more conventional hagiographical narrative, complete with miracle stories and didactic messages.[4] As historical personalities, both Áed and Muirchú are attested independently of the Life of Patrick. Both appear as signatories to a text known as the Law of Innocents (also *Cáin Adomnáin*), to which I shall return. But Áed is known also from the *Additamenta*, where the following is said of him: 'Bishop Áed dwelt in Sleaty. He went to Armagh. He brought his testament to Ségéne of Armagh. Ségéne returned the testament to Áed, and Áed made a grant of his testament and his kin and his church to Patrick until Doom. Áed left the testament with Conchad. Conchad went to Armagh, and Flan Febla gave his church to him and took him himself as abbot'.[5] This passage is worth pausing on, because it reveals much about the way in which Patrick's patronage of Armagh was being played out at this time and about the way in which property interests were expressed in hagiographical idiom. Sleaty was the chief episcopal see of the kingdom of the Uí Bairrche Tíre kin group in the south of the medieval province of Leinster. It was a proprietary church, a concept described in detail in chapter 2, on Patrick's Irish background. In the passage just quoted, Áed pledges his church to Armagh in perpetuity, possibly—as Francis John Byrne suggested—in order to avoid being incorporated into the ecclesiastical ambit of Armagh's rival, Kildare, which was under the control of the Uí Dúnlainge, the dynasty to which the Uí Bairrche were subjected. We are able to date Áed's dedication with relative precision because we know Ségéne's years in the abbacy, between 661 and 688. The pledging of a church to another, greater church would have had both spiritual and economic implications. On the spiritual side, Sleaty would have committed itself to the veneration of Armagh's patron saint and to observing rites that were connected with his cult, including praying for the saint and for various figures related to him or the church of Armagh and participating in the adoration of contact relics—objects that are said to have come into contact with the saint. On the economic side, Sleaty would have owed a certain tax to Armagh, paid in kind, although the rate is not specified. Finally, Sleaty, as one of many daughter houses in the ecclesiastical network of Armagh, would also have owed loyalty to its mother church, helping to safeguard its interests against those of its rivals, Kildare and Clonmacnoise. In return, Armagh would extend its protection over its daughter churches and also allow them to partake in the fruits of its economic prosperity. The passage quoted also gives us an idea of the ritualised manner in which the granting of a church took place, and of the manner in which such a grant had to be confirmed by the successors of both Áed and Ségéne—namely, Conchad and Flan Febla, respectively. The description of Conchad as abbot rather than bishop of Sleaty ought not seem strange because the fusion of the offices of abbot and bishop was not unusual in contemporary Ireland. At any rate, it is clear that the appointment of the head of the church of Sleaty had to be ratified by the head of the church of Armagh; this was one of the prerogatives of a mother church. This, then, is the background for Muirchú's writing of the Life of Patrick, an undertaking for which he was commissioned by Áed, who was promoting the cult of the patron saint of the mother church to which he committed himself and his kindred.

The inclusion of both Áed and Muirchú among the guarantors of the so-called Law of Innocents, promulgated in 697 at Birr (County Offaly), invites some attention. This was a law that secured the safety of noncombatants, and in particular women and children, in times of war. The instigator of the law, Adomnán (d. 704), ninth abbot of Iona, was himself a member of the Cenél Conaill branch of the powerful northern Uí Néill dynasty. A statesman and scholar as well as abbot, Adomnán not only led diplomatic missions to Northumbria but also wrote a Life of Columba, the founding saint of Iona, and authored a popular work on sites of Christian veneration in the Near East, titled De locis sanctis. His Law of Innocents received the backing of no fewer than ninety-one guarantors, churchmen and kings from all over Ireland. The extent of support testifies to the weight that Adomnán's authority had throughout Ireland and to the willingness of churchmen from the north and south of the island to collaborate despite the ongoing disagreement with Iona over the dating of Easter. Those who gave their names as guarantors must also have been regarded as men of note whose individual authority could guarantee that the law be upheld. It is therefore of some significance to find Áed and Muirchú among them, even if no further biographical details can be adduced.

The narrative of Muirchú's Life of Patrick, as has been observed by several modern commentators, revolves around the climax of Patrick's celebration of the first Easter in Ireland and subsequently overcoming the druids of the legendary pagan king of Tara, Lóegaire mac Néill. Put simply, these events signify the triumph of Christianity over paganism. None of the details from this episode has any roots in Patrick's own writings, which make no mention of druids and only refer to Easter obliquely, as we have seen in chapter 3, on captivity. Nevertheless, Muirchú did draw on Patrick's writings for some biographical material, and he had other historical sources at his disposal, including the Chronicle of Prosper of Aquitaine, which told him about Palladius's mission. In Muirchú's account, after Patrick's escape from his captivity in Ireland, he reaches his home in Britain but then decides, at the age of thirty, to embark on a journey to Rome, where he hopes to be trained as a missionary. The age is significant, because thirty is the minimum canonical age for being ordained a priest. However, Patrick is distracted, and instead of continuing on this route, he stays for many years in Gaul with Bishop Germanus of Auxerre, whose mission to Britain has been discussed in chapter 5, on the missionary life. Germanus sends Patrick as a missionary to Ireland, but the role of chief missionary is reserved for Palladius (see, again, chapter 5), who was selected to lead the mission by Pope Celestine. However, while en route to Ireland, Patrick hears of Palladius's failure to convert the Irish and of his untimely death in Britain. The story then races towards its climax, as Patrick is about to celebrate the first Easter. From this point, Muirchú's account is framed with reference to the book of Exodus, signifying the transition from pagan bondage to Christian emancipation while portraying Patrick as an apostle and saviour in the image of Moses: 'In those days Easter was approaching, the first Easter to be offered to God in the

Egypt of this our island.'[6] Patrick chooses to celebrate Easter publicly and provocatively in the plain of Brega while the druids,
magicians, and fortune-tellers gather for their great annual celebration of idolatry. The tension between the two groups builds
up, and Patrick is then said to openly challenge the taboo that
no one may light a fire on the night of the great pagan feast before the king has lit his fire at his royal seat of Tara. By lighting
his own fire, Patrick shows disregard for his own life because the
punishment for disobedience was death. Meanwhile, at the king's
court, which is portrayed as Nabuchodonosor's Babylon, the elders (*seniores*), seeing Patrick's fire, exclaim, 'Unless this fire
which we see, and which has been lit on this night before the
fire was lit in your house, is extinguished on this same night, on
which it has been lit, it will never be extinguished at all.'[7] With
these words, in effect, the elders prophesy Christianity's eventual triumph and its perpetual observance in Ireland. The
narrator then shifts from identifying Lóegaire with Nabuchodonosor to identifying him with one of the chief villains of the New
Testament, Herod. Speaking as a second Herod, Lóegaire has the
following words placed into his mouth: 'We shall go and see what
is going on, and restrain and kill those who are doing such a
wicked thing against our kingdom.'[8] Lóegaire then orders twenty-
seven battle chariots to be prepared and heads towards the plain
of Brega with his two chief druids, Lucet Máel and Lochru. But,
for fear of violating another taboo, they dare not enter the pe-
rimeter within which Patrick is worshipping but rather perch
themselves outside as Patrick is summoned to the king. At Patrick's arrival, the pagans refuse to rise in his honour, except one
Erc mac Dego, who shows respect by standing and who is subsequently converted to Christianity. The narrator says that Erc's
relics are revered to his own day as patron saint of Slane (County
Meath), thus giving the readers a background story, or etiology,
for the relics at Slane. Then begins the contest between Patrick

and Lóegaire's druids, which is made to echo the contest between Moses and Pharaoh's magicians (there are also inconclusive attempts by scholars to draw parallels with apocryphal biographies of the apostles). It opens with a series of insults hurled by Lochru at Patrick and the Christian faith, to which Patrick responds by uttering an invocation that causes the druid to be lifted into the air and subsequently dropped at once, cracking his skull and causing great panic among the pagan spectators. In response, the king rises to kill Patrick, but the saint, again, makes an invocation, this time citing Psalm 67:2: 'Let God arise and let His enemies be routed and His illwishers flee from His face.'[9] At this, darkness descends on the pagans and they plunge into battle against one another, killing fifty men and sowing fear among the survivors, so much so that the king, in terror, feigns his own conversion, but secretly vows to pursue Patrick and kill him.

The following episode, which takes place on the next day, sees a meeting between Patrick and the poet Dubthach maccu Lugair in Lóegaire's court at Tara. Unlike the reception at the king's camp, on this occasion Dubthach and all those assembled arise in Patrick's honour and they are all converted. At this point we hear once again of the veneration of relics in the age of Muirchú, this time of Fíacc's, a young poet who was present at the scene. The noun 'poet', commonly used to describe the likes of Dubthach and Fíacc, is the standard English translation for the Old Irish *fili*, plural *filid*. The *filid* were members of a professional learned class patronised by aristocrats, whom they served as teachers, praise poets, genealogists, and legal experts. Irish law ranked a career as a *fili* on a par with an ecclesiastical or a political career for the purpose of attaining and retaining noble status. For example, the eighth-century *Uraicecht Becc* (Small Primer), states that the honour price of the highest grade of scholar, *ollam*, is equal to that of a king. The relatively high legal status (or 'honour price') associated with scholarship and the social prestige that it brought suggest that becoming a *fili* would have been a very desirable pursuit. Although access to the ranks of the *filid* was restricted by hereditary right, scholarly merit would have allowed some learned men to join as low-ranking members. Thomas Charles-Edwards has argued that Irish law seems to have recognised a single hereditary aristocracy, whose members were royals, high-ranking ecclesiastics, or prolific scholars.

The encounter between Patrick and Dubthach is a frequent motif in early Irish literature, usually representing the conversion of the old pagan elite and its submission to the influence of the church. A famous case in point is the text known as the pseudo-historical prologue to the late seventh- or eighth-century Irish legal compilation *Senchas Már*.[10] This prologue describes a meeting at Tara between Lóegaire, Dubthach, and Patrick, at which it is established that the 'law of nature', the vernacular law that prevailed in pre-Christian Ireland, was not wholly incompatible with the Christian 'law of the letter', which Patrick introduced. Insofar as apparent contradictions did occur, they were overcome by Patrick such that the two laws were harmonised.

The meeting between Patrick and Dubthach at which the poets were converted—thereby signifying the Christianisation of the scholarly class—is the backdrop for the final showdown between Patrick and the last of Lóegaire's chief druids, Lucet Máel. The two embark on a fated magic contest (evocative of Moses and Pharaoh's magicians again), at the end of which the druid is burned alive. Patrick then threatens the king, who has witnessed the event, with death if he refuses to convert. The threat doesn't seem to leave the king with much of a choice, but he nevertheless takes counsel with his elders and comes to the only rational (and possible) conclusion under the circumstances,

which is that 'it is better for me to believe than to die'.[11] The irony
appears to be lost on the narrator, who does not seem concerned
that Patrick won on the strength of his threats rather than his
powers of persuasion, or that the king's motive for conversion
was rather lame. The entire episode, when contrasted with the
episode of the conversion of the poets, can be read as an allegory
for the different fates that, according to the hagiographical narrator, befell two of the most important pre-Christian classes in
Ireland: on the one hand, the poets were allowed to retain their
social position and continue practising their craft so long as they
converted, and on the other hand, the druids, whose main function was the practice of pagan religion, became obsolete and
perished.

Following a few twists and turns in the plot, which sees the
story shift more and more towards the miraculous, the account
then turns to Patrick's final days. In Muirchú's account, Patrick's
impending death is foretold by an angel, at which point he leaves
Saul (County Down; called Sabul in Muirchú's text), where he
is understood to have had a church, and heads towards his foundation of Armagh, which he is said to have built on land granted
him by 'a wealthy and honoured man' (*homo dives et honorabi-
lis*) named Dáire.[12] However, an apparition of an angel from a
burning bush (yes, evoking Moses again) bids him to return to
Saul and die there. Patrick is then granted four requests, the most
political of which is that Armagh should be held in special honour even though he will not be buried there. Instead, Muirchú
tells us he was buried at Downpatrick (Old Irish Dún Lethglaise),
dying on 17 March at the age of 120. The text gives no calendar
year, and as discussed at different points throughout this book,
modern historians have no secure way of fixing his death date
with certainty. Speculation has usually revolved around the two
conflicting years given in the Irish annals, 457 and 493, both of

which were entered into the annals retrospectively.[13] In chapter 2, we have already seen how the additional notes appended to Tírechán's writings in the Book of Armagh bear witness to an early tradition that tried to resolve the conflict by inventing two Patricks, one of whom was identified rather clumsily with Palladius.

Patrick's burial at Downpatrick marks a turning point in Muirchú's narrative, which continues with the subject of competition over Patrick's relics. Relics, which have made appearances in other contexts in Muirchú's text, were central to early medieval Christian culture in Ireland and indeed elsewhere. Often ascribed with healing powers and talismanic properties, relics also served as markers of identity for the churches that possessed them, corresponding to the saints they venerated. Our sources from the period suggest that contact relics were more common than corporeal relics—physical remains of the saint, such as bones, teeth, or hair. In fact, nearly all early medieval manuscripts that survive from Ireland, about fifteen altogether, owe their survival to their having been venerated as contact relics. For instance, the Cathach 'battler' (Royal Irish Academy MS 12 R 33), a psalter dating circa 600 that was believed to have been written by Saint Columba, was treated as a contact relic and kept in a reliquary (*cumdach*) between the eleventh century and 1813.

The absence of Patrick's relics at Armagh was therefore no trivial matter, since it threatened to undermine Armagh's status as Patrick's cult centre. It was the inventiveness of hagiography that was called on to produce an etiology for redressing this deficit. Thus, we later learn from Tírechán that Armagh had other powerful relics, which it received from Rome, in particular the relics of Peter, Paul, and the martyrs Stephen and Lawrence. The *Liber Angeli* adds that there was also a cloth soaked with the blood of Christ.[14] Hence, with or without Patrician relics, Armagh could claim a direct link with Rome and reinforce its primatial identity.

Although our sources from the period suggest that contact relics were more common than corporeal relics, Muirchú is definitely concerned with the latter. The level of attention Muirchú devoted to Patrick's corporeal relics indicates they remained a contentious subject in his day. We are told that the angel Victor gave instructions that Patrick's remains be covered by a thick layer of soil of no less than one cubit, 'lest thy relics be taken away from that place'.[15] Here, the text is alluding to the theft of relics, not an uncommon practice in the medieval world and also attested in early Irish saints' Lives. Theft was sometimes occasioned because different churches would contest the ownership of relics, as each could claim the same saint as its patron and source of status. It is precisely such a competition over relics that is described in the remainder of Muirchú's text. As the story goes, the Uí Néill, together with another group of northern dynasties collectively known as the Airgíalla, contested the Ulstermen's (Ulaid's) claims for the right to possess Patrick's body. On two occasions the confrontation was about to escalate into violence, which was miraculously defused. That violence was avoided is no small matter, for the outcome of interchurch conflict, usually over land or as part of a dynastic struggle, was not always peaceful. For example, in an episode in Tírechán's text, we learn that Clonmacnoise occupied 'by force' (*per vim*) churches that are said to have rightfully belonged to Armagh.[16] Likewise, chronicles are unequivocal about the presence of fighting men on the premises of settlements that housed churches, sometimes major churches. The Irish annals record nineteen incidents between 759 and 836 in which settlements that are commonly accepted to have been ecclesiastical were involved in violence, often against other ecclesiastical settlements.[17] The fighters are said to have been members of the *familia* (Old Irish *muinter*), probably a reference to lay tenants residing on the premises. The bloodiest incident took place in 764, when we hear of a battle between the *familiae* of Durrow and Clonmacnoise in which two hundred men are said to have died.

From Muirchú's description of the contention over relics and the annalistic record of intermonastic fighting, we now turn to Tírechán and the way in which his text figures in relation to Muirchú's. Muirchú's text and its background are rather different from Tírechán's, which is commonly known as the *Collectanea*, a title coined by James Ussher, archbishop of Armagh between 1625 and 1656. Tírechán, a bishop of an unspecified see, does not appear to have been aware of Muirchú's text and vice versa, although they appear to have been relying on a common source for some of their material, a book by Bishop Ultán (d. 657) of Ardbraccan, in Brega (Old Irish Ard Breccáin; in modern County Meath).[18] Scholarship usually dates Tírechán's work before Muirchú's but definitely after 688, the year of 'the recent plague' mentioned in the text, which can be dated, thanks to other sources.[19]

Muirchú's and Tírechán's texts both portray Patrick as a successful missionary, though the way in which the conversion process is described by each varies a great deal. For one thing, Muirchú's narrative is more firmly couched in the north of the island, whereas Tírechán's focus is on the west country, Connacht, which is where his kindred, the royal dynasty of Uí Amolngid, hails from. Tírechán himself did not spend his entire life in Connacht but moved to Ardbraccan, where he studied with Bishop Ultán, the author of the book from which both he and Muirchú drew material on Patrick.

But Tírechán remained loyal to his place of origin. His loyalty is evident from the manner in which he highlights the subjection of his own kin to the Patrician church and from his description of the foundation of a church at the Wood of Voclut, Patrick's presumed place of captivity in Ireland, in the territory of the dynasty of Amolngid.[20] Another church that Tírechán holds in special regard is Donaghpatrick (Old Irish Domnach Pátraic) in County Meath, which figures in his narrative in connection with two other sites of major importance: Tailtiu, where a great annual assembly and fair took place under the auspices of the Uí Néill kings, and Ráith Airthir, which was the royal centre of Brega and seat of Finsnechtae Fledach (d. 695), king of Tara, the symbolic seat of the High Kingship. According to some interpretations, Tírechán wished to see the Uí Néill kings of Brega ruling over Ireland with the backing of the churches affiliated with Patrick, though not necessarily under the headship of Armagh but rather that of Donaghpatrick.

Tírechán takes the reader on a circuit of the island, following what he wished his readers to believe was Patrick's route, from the lands of the southern Uí Néill in Brega, westwards into Connachta territory across the Shannon, then northeast into present-day County Antrim, then south to Armagh, and eventually concluding the journey in Brega again. There is also a brief detour to Leinster and Munster, where Patrick is said to have visited the royal centre of Cashel.

Tírechán is more utilitarian than Muirchú in his use of the figure of Patrick and the events connected with him, frequently drawing on them as a means of asserting contemporary property claims, of the kind that was quoted earlier from the *Additamenta* concerning Áed of Sleaty. Likewise, Tírechán's text is replete with stories relating how land was made over to the Patrician church (with its head at Armagh) or how certain individuals (sometimes associated with his own kindred) were granted land by the saint's intervention. In the absence of a formal charter tradition in contemporary Ireland, which could have recorded land transfers in

written documents, hagiography sometimes fulfilled this purpose, serving as a form of quasi-charter. This had contemporary
parallels elsewhere, even in places where charters were known—
for example, in eighth-century England, where the contemporary
Life of Saint Wilfrid of York by Stephanus exalts the saint's
properties.

A typical text in which Tírechán describes how land was trans-
ferred to the church is his account of the submission of his own
kin, the Uí Amolngid, to the Patrician church: 'Six sons of Amolngid came before Lóegaire for judgement, and opposing them
Éndae alone and his small son and Patrick before them, and they
examined the case of their inheritance, and Lóegaire and Patrick
passed judgement that they should divide their inheritance into
seven parts. And Éndae said: "I offer my son and my share in the
inheritance to Patrick's God and to Patrick". It is for this reason,
some say, that we are servants of Patrick to the present day'.[21] This
story is a retrospective justification of the fact that Armagh holds
a seventh of the land of the kin of Amolngid. Such a division
was not uncommon in early medieval Ireland, where kindreds
would often dedicate one of their branches to the church as a
form of proprietary holding, of the kind that was described in
chapter 2.

Descriptions of foundations of churches can often be found
incorporated into rather elaborate etiological tales that revolve
around a narrative of religious conversion. One of the more in-
ventive tales tells of the conversion of the daughters of King
Lóegaire.[22] I shall visit it here at some length because it offers a
useful and fascinating case study of the value of etiological tales
as sources for the historian, thanks to its allusions to contemporary political and social realities. This episode, as will be
seen, can be read on a number of levels: as a straightforward
legend about the conversion of two princesses, as a didactic story

about the correct observance of Christianity, as a political and social commentary on the author's times, and as a store of intertextual references that range across hagiography and other genres.

The story of the princesses is, of course, not a historical account, and certain elements from it recur in an episode concerning the British princess Monesan, as told by Muirchú, suggesting that some of the narrative derives from common topoi.[23] It does not in any way reflect the circumstances of the fifth century in which Patrick operated; rather, it reflects the author's own contemporary reality. As such, it provides insights into Tírechán's world and into his contemporaries' perspective of an imagined pagan past. The story begins with the arrival of Patrick and his company of bishops to a well called Clébach, in Connacht, near the Iron Age cult site of Crúachain, the chief pagan cult site in the province of Connacht, which continued to be used for ritual purposes into the early Middle Ages. The ritualistic significance of both Crúachain and the well (as sacred water feature) would not have been lost on the early medieval readers of the *Collectanea*, since wells and other water features were frequently sites of ritual activity from pre-Christian times and into the Christian era, so much so that approximately three thousand holy wells with saintly associations persist today. We can see, therefore, that from the outset, the scene is being set for a mighty confrontation that is about to unfold between pagan and Christian forces. Beside the well, the troop of holy men encounters the two daughters of King Lóegaire, Ethne and Fedelm. The girls' names, too, have pagan resonances, because they are known from Irish mythological tales: they both appear in the Ulster Cycle (see chapter 4, on religion). Although, in its written form, the Ulster Cycle is known only from the eleventh or twelfth century, the earliest strata of the tales go back to the seventh century, and, as John Carey has noted, Muirchú might have been familiar with an early version of a tradition that fed into this epic. In the Ulster Cycle, Ethne and Fedelm are, respectively, the sister of the Connacht queen Medbh and a prophetess.[24] Astonished by the sight of bishops, men of a kind that Ethne and Fedelm had never seen before, the two princesses grow curious: 'And they did not know whence they were or of what shape or from what people or from what region, but thought they were men of the other world or earth-gods or a phantom; and the maidens said to them: "Whence are you and whence have you come?" and Patrick said to them: "It would be better for you to profess our true God than to ask questions about our race".'[25]

At this point the princesses follow Patrick's command and direct their attention to the Christian God. In Tírechán's portrayal of them, they are stereotyped rather pejoratively as ignorant pagans whose interest in the materiality of supernatural forces undermines their ability to concentrate on the spiritual and, according to Tírechán, correct way of perceiving the Divinity: 'The first maiden said: "Who is God and whose God is he and where is his dwelling-place? Has your God sons and daughters, gold and silver? Is he ever-living, is he handsome, have many fostered his son, are his daughters dear and beautiful in the eyes of the men of the earth? Is he in the sky or in the earth or in the water, in rivers, in mountains, in valleys?"'[26] Some of these questions, such as the ones about good looks and the number of foster children, may seem at first odd or even satirical, but they make perfect sense in Tírechán's social context, as we shall see shortly. Let us, however, begin with the opening questions. These are rather predictable, coming from stereotyped pagans who expect their deities to inhabit a fixed place in the landscape. The questions then continue with what contemporary noblewomen might ask when evaluating whether a nobleman is worthy of their esteemed company: Does he have heirs, and is he wealthy? This is followed by a question about immortality, which the princesses are keen to affirm in order to ensure that God does not fall short of the demigods of the Túatha Dé Danann, which was the closest thing that early Irish culture had to a pantheon. These races of demigods were distinguished from humans by their extraordinary powers, exceptional longevity, and sometimes even immortality. Then come the questions concerning God's appearance and his foster children. These lead the reader straight into the core trappings of seventh-century Irish aristocratic society. Appearance—not only in Ireland but more broadly in antique and late antique societies—was seen as a reflection of one's inner qualities: a beautiful woman or a handsome man would be perceived as morally superior to a deformed or ugly person. Physical well-being was also the preserve of those who were wealthier and had access to a more balanced diet, did not wear themselves out through hard labour, and could enjoy the best medical attention available. Hence, 'beautiful' meant being better off and therefore good marriage material. However, more specifically to Irish political culture, physical perfection was a requisite for kingship: those who were physically blemished or deformed were, in principle, excluded from kingship, as we find in a tradition concerning Congal Cáech (d. 637), the king of Tara who lost an eye to bee stings.[27] And then we come to the princesses' concern with fosterage, an institution that also played a central role in contemporary Irish society. The reciprocal fosterage of children among aristocratic families was common practice. It was a means of reinforcing social ties, solidifying bonds between kindreds, and vindicating one's own high status or ambition to attain social prestige, especially when fostering highborn children. For example, in this very episode from Tírechán's *Collectanea* concerning Lóegaire's daughters, we learn that one of the daughters was fostered by the druid Caplit. The bond established between fosterer and fosterling could be as strong as a father-child relationship and could lead to certain conflicts of interests, as it does in the epic tale *Táin Bó Cúailnge*, where the protagonist, Cú Chulainn, and his foster father, Fergus, persist in their sympathy for one another despite fighting on opposite sides. An early Irish law tract, *Cáin Íarraith* (Law of Foster Fee), gives details of the entitlements of foster children, from humble commoners to princes. The fee that a king (*rí*) paid to have his children reared by a fosterer could be ten times higher than what an ordinary commoner (*ócaire*) paid to have his fostered. The higher the status of the child, the more foster parents he or she was expected to have had, as the child rotated between noble families who wished to put themselves in good stead with his or her parents. Highborn children were expected to be reared in a manner befitting their rank, such that their fosterers equipped them with a horse, appropriate clothing, and education consisting of learning the skills for board games and hurling.

Patrick responds to the princesses' questions with an affirmation of the transcendentality of the Christian God, who is unlike pagan gods, which are said to dwell in earthly abodes. The Christian God, Patrick continues, created the physical universe; he is omnipresent and omnipotent. There follows a sombre proclamation: 'He has a son, coeternal with him, similar to him; the Son is not younger than the Father, nor is the Father older than the Son, and the Holy Spirit breathes in them; the Father and the Son and the Holy Spirit are not separate'.[28] In placing these words in Patrick's mouth, Tírechán is affirming the saint's rejection of heresy and commitment to Orthodox Christianity, as established in the Nicene Creed (325), which declares, 'We believe in one Lord, Jesus Christ, the only Son of God, eternally begotten of the Father, God from God, Light from Light, true God from true

God, begotten, not made, consubstantial of one Being with the Father'. In making Christ equal to the Father and coeternal with him, the creed ensured that Christ would not be numbered among the created beings but rather be positioned strictly above them, as a creator, with no beginning and no end. This also placed him firmly in contrast to the Túatha Dé Danann, which, despite comprising immortals, consisted of beings that had a beginning and were therefore of the created order.

The dialogue between Patrick and the princesses reaches its conclusion when, in a curious twist of the plot, the princesses are joined to the Son of God in spiritual marriage after they profess their commitment to the faith. This they do by swearing that they believe that baptism purges inherited sins, that sin can be overcome by penance, and that the dead will be resurrected on the day of judgement. In quoting these pledges, Tírechán reveals to us the benchmark for being accepted as Christian in his contemporary Ireland: the ability to recite these basic articles of faith. Following this profession of faith, the daughters are baptised while wearing the signature white garment of the catechumens (on which see chapter 5), and subsequently they demand to see the face of Christ. In response, Patrick warns them that 'unless you taste death you cannot see the face of Christ, and unless you receive the sacrament'. Undeterred, the princesses reply, 'Give us the sacrament so that we may see the Son, our bridegroom'.[29] Their wish is granted as they are given the sacrament and die. In their coming to a sticky end, the moral of the story becomes apparent: paganism, as represented by the dying princesses, is eradicated when Christianity takes hold.

Their death, however, is not the end of the story but only a lead-up to its final phase, in which the narrative threads reach into Tírechán's own time. After their death, the daughters are said to have been placed in a bed, covered with their own garments, while their friends 'made a lament and great keening' (*fecerunt ululatum et planctum magnum*).[30] The lament described here is a ritual lamentation, which Tírechán would have expected his readers to be familiar with despite its being proscribed by seventh-century Irish canonical rulings like the following: 'The penance for wailing after the death of a layman or a laywoman, fifty days on bread and water.'[31] Such ritual keenings, for which professional women keeners were employed at funerals, were perceived to be in competition with Christian practices of bereavement, although, unfortunately for us, the approved rituals are not well attested in Ireland for the early medieval period.

The bereavement episode of the story continues with Patrick's baptism of the druid Calpit (who, as will be remembered, fostered one of the princesses) and his brother Máel, both of whom have their hair shorn, thereby losing one of the signature traits of the druid's appearance. And then, after a number of 'days of mourning', the princesses are buried beside the well of Clébach.[32] Although the number of days of mourning is not specified, it is likely to have lasted three days, which is the period for which the Life of Columba says that the saint's body was retained before burial.[33] The princesses are said to have been buried in a grave with a circular ditch around it, 'after the manner of a *fert*, because this is what the heathen Irish used to do'.[34] A *fert*, discussed in chapter 4, was a family cemetery in which families looked after the burial of their own dead. Such places could also be sites at which the dead ancestors were worshipped as gods. The pagan associations are, therefore, obvious. And it is for this reason that Tírechán is quick to remark that although their burial site was once called a *fert*, at present 'we call it *relic*, that is, the remains of the maidens'.[35] Tírechán says that a church was then built on the site, which was dedicated to Patrick, and the remains (relics) of the princesses continue to be venerated there, purged of pagan impurities.

The story, which comes to an end here, is one of many stories in which Tírechán describes how the old features of a pagan landscape were converted into places of Christian worship, usually with the foundation of a church to finalise the transition. But it also has an etiological thrust, in which we are shown how paganism withdrew in the face of Christianity and how profane personalities (Fedelm and Ethne), whose veneration has pagan undertones, were given Christian alter egos to allow Christians to revere them. We are also shown the demise of the pagan priesthood, the submission of the druids to the apostle of the new religion, the conversion of the druids, and the ultimate undisputed triumph of Christianity on all fronts. At the same time, the story has more mundane objectives: to exhibit Patrick's Orthodoxy, to articulate the basic articles required of a Christian when professing his or her faith, and—as we have seen in other examples before—to stake a claim for the subjection of a certain church to Armagh, in this case the church beside the well of Clébach. Clearly, a contextual and attentive reading of such loaded episodes can be quite rewarding.

Tírechán's and Muirchú's texts established some fundamental commonplaces for the legend of Patrick that exerted an influence on subsequent hagiographical compositions. The Lives of Patrick in the Book of Armagh were followed in the second half of the eighth century by another Life, now lost, which was the basis for a surviving early tenth-century Life known as the Tripartite Life of Patrick, comprising three homilies on the saint.[36] The most conspicuous difference between the Tripartite Life and the seventh-century Patrician dossier is its language: it is mostly in Irish. It is also significantly longer than the earlier Lives, but much of its core material can be traced to the writings of Patrick himself and to those of Muirchú, but also to traditions known to both Muirchú and Tírechán. This core is augmented by copious legendary material, much of which (as in Tírechán's text and the

Additamenta) is intended to reinforce contemporary property claims and proclaim high status for certain places. For example, when incorporating a translated version of Tírechán's episode concerning the conversion of the daughters of Lóegaire, the text adds that the place in which they died is called the 'Old Church of Mag nÁi' (Sendomnach Maige Ái) and that 'some say' (*asberat alaili*) that the remains of the princesses were brought to Armagh.[37]

Some of the legends on which the Tripartite Life draws were said to have been handed down orally, and the text even recounts a pedigree of informants who transmitted the tales from the mouth of the original 'witness' to the author's present time. In one place, for example, some miraculous deeds are introduced as follows: 'These are the miracles which the elders of Ireland declared, and connected with a thread of narration. Colum Cille, son of Fedlimid, first declared Patrick's miracles and composed them. Then Ultán son of Conchobor's descendant, Adomnán, grandson of Tinne, Ailerán the sage, Ciarán of Belach nDúin, bishop Airmedach of Clochar, Colmán Uamach, presbyter Collait of Druim Róilgech.'[38] The chain of informants comprises historical personalities, most of whom can be identified by cross-referencing with the Irish annals and whose reputations were meant to lend credence to the miracle tales. Thus, Colum Cille (d. 595 or 597) is the famous aristocratic founder of the monastery of Iona, Ultán (d. 657) is the bishop of Ardbraccan and author of a book on Patrick that has already been mentioned, Adomnán (d. 704) is the ninth abbot of Iona and author of a Life of the founding abbot, Ailerán (d. 665) is a sage of great renown, and so on.[39]

The text follows Patrick on a journey of church foundation, during which he overcomes threats, defeats adversaries, and converts individuals as well as kindreds. It is the earliest instance in which his biography is reconfigured to intersect with that of Saint Martin (d. 397) of Tours, the most prominent Gallic saint, hitherto only indirectly connected with Patrick through the inclusion of his Life alongside Patrick's in the Book of Armagh. The two are said to be relatives, and this apocryphal connection continued to be asserted throughout the Middle Ages, most famously in Jocelyn (d. 1214) of Furness's Life of Patrick, which was widely read. The Gallic roots that Patrick is given in the Tripartite Life are due to his mother: 'Concessa was the name of his mother: of the Franks was she, and she was a kinswoman of Martin's'.[40] But the attribution of Gallic associations to Patrick has a longer history, going back—as we have seen—to Muirchú and his account of Patrick's sojourn with Germanus of Auxerre. The name of his mother is also first given by Muirchú, who does not attempt to connect her either with the Gauls or with the Franks.

It has been suggested by Ludwig Bieler that an early, 'primitive Life', perhaps dating as early as the sixth century, lay at the base of the earliest version of the Tripartite Life, of Muirchú's Life, of parts of Tírechán's Life, and of two Lives of a later (yet disputed) date commonly referred to as *Vita Secunda* and *Vita Quarta*. The last two Lives, which are closely textually related, originated in Ireland but were augmented as they were transmitted in Continental Europe. The dating bracket that is assigned to them is rather broad: later than the first half of the eighth century but earlier than the eleventh century. Of the two, the *Vita Quarta* is exceptional in the lengths it goes to in order to cast Patrick in the figure of Moses, the ideal-type proselytiser. This analogy is also made briefly by Muirchú in an episode in which the angel Victor appears from a burning bush, and by Tírechán, who lists four aspects in which Patrick is similar to Moses: he heard a voice from a burning bush, he fasted for forty days and nights, he lived to be 120 years old, and his place of burial is unknown.[41] But the *Vita Quarta* devotes its entire preface to establishing the parallels with Moses and with the biblical Exodus: there is the captivity, the liberation from enslavement, and the introduction of a new faith (to the Israelites and to the Irish). And of all the Lives of Patrick, the *Vita Quarta* is the only one to attribute Jewish origins to Patrick in its first chapter, claiming that his ancestors were among the Jews who were exiled by the Romans in AD 70. This is followed by a fanciful description of a journey that led them to Armorica (present-day Brittany), but the author then appears to confuse Armuircc Letha, which is Brittany, with Letha, in Italy, when he states that Armorica is near the Tyrrhenian Sea. Ironically, the end point of this meandering journey is Strathclyde, where Patrick's parents are said to have hailed from. Traditions about Patrick's origin from Armorica continued to circulate and develop throughout the Middle Ages, some persisting into the modern era. One such tradition, from the area of Château de Bonaban near Saint-Malo in Brittany, was the basis for a controversial book, *Rediscovering Saint Patrick*, by Marcus Losack, published in 2013, which reasserted Patrick's Breton origins.

Patrick's fame was not restricted to Ireland. In the early Middle Ages his renown spread beyond Ireland, and as early as the eighth century he was commemorated among the saints listed in the liturgical calendar of the Anglo-Saxon missionary Willibrord (d. 739).[42] Born in Northumbria, Willibrord was sent to evangelise Frisia in 695 with the pope's blessing, becoming abbot of Echternach and the first bishop of Utrecht. The calendar, composed at Echternach, is one of our best contemporary guides to saints who were venerated throughout Christendom at the time. The calendar also opens the possibility that Patrick's renown reached Anglo-Saxon England at the time, because Willibrord was of Anglo-Saxon origin and is known to have maintained contacts with his native land. If so, then Patrick is more than likely to have been known to Bede, a contemporary of Willibrord's and a Northumbrian compatriot who reported on Willibrord's activities in his Ecclesiastical History. Nevertheless, Patrick is omitted from Bede's account, which, instead, gives Palladius centre stage as evangeliser of Ireland. In light of the connection with Willibrord and the fact that Patrick's cult was already well established in Ireland, Bede can be assumed to have omitted Patrick on purpose. The suppression of Patrick from Bede's narrative may not have anything to do with Patrick himself or what he stood for but rather may have been a product of Bede's predilection for all things Roman and his unflinching deference to papal authority. Palladius, of course, was an emissary of the pope, and as such qualified as the perfect Roman. But Patrick had no direct connection with Rome.

Patrick is mentioned in other calendars apart from Willibrord's. Nineteen of these, dating before 1100, are found in the monastery of Saint Gallen, founded by a disciple of the Irish abbot Columbanus, where we also find the genealogy of Saint Patrick in a ninth-century manuscript (the sole manuscript to contain the Life of the founder), alongside a number of saints' Lives and the genealogies of Gallus and Brigit.[43] In the genealogy, the names of Patrick's parents, Calpornius and Concessa, are followed by a note that strikes an ironic cord, because the author of the genealogy was ignorant of a crucial biographical detail—namely, that Patrick was born to a deacon father: although he correctly ascribes Patrick's origin to Britain and credits him with the conversion of the Irish, he also tells the impossible tale that Patrick brought about the conversion of none other than his own father, who subsequently became a monk.[44]

Continuing with Patrick's fame abroad, we find a Life that was argued by F. J. Byrne and Pádraig Francis to have been written at Lismore (County Waterford) for the abbey of Landévennec in the west of Brittany. The *Vita Tertia* is dated by some between the seventh and eighth centuries, but a note in the Life concerning 'barbarian' rule of Ireland, which J. B. Bury interpreted as Scandinavian rule, has led him and Bieler to conclude that the Life must date after the eighth century. For his material, the author drew directly on Patrick's *Confessio*, Muirchú, Tírechán, and a version of the Tripartite Life. The *Vita Tertia* was modified at Glastonbury and in Germany, where it circulated widely. It enjoyed a great deal of popularity in the Middle Ages, and it survives in more manuscripts than any other Life of Patrick. Their distribution ranges from England to Trier, Munich, and Austria. It was the source for a later Life of Saint Patrick, now lost, by William of Malmsbury (d. 1143), parts of which are incorporated into his *De antiquitate Glastoniensis ecclesiae*. This text tells the history of the church at Glastonbury, where, according to the tenth-century Life of Saint Dunstan, a cult of Patrick flourished and attracted scores of Irish pilgrims, owing to the belief that the saint was abbot of Glastonbury and died there in 472.[45] Therefore, whatever view one may hold about the exact dating of the text, clearly the *Vita Tertia* must date before William's time. A Life that is not of Irish origin is the Life by a certain Probus, of whom nothing is known. It has been argued to date from the 970s, perhaps written in England under King Edgar (d. 975), and is largely based on Muirchú. It seems to assert that Patrick was patron saint not only of Ireland but also of Britain. It has been observed by Bieler that Probus freely modified episodes he found in Muirchú's Life in order to suit his own agenda. Most crucially, he diminished Ireland's role in Patrick's biography, such that Patrick's place of captivity is not said to have been Ireland. No alterative place of captivity is specified, which would have allowed the reader to infer that he may have been abducted within Britain. This, as the hypothesis goes, would have supported a case for Patrick's relics belonging in Britain.

By the early thirteenth century, the cult of Patrick had struck deep roots in England, and the Patrician legend became augmented with additional anecdotes that would become a staple of the image of Patrick for future generations. Of these, the most famous is probably the story of Patrick banishing all venomous reptiles from Ireland. It is found in three near-contemporary texts: the *Topographia Hiberniae* by Gerald (d. 1223), the Life of Patrick by Jocelyn, and an anonymous fragmentary Life of Patrick.[46] Of the three texts, Gerald's expresses scepticism about Patrick's contribution to ridding Ireland of venomous creatures. He begins by confirming that, indeed, there are no serpents, snakes, toads, or any venomous creatures in Ireland, but then he continues, 'Some indulge in the pleasant conjecture that Saint Patrick and other saints of the land purged the island of all harmful animals. But it is more probable that from the earliest times and long before the foundation of the faith, the island was naturally without these as well as other things.'[47]

However, unlike Gerard, Jocelyn is not so cautious in his assessment and offers a picturesque account of Patrick's triumph over the reptiles:

Even from the time of its original inhabitants, did Hibernia labour under a threefold plague: a swarm of poisonous creatures, whereof the number could not be counted, a great concourse of demons visibly appearing, and a multitude of evil-doers and magicians ... and the most holy Patrick applied all his diligence unto the extirpation of this threefold plague; and at length by his salutary doctrine and fervent prayer he relieved Hibernia of the increasing mischief. Therefore he, the most excellent pastor, bore on his shoulder the staff of Jesus, and aided of the angelic aid, he by its comminatory elevation gathered together from all parts of the island all the poisonous creatures into one place; then compelled he them all unto a very high promontory, which then was called Cruachán Aigle, but now Cruachán Phádraig; and by the power of his word he drove the whole pestilent swarm from the precipice of the mountain headlong into the ocean. ... Then turned he his face toward the isle of Man, and the other islands which he had imbued and blessed with the faith of Christ and with the holy sacraments; and by the power of his prayers he freed all these likewise from the plague of venomous reptiles. But other islands, the which had not believed at his preaching, still are cursed with the procreation of those poisonous creatures.[48]

Jocelyn's rather elaborate tale makes an obvious analogy between serpents, demons, and evil. The converse of this depraved state is presented as the Christian faith, which is said to have struck root in Ireland (and the Isle of Man) at a relatively early stage in comparison with neighbouring places. Unfortunately for the places that were slower to convert, they were not freed from the scourge of venomous reptiles. By implication, one such place was, ironically, Jocelyn's Britain.

Whereas the medieval myth of Patrick as saintly pest controller who drove out snakes from Ireland can be traced—in its written form—to the early thirteenth century, the notion of Ireland as a reptile-free landscape goes back a long time, as indeed Gerald's sceptic comment implies. The earliest mention in a hagiographical text of an Irish saint driving away snakes is found in Adomnán's late seventh-century Life of Saint Columba.[49] But one can go even further back in time and trace the evolution of this idea from a passing remark in a third-century text, which we will soon probe, to the eighth century, when this remark was taken out of context and placed in Bede's depiction of Ireland. Bede presents Ireland as noxious to serpents:

> No reptile is found there nor could a serpent survive; for although serpents have often been brought from Britain, as soon as the ship approaches land they are affected by the scent of the air and quickly perish. In fact almost everything that the island produces is efficacious against poison. For instance, we have seen how, in the case of people suffering from snakebite, the leaves of manuscripts from Ireland were scraped, and the scrapings put in water and given to the sufferer to drink. These scrapings at once absorbed the whole violence of the spreading poison and assuaged the swelling.[50]

The ending of this text, with its mention of books being used as healing relics, is a remarkable example of the power of contact relics from Ireland. But the opening of the text is also significant because it can be shown to have had a long pedigree. Bede borrowed it from Isidore's (d. 636) description of the Isle of Thanet in his Etymologies: 'Thanet is an island in the Gallic [that is, English] channel, separated from Britannia by a narrow estuary, with fruitful fields and rich soil. It is named Thanet [Thanatos] from the death [*thanatos* in Greek] of serpents. Although the island itself is unacquainted with serpents, if soil from it is carried away and brought to any other nation, it kills snakes there.'[51]

Isidore himself was not the original source for this text, which he borrowed from the *Collectanea rerum memorabilium* by the third-century grammarian Solinus. Solinus appears to have had a particular penchant for snakes. In his account of universal curiosities, he frequently mentions whether certain places had snakes, how many, or how few. Thus, according to him, there are no snakes on Thanet, nor in Italy, nor in Sardinia, nor in Ibiza. But the Spanish coast (at Portus Sucronis, which faces Ibiza) is infested with snakes, and so are Egypt and Africa more generally.[52]

We can see here serendipity in action by following the vicissitudes of a rather trivial anecdote told by Solinus, an anecdote that eventually found its way, through Isidore's inadvertent mediation, to Bede, who translated it into a very different context from the one in which it was first conceived. The connection between saintly power and the absence of snakes in Ireland is implied by Bede in his advice for curing snakebite with relics in the form of manuscript scrapings. That Patrick should eventually be given credit for purging Ireland of snakes has something of the poetic justice to it, because in retrospect it compensates for the fact that Bede omitted Patrick entirely from his narrative of the conversion of Ireland. There is no obvious line of transmission that connects Isidore's or Bede's snake tales with the myth of Patrick's miraculous reptile-repelling powers. As may be inferred from Gerald, the anecdote about saintly pest control circulated orally and might have had oral roots. Nevertheless, it is remarkable to see how an anecdote about the absence of snakes in Ireland is appropriated by folklore and hagiography and becomes synonymous with the saint. The snakes then cease to be mere reptiles and become the ousted forces of evil, while Patrick is hailed as the triumphant hero in the hagiography, eminently worthy of the title of Ireland's patron saint, on which more in the next chapter.

Notes

1. Bede, *HE* 2.9, ed. and trans. Colgrave and Mynors, 200–203.

2. M. Walsh and D. Ó Cróinín, eds., *Cummian's Letter 'De controversia pachali'* (Toronto, 1988), 56–97.

3. Walsh and Ó Cróinín, *Cummian's Letter*, 84, 85.

4. On Muirchú's veneration, see the entry for 8 June in the eighth- or ninth-century *Félire Óengusso*, in *The Martyrology of Oengus the Culdee*, ed. and trans. W. Stokes (London, 1905), 139.

5. *Additamenta* § 16, in Bieler, *Patrician Texts*, 178, 179.

6. Muirchú, Life of Patrick I.13, in Bieler, *Patrician Texts*, 82, 83.

7. Muirchú, Life of Patrick I.15, in Bieler, *Patrician Texts*, 86, 87.

8. Muirchú, Life of Patrick I.16, in Bieler, *Patrician Texts*, 86, 87.

9. Muirchú, Life of Patrick I.18, in Bieler, *Patrician Texts*, 90, 91.

10. Translated by D. A. Binchy, 'The pseudo-historical prologue to the *Senchas Már*', *Studia Celtica* 9–10 (1975–76): 15–28, at 23–24.

11. Muirchú, Life of Patrick I.21, in Bieler, *Patrician Texts*, 96, 97.

12. Muirchú, Life of Patrick II.24, in Bieler, *Patrician Texts*, 108, 109.

13. Chronicle of Ireland 457.3, 493.4.

14. Tírechán, *Collectanea* II.3.5, in Bieler, *Patrician Texts*, 122; *Liber Angeli* § 19, in Bieler, *Patrician Texts*, 186.

15. Muirchú, Life of Patrick II.12, in Bieler, *Patrician Texts*, 120, 121.

16. Tírechán, *Collectanea* 25(2), in Bieler, *Patrician Texts*, 142.

17. Chronicle of Ireland 719.9, 757.5, 759.2, 760.10, 762.2, 764.6, 775.6, 776.12, 783.6, 789.8, 789.10, 793.4, 799.3, 805.8, 807.9, 817.6, 817.7, 819.5, 828.6, 828.9, 831.7, 831.8, 833.5, 833.6, 836.3.

18. Ultán's book is mentioned in Muirchú, Life of Patrick, B Prologue, in Bieler, *Patrician Texts*, 62, 63; and Ultán is also named as Tírechán's fosterer and teacher in Tírechán, *Collectanea* 18, in Bieler, *Patrician Texts*, 138, 139.

19. Tírechán, *Collectanea* 25(2), in Bieler, *Patrician Texts*, 142.

20. Tírechán, *Collectanea* 15, 42, in Bieler, *Patrician Texts*, 134–36, 156.

21. Tírechán, *Collectanea* 15, in Bieler, *Patrician Texts*, 134, 135. The translation is Bieler's, with minor emendations.

22. The entire episode is related in Tírechán, *Collectanea* 26, in Bieler, *Patrician Texts*, 142–45.

23. Muirchú, Life of Patrick I.27, in Bieler, *Patrician Texts*, 98–100.

24. The two are mentioned, for example, in the *Táin Bó Cuailnge*: *Táin Bó Cuailnge: Recension 1*, ed. and trans. Cecile O'Rahilly (Dublin, 1976), 1, 6–7.

25. Tírechán, *Collectanea* 26, in Bieler, *Patrician Texts*, 143.

26. Tírechán, *Collectanea* 26, in Bieler, *Patrician Texts*, 143.

27. As recorded in a mid-seventh-century law tract on beekeeping: *Bechbretha: An Old-Irish Law-Tract on Bee Keeping* §§ 31–32, ed. and trans. T. M. Charles-Edwards and F. Kelly (Dublin, 1983), 68, 69, 123–26n.

28. Tírechán, *Collectanea* 26, in Bieler, *Patrician Texts*, 143.

29. Tírechán, *Collectanea* 26, in Bieler, *Patrician Texts*, 145.

30. Tírechán, *Collectanea* 26, in Bieler, *Patrician Texts*, 145.

31. *Canones Hibernenses I* § 26, in *The Irish Penitentials*, ed. and trans. L. Bieler (Dublin, 1963), 162, 163.

32. Tírechán, *Collectanea* 26, in Bieler, *Patrician Texts*, 145.

33. Adomnán, Life of Columba 3.23, in *Adomnán of Iona: Life of St Columba*, trans. R. Sharpe (Harmondsworth, 1995), 231.

34. Tírechán, *Collectanea* 26, in Bieler, *Patrician Texts*, 145.

35. Tírechán, *Collectanea* 26, in Bieler, *Patrician Texts*, 145.

36. *Vita Tripartita*, ed. and trans. Whitley Stokes, *The Tripartite Life of Patrick, with Other Documents Relating to That Saint*, 2 vols., Rerum Britannicarum Medii Aevi Scriptores 89 (London, 1887).

37. *Vita Tripartita*, ed. Stokes, *Tripartite Life*, 1:104, 105.

38. *Vita Tripartita*, ed. Stokes, *Tripartite Life*, 1:60, 61.

39. See, respectively, Chronicle of Ireland 595.1 (and n. 3), 657.1, 704.4, 665.3.

40. *Vita Tripartita*, ed. Stokes, *Tripartite Life*, 1:8, 9.

41. Muirchú, Life of Patrick II.5.1, in Bieler, *Patrician Texts*, 116; Notes Supplementary to Tírechán, 54, in Bieler, *Patrician Texts*, 164.

42. The calendar is now Paris, Bibliothèque Nationale de France, MS Lat. 10837, fols. 34–41.

43. Emmanuel Munding, *Die Kalendarien von St. Gallen aus 21 Handschriften*, 2 vols. (Beuron, 1948–51), 1:7, 45.

44. St. Gallen, Stiftsbibliothek, MS. 553, p. 164.

45. Life of Saint Dunstan 5.3, in *The Early Lives of St Dunstan*, ed. and trans. M. Winterbottom and M. Lapidge (Oxford, 2012), 18.

46. Gerald of Wales, Topography of Ireland, trans. J. J. O'Meara, in *The History and Topography of Ireland* (Harmondsworth, 1982), 1–122; a translation of the Life by Jocelyn of Furness is by Edmund Swift, *The Life and Acts of St Patrick the Archbishop, Primate and Apostle of Ireland: Now First Translated from the Original Latin of Jocelin* (Dublin, 1809), reprinted in James O'Leary, *The Most Ancient Lives of Saint Patrick, including the Life by Jocelin Hitherto Unpublished in America and His Extant Writings* (New York, 1904), 132–347; an edition of the Latin text is by J. Colgan, *Vita Sexta*, in *Triadis Thaumaturgae seu Diuorum Patricii Columbae et Brigidae . . . Acta* (Louvain, 1647), 64a–108b; the fragmentary Life is edited by L. Bieler, *Andecdotum Patricianum*, in his *Studies on the Life and Legend of St Patrick* (London, 1986), XIX.222–29.

47. Gerald of Wales, Topography of Ireland 21, trans. O'Meara, 50.

48. Jocelyn, Life of Patrick §§ 169–70, trans. O'Leary.

49. Adomnán, Life of Columba 2.28, 3.23, trans. Sharpe, 177, 225.

50. Bede, *HE* 1.1, ed. Colgrave and Mynors, 18–21.

51. Isidore, Etymologies 14.6.3, in *The Etymologies of Isidore of Seville*, trans. S. A. Barney, W. J. Lewis, J. A. Beach, and O. Berghof (Cambridge, UK, 2006), 294.

52. See, respectively, Solinus, *Collectanea rerum memorabilium*, ed. Theodor Mommsen, 2nd ed. (Berlin, 1895), 22.8, 2.31, 4.2, 23.10 (×2), 32.32, 17.28.

Remembering Saint Patrick

SINCE THE HIGH MIDDLE AGES and until the present day, Patrick's renown spread primarily through rituals of veneration, myths, and legends that developed around his personality, many of which were transmitted orally. Few of these bear any relation to the historical Patrick or to the hagiographical image that took shape in the seventh-century dossier associated with Armagh. In fact, the *Confessio* and Letter to the Soldiers of Coroticus seem to have vanished from sight during the Middle Ages, reappearing only in the seventeenth century. They were rediscovered by James Ussher (d. 1656), archbishop of Armagh, and James Ware (d. 1666), the Dublin politician and antiquarian who published a first edition of Patrick's writings (*Opuscula Sancto Patricio Adscripta*) in 1656 while in exile in London.

The medieval cult of Patrick had no central texts around which it revolved, nor was it submitted to oversight by any religious authority. Instead, it flourished locally, as did most contemporary saints' cults, becoming ensconced in local identities and at the same time contributing to their continual formation. Cults were also strongly landscape based. A saint's life and deeds were commemorated in places in which she or he was believed to have been born, to have trodden, performed miracles, and died. Saints' memories were reinforced through the landscape and material culture, such that their deeds were often told in conjunction with a display of their relics at churches. They were also remembered at holy wells, groves, and various other prominent features in the landscape, many of which were previously associated with pagan deities. Numerous sites of pilgrimage were connected with Patrick, some going back to his hagiography—for example, Croagh Patrick, mentioned in the Tripartite Life, a mountain in County Mayo at which the saint was visited by an angel. Patrick's name became associated particularly with holy wells, at which healing miracles could happen, such as at Clonfad (County Monaghan), Struell (County Down), Downpatrick (County Down), Davagh Patrick at Belcoo (County Fermanagh), and many others that are mentioned in travellers' tales, the bulk of which date from the eighteenth century.

The Irish landscape had been transformed into a landscape of saints. By the early modern period, popular local traditions concerning individual saints were rife, and a measure of the extent of the proliferation of diverse accounts of saints' Lives can be gained from a 1645 tally that the scholar of hagiography John Colgan made of written genealogies of saints: 12 Brigits, 14 Brendans, and 120 Colmans.[1]

The Protestant Reformation and Catholic Counter-Reformation saw both Catholics and Protestants attempting to moderate the centrality of the veneration of saints in Ireland. Protestants, generally speaking, rejected local saints' cults altogether, dismissing them as idolatry and superstition, while protagonists of the Counter-Reformation sought more control for church authorities over popular expressions of piety. An interesting description of a typical 'popular' ritual is found in a vituperative text by the Protestant rector of the church at Belturbet (County Cavan), John Richardson, who was a strong advocate of the conversion of Irish Catholics by means of gradually reforming their rites and intervening in the education of their children. In 1727 he recounted the veneration that took part beside a holy well:

> The pilgrims to this place first kneel at the north side of the well, salute St Patrick and say fifteen paters, and one credo. They rise up, bow to him, walk thrice round the well, and drink of the water every round at the place where they began. From thence they go to the heaps of stones, bow to the cross, kiss the print of St Patrick's knee, and put one of their knees into it. Then they go thrice round the heap on their knees, always kissing the stone that hath the print of St Patrick's knee, when they come to it. They rise up and bow to it, and walk thrice round, bowing to the said stone when they come before it, and the last time kiss it. From the heap of stones they go to the alder tree. They begin at the west side with bowing to it, they go thrice round and bow to it from east and west, and conclude their great superstition and idolatry with fifteen paters and one credo.[2]

At the same time as Protestants condemned such 'idolatries' and Catholics sought to tame the cults associated with Patrick and other saints, both sides appropriated Patrick to vindicate starkly contradictory positions. Consequently (and paradoxically), his figure marked a cultural divide despite being venerated on both sides. Each camp claimed to trace the origins of its institutions and doctrines to the days of what it believed was an early church established by Patrick. Protestants took Patrick as proof that the church in Ireland was always independent, especially from Rome. Catholic reformers, on the other hand, emphasised Patrick's putative connections with Rome as they attempted to transform his figure into one that was more informed by biblical imagery and less by miracle working. Nevertheless, despite the efforts on both sides to clamp down on popular forms of veneration and to control the cult of Patrick, grassroots piety continued to flourish.

A well-known symbol of the popular commemoration of Patrick is the shamrock. Like all traditions that spring from below, its history is difficult to trace. However, Bridget McCormack shows that some of the earliest surviving records of the saintly connections of the plant go back to the 1680s, when coins were minted depicting Patrick clutching a shamrock. There are also German statues of Patrick from the early eighteenth century that sport a shamrock. The earliest account of the tradition that Patrick used the shamrock as an aid in a symbolic show-and-tell to explain the mystery of the Holy Trinity comes from the 1727 *Synopsis stirpium Hibernicum* by the botanist Caleb Threlkeld. In an entry on *Trifolium pratense*, the technical botanical name for the plant, he mentions the tradition associated with it and does not spare Irish Catholics from an insult: 'The plant is worn by people in their hats upon the 17 day of March yearly, which is called St Patrick's Day. It being a current tradition that, by this three leafed grass, he [Saint Patrick] emblematically set forth to them the mystery of the Holy Trinity. However that be, when they wet their *seamar-oge* [shamrock], they often commit excess of liquor, which is not a right keeping of a day of the Lord'.[3]

For Catholic leaders, the veneration of Patrick could also be a means for promoting the Irish church to a more prominent place on the international stage of Roman Catholicism. When a new breviary for the universal church was being prepared, Irish bishops campaigned to have Patrick commemorated in it. This was achieved with the help of the Irish Franciscan Luke Wadding, who was a member of the commission charged with reforming the breviary, which eventually included Patrick when it was published in 1632. Later, in 1687, Pope Innocent XI proclaimed 17 March as a 'double rite with nine lessons', which was a way of emphasising the significance of a certain day over other days of commemoration. In a study of the veneration of saints during the Catholic Counter-Reformation, John McCafferty shows that despite popular adherence to Irish saints throughout Europe and despite the contemporary image of Ireland as the 'island of saints and scholars', official Catholic publications accorded Irish saints a relatively minor place. For example, the Roman martyrology of 1627 (in its English translation) lists Brigit last on 1 February, Patrick appears in the second half of the entry for 17 March, and Columba (Colum Cille) is second to last on 9 June.[4]

The Protestant Reformation in Ireland from the 1530s onwards and the later enactment of the penal laws from the 1690s into the early eighteenth century, which restricted, and in certain cases outlawed, the practice of Catholic worship and education in Ireland, drove Catholic scholars and clergy to establish themselves outside Ireland. It is in this context that we meet Colgan again, who, in 1647, published seven Lives of Saint Patrick while at Saint Anthony's College in Louvain, where exiled Irish Franciscans had settled.[5] The publication of these Lives, alongside Lives of Brigit and Colum Cille (all in Latin), was intended primarily to bolster the image of Catholic Ireland abroad, especially among Catholics on the European Continent. It provided a complement to the already existing popular practices of the cult of Patrick in Continental Europe.

However, by far the most famous and resilient form of popular piety commemorating Saint Patrick is the pilgrimage to Saint Patrick's Purgatory, which attracted devotees from all over Europe and continues to the present day. The first written records of Saint Patrick's Purgatory can be found from as early as the late twelfth century, around the same time as the myth of Patrick's overpowering of snakes was first committed to writing (see previous chapter). Saint Patrick's Purgatory, a place on Station Island in Lough Derg (County Donegal), is believed to be an entrance to Purgatory that was revealed to the saint by Christ. It is unknown when the site began to be frequented by pilgrims, but the earliest written account of it—and also the most popular account, since it survives in over 150 copies and hundreds of adaptations—is Henry of Saltry's *Tractatus de purgatorio Sancti Patricii*, which dates from around 1170.[6] It tells the story of the Irish knight Éoghan, who descended to Purgatory. Henry's source for the tradition about the passage to Purgatory was Gilbert, a monk from Lincoln, who relied on Éoghan as his interpreter on a trip to Ireland in 1148. Éoghan's tale is a harrowing account of a penitential voyage through Purgatory, to which he descended by the route through which Christ instructed Patrick to guide those wishing to atone for their sins. According to the text, Christ appeared to Patrick, gave him a book of Gospels and a staff, and showed him an entrance to Purgatory. He then told him that those who are sincere in their intention to perform true penance would be absolved of their sins if they spend a day and a night in Purgatory, where they will witness the torment of the wicked and the eternal joy of the blessed. Patrick is said to have founded a church by the entrance to Purgatory on Station Island, and in the 1130s or thereabouts, Augustinian canons established themselves there.[7] Other accounts of Saint Patrick's Purgatory, like the one contained in Peter of Cornwall's *Book of Revelations*, can be more audacious and include descriptions of pain inflicted on the genitals of lustful men. In the following excerpt, we hear of a knight's ordeal in

Saint Patrick's Purgatory, as a certain King Gulinus tests the knight's love for his daughter.

> And [Gulinus] ordered a servant to prepare a bed for them in a chamber. And this was done. And, lo, when the knight believed he was about to enjoy sex with this girl, his eyes were opened and he saw a most ancient, arid, and misshapen trunk lying between his arms, and his male member was squeezed into a certain hole made in that trunk, which a servant deputed to the task by Gulinus shredded and weakened by striking a nail with a hammer vigorously and very frequently, confining his virile member in that hole, so that the knight desired a hundred times to incur death, if it were possible, rather than sustain such agony even for a brief while. When the foresaid servant had very frequently repeated the blows on the nail with the hammer, and, more narrowing compressing the knight's penis, had dashed, smashed, battered, and pounded it, and when this knight had suffered these dire straits of tortures and cried out and wailed for the great part of the day, and was exhausted to death, Gulinus said to his ministers, 'How's that knight, our son-in-law, getting on?'[8]

Testimonies, both oral and written, of the experience of descending into Purgatory via Station Island continued to proliferate. Among the most influential is perhaps the mid-thirteenth-century *Legenda Aurea*, a 'best-selling' compendium of saints' Lives attested in over a thousand manuscript copies that devotes nearly its entire entry on Patrick to a graphic description of a descent into Purgatory.[9] In time, the site of Saint Patrick's Purgatory became a major attraction for pilgrims, who were given hospitality by the friars. Before spending twenty-four hours in the cave on the island, the pilgrims were required to perform two

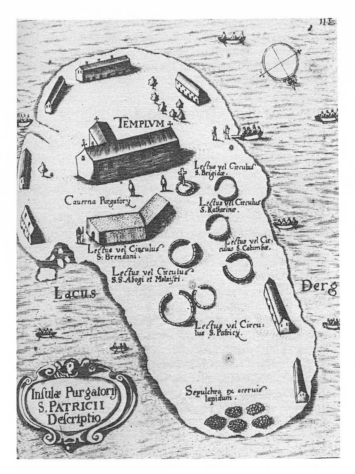

FIGURE 8. Map of Saint Patrick's Purgatory on Station Island.
After Thomas Carve, *Lyra sive Anacephalaeosis Hibernica*,
2nd ed. (Sulzbach, Germany, 1666), between pp. 112–13

weeks of penitential preparation at a nearby site, fasting and
praying under the guidance of the friars. The cave has been closed
since 1632, the year in which the monastery was dissolved (see
Figure 8). However, in the early eighteenth century, the site was
handed over to the Franciscans, eventually passing in 1960 to

the Catholic Diocese of Clogher, which maintains it to this day. It continues to attract pilgrims, though a harsh penitential regime is no longer prescribed to those who attend.

Objects venerated as relics of Saint Patrick are attested mainly from the High and Late Middle Ages. The stories connected with them do not always respect the tradition of Patrick's burial at Downpatrick, although one of the earliest certainly does: in 1185 the remains of Saints Patrick, Brigit, and Colum Cille were 'discovered' by John de Courcy (d. 1219), the Anglo-Norman conqueror of Ulster who also commissioned a Life of Patrick from Jocelyn of Furness. The discovery of the relics was reported by a contemporary author, Gerald of Wales, who believed that de Courcy's conquest happened in fulfilment of a prophecy. Other relics that circulated in later centuries included the tooth of Patrick at the church of Killaspugbrone (County Sligo); another tooth at Kilfeacle (County Tipperary), which literally translates as 'church of the tooth'; and pieces of Patrick's arm and head in ornamented fifteenth-century reliquaries made in all likelihood on the Continent (the former now at the Ulster Museum in Belfast and the latter at the Hunt Collection, Limerick). The patron of the head shrine was James Butler (d. 1452), Earl of Ormond, also known as the White Earl, renowned for his learning and literary patronage. And there were also contact relics, such as Saint Patrick's Bell, whose twelfth-century shrine, commissioned by King Dmonall Ua Lochlainn, is preserved to this day in the National Museum of Ireland (see Figure 9). Several other relics and shrines existed, but many are likely to have been destroyed during the Protestant Reformation in Ireland. A well-recorded instance of public relic destruction is the burning in 1538 of the tenth- or eleventh-century Bachall Ísu (Staff of Jesus), allegedly containing a splinter from the True Cross but denounced as superstition by reformers.

FIGURE 9. Shrine of Saint Patrick's Bell, National Museum of Ireland. Sketch by Margaret Stokes, in James Ward, *Historic Ornament: Treatise on Decorative Art and Architectural Ornament*, 2 vols. (London, 1897), 2:172

Throughout the early modern and modern periods, Patrick's image continually changed in tandem with the political vicissitudes of Ireland and the oscillating fate of the Catholic majority under Protestant rule. As Catholic campaigners were becoming more assertive in the early nineteenth century—and especially the 1820s—in suing for Catholic emancipation, Protestants could be seen to feel less comfortable than they had in the previous century with associating themselves with Patrick. In 1800, the year of the Acts of Union, which abolished the Irish Parliament and created the United Kingdom of Britain and Ireland (from 1 January 1801), an anonymous poem was published titled *Saint George and Saint Patrick*.[10] This was a polemical Catholic text that pitted the two national patron saints against each other. An extraordinary piece of satirical hagiographical science fiction, it tells of a debate between Patrick and George that is said to take place on the planet Mars, in the course of which Patrick demands that the Irish be given the right to live as free men and women. The poem opens with an invitation:

> He wrote to the patron of England this message:
> Most potent, most warlike, fleet-vanquishing Saint,
> your brother, St Patrick, has cause for complaint;
> We therefore dispatch this note unto you, greeting—
> Entreeting your Saintship will grant us a meeting;
> We further request, Saint, you will not suppose
> That we come, like St Denis, to cut off your nose.[11]

But towards the end of the poem, the threat of nose cutting resumes, as the two argue over the union:

> St George reply'd, 'Yes, be it understood,
> The measure's intended alone for your good',
> 'Be it so', cried St Patrick, 'look sharp to your nose,
> Since you are determin'd on coming to blows'.[12]

The clash between the saintly rivals was, alas, irreconcilable, as was the split in public opinion around the time of the union. Nevertheless, then, as before, both sides claimed an exclusive connection with Ireland's patron saint.

A commemoration of Patrick that was observed by both Catholics and Protestants, albeit separately, was Saint Patrick's Day, celebrated on 17 March. Tracing its changing fortunes over the years offers a useful yardstick for measuring both the popularity of the saint among the various groups in Ireland and the temperature of Catholic-Protestant relations. Private and local events to mark the saint's feast day were held throughout the Middle Ages in Ireland and abroad. It is only in 1607 that we find a record of its being officially recognised in the Irish legal calendar.

In the eighteenth century there are also records of Saint Patrick's Day celebrations in England, in particular among Irish soldiers billeted abroad, and the earliest recorded Saint Patrick's Day celebration in America comes from 1737, when a group of merchants and gentlemen gathered in Boston under the banner of the 'Charitable Irish Society'.

But the saint's feast day retained an air of controversy. Following the deposition of the Catholic James II and the ascent of William III (of Orange), a law passed by the second Williamite Parliament in 1695 revoked many feast days of saints venerated by Catholics, replacing them with twenty-nine holidays of Anglican aspect, none of which was connected to Patrick. During the eighteenth century, however, the mood appears to have changed, and records appear of Saint Patrick's Day celebrations at Dublin Castle, the seat of English rule in Ireland. By the last quarter of that century, celebrations at the castle became a regular annual affair. This exclusively Protestant event consisted of a ball and feast, which was attended by the Lord Lieutenant (also styled Viceroy), as well as members of the Protestant Ascendancy, comprising notables and the landed nobility that formed the ruling elite. The urban Protestant population participated in celebrations throughout the town that, as observed by Bridget McCormack, were the preserve of merchants, artisans, professionals, and generally well-to-do people. By 1760 it became a holiday for bank employees in Ireland, perhaps in recognition of an existing situation in which many in the finance sector were already absent from work that day.

On the whole, however, the observance of Saint Patrick's Day remained primarily a rural and Catholic matter, with the Catholic majority tending to congregate at provincial towns for fairs, whereas for Protestants the chief festival in the calendar was

4 November, the birthday of William III, the victor of the Battle of the Boyne in 1690 and suppressor of Catholic resurgence in Ireland. Indeed, Protestants also celebrated the anniversary of the battle on 12 July.

As the penal laws gradually began to be repealed from the 1770s onwards, and as Catholic activists of the early nineteenth century were stepping up their efforts to achieve full emancipation, a noticeable rise in friction between Catholics and defensive Protestants also found an expression in the happenings on the national days of commemoration: Saint Patrick's Day and the dates of the Williamite anniversaries. Incidents of violence and mutual bullying reoccurred until, eventually, after 1822, it was the Williamite celebrations that became de facto banned in an effort to reduce tensions. Saint Patrick's Day, on the other hand, received a rejuvenating boost when, in 1829, weeks before the passing of the Catholic Relief Act, which repealed the last vestiges of the penal laws and secured emancipation, the Lord Lieutenant not only addressed the crowds gathered outside Dublin Castle but did so wearing a shamrock, previously considered an emblem of vulgar Catholic popular piety and despised by the likes of Threlkeld, whose reproof we saw earlier. Thereafter the appearance before the crowds became an annual tradition.

But it was not until 1903 that Saint Patrick's Day became an official public holiday in Ireland, thanks to the Bank Holiday (Ireland) Act passed at Westminster following the campaigning of the Irish Member of Parliament James O'Mara. Another law passed subsequently required all public houses not to open on 17 March as a measure to prevent public disorder due to excessive drinking. It remained in force until 1961, when news of the repealing of the law made it as far as the *Quebec Chronicle Telegraph*, which sarcastically commented on 17 March that, for the first time, 'bars were open, legally, that is'.

The year 1903 also saw a procession take place in Waterford, on Sunday, 15 March, as part of an Irish language week organised by the Gaelic League, the society for the promotion of Irish culture and language. This procession is the earliest recorded event that can be described as a Saint Patrick's Day parade, even though it did not take place on the saint's day itself.

In Dublin, parades are recorded in 1915 and 1916, and the two could not have been more starkly different. The protagonists of both parades were the members of the Irish Volunteers, a militia of Irish nationalists founded in 1913 in response to the formation of the Protestant Ulster Volunteers. However, in 1915 those marching belonged to the majority group that split from the Irish Volunteers and that called itself the National Volunteers, among them approximately twenty-five thousand who enlisted in the Irish regiments of the British army and were stationed in the city ahead of being dispatched to the front. But in 1916 the marchers were members of the original Irish Volunteers who were among the ten thousand or so who chose to remain in Ireland in pursuit of the cause of home rule.

In 1915 soldiers paraded through the streets in full military uniform before large crowds of spectators, many of whom simply took advantage of the good spring weather to enjoy a recreational day out, undaunted by the cold winds of war blowing in the distance. The newspapers reported record attendance at the Dublin zoo and botanic gardens, as well as crowded trains heading to the seaside town of Bray. Visitors also flocked to the barracks of the Irish regiments, which opened their gates to the public.

The parade in 1916 was an altogether different affair, held, as it was, a little over a month before the Easter uprising, when nationalist sentiment was peaking. The following day, the *Irish Times* reported on the parade with open apprehension:

'Yesterday some thousands of able-bodied Irishmen, who refuse to help their country in the present war, paraded the streets
of Dublin and Cork. The existence and designs of these people
are not negligible; on the contrary, they demand a far closer
attention than they are getting from the absentee Chief Secre-
tary for Ireland'.

According to records of the Royal Irish Constabulary (examined by Mike Cronin and Daryl Adair), thirty-eight parades
took place that day in Ireland, in which 5,995 marchers took part
altogether, 2,637 of whom were armed. The largest parade was
held in Cork, numbering 560 armed marchers and 520 unarmed
marchers, who paraded before a crowd of two thousand onlookers. Such displays of nationalism and increasing politicisation
continued to colour the Saint Patrick's Day parades for decades
to come, drawing the focus of the day more and more towards
the politics of identity and away from the figure of the saint
himself.

It is at this turning point, as the legacy of Patrick enters its
modern phase, that this book comes to a close. Like the parades,
the popular venerations, and the legendary traditions, this very
book also makes a contribution, albeit modest, to the enduring
memory of Saint Patrick. There are a variety of reasons why individuals and communities will choose to remember Patrick in
the present day: the romantic patriot will seek to vindicate her
or his proud narrative, the religious devotee will absorb the es-
sence of the Christian messages in Patrick's writings, the school-
teacher will reinterpret them to distil their didactic hue, and the
enthusiast of late antique or medieval literature will cherish the
first-person accounts by the saint for their unique value as testimonies of an otherwise dark age but also for their entertainment value. For the purpose of the present book, however, the

writings by Patrick and the medieval writings concerning him
have been, in the first place, a spur for thinking about the challenges of interpretation, the contemporary and retrospective
construction of memory, the shaping of identities, the limitations
of reverence, and also the utility of irreverence as a requisite for
analytical probing. Although it is not possible to tell Patrick's
story 'as it was' (if this is ever possible of anything), the modern
reader can nevertheless aspire to be attuned to the saint's words
and draw as much as possible from the different levels of interpretation that they support. Up to a point, these words can be
taken at face value, whence the general outline of a narrative
emerges but also many questions arise, in particular regarding
the two rival accounts that are revealed in Patrick's autobiographical comments: his own righteous version and the version of his
detractors, who accused him of leaving Ireland for personal gain,
put him on trial, and condemned him. With these two in view,
we may choose to depart from the plain wording of Patrick's texts
and to read them with a heightened awareness of their historical
context. Such a context can be formed by drawing on certain concepts of Roman law or by piecing together information from
other forms of evidence, especially archaeology, which may shed
light on Patrick's immediate background in both Britain and Ireland. However, in reading Patrick contextually, we have seen
that it is necessary to have recourse to a certain degree of speculation in order to connect events from his own life with events
and phenomena from the history of contemporary Britain and
Ireland. A similar observation was eloquently made by Daniel
Binchy, who, in surveying the state of the art on Patrick, wrote,
'I feel strongly that scholars who offer to supply the gaps in our
knowledge are not entitled to claim that they can give us more
than conjectures, which—like all of those put forward in this

study—may very well be refuted by subsequent research'. The same holds true for my own attempts in this very book to supply gaps in our knowledge.

In addition to using Patrick's writings for the sometimes frustrating exercise of filling in gaps, we may also choose to read them as literature and appreciate the author's rhetorical ingenuity. As we gain more appreciation for his style, which exhibits familiarity with the Bible, biblical exegesis, and the rudiments of classical rhetoric, we can begin to look behind the literal meaning of his texts and catch glimpses of another, latent, narrative dimension. The image of Patrick that then emerges, or indeed the images that emerge, may be at first sight contradictory. But if we suspend judgement, we may accept that there is no real contradiction in seeing him as both a missionary and a slave owner or even slave trader. We may also come to accept that a pious preacher could have been a sinner earlier in life and could even have failed his community when absconding from his duties as an imperial official. The least that we, as readers, will achieve by straddling these perspectives, which are informed by both fact and speculation, is to humanise a personality who is too often mystified by the distance of time and reverential deference.

Notes

1. John Colgan, *Acta Sanctorum veteris et maioris Scotiae, seu Hiberniae sanctorum insulae* (Louvain, 1645); reference from John McCafferty, 'The communion of saints and Catholic Reformation in early seventeenth-century Ireland', in *Community in Early Modern Ireland*, ed. Robert Armstrong and Tadhg Ó hAnnrachín (Dublin, 2006), 199–214, at 201n6.

2. John Richardson, *The Great Folly, Superstition and Idolatry of Pilgrimages in Ireland* (Dublin, 1727), 67.

3. Caleb Threlkeld, *Synopsis stirpium Hibernicum siue commentario de plantis indigenis praesertim Dublinensibus instituta* (Dublin, 1727), 7.

4. *The Romane Martyrologe according to the Reformed Calendar* (Saint Omer, France, 1627), cited by McCafferty, 'Communion of saints', 203nn15, 16.

5. John Colgan, ed., *Triadis Thaumaturgae seu Diuorum Patricii Columbae et Brigidae . . . Acta* (Louvain, 1647).

6. Robert Easting, ed., *St Patrick's Purgatory: Two Versions of 'Owayne Miles' and 'The Vision of William of Stranton' Together with the Long Text of the 'Tractatus De Purgatorio Sancti Patricii'* (Oxford, 1991), 121–54.

7. Henry of Saltry, *St Patrick's Purgatory*, ed. Robert Easting (Oxford, 1991), 124.

8. Peter of Cornwall, *Book of Revelations*, ed. Robert Easting, 'Peter of Cornwall's account of St Patrick's Purgatory', *Annalecta Bollandiana* 97 (1979): 397–416, repr. in *Peter of Cornwall's Book of Revelations*, ed. Robert Easting and Richard Sharpe (Toronto, 2013), 130–41, at 137.

9. Iacobus de Vorgine, *Legenda Aurea*, ed. Theodor Grässe (Leipzig, 1846) § 50, trans. W. G. Ryan, *The Golden Legend*, 2nd ed. (Princeton, NJ, 2012), 193–96.

10. *Saint George, and Saint Patrick, or the Rival Saintesses: An Epic Poem of the Eighteenth Century* (Dublin, 1800).

11. *Saint George, and Saint Patrick*, 6.

12. *Saint George, and Saint Patrick*, 29.

CITED SCHOLARSHIP AND
FURTHER READING

Introduction: Patrick of Legend and History

There are numerous editions and translations of Patrick's writings. The following are the principal modern ones, first of Patrick's *Confessio*: Ludwig Bieler, ed., *Libri Epistolarum Sancti Patricii Episcopi*, 2 vols. (Dublin, 1952), 1:56–91; Richard P. C. Hanson with C. Blanc, eds. and trans., *Saint Patrick: Confession et lettre à Coroticus*, Sources Chrétiennes 249 (Paris, 1978), 70–133; David R. Howlett, ed. and trans., *The Book of Letters of Saint Patrick the Bishop* (Dublin, 1994), 51–93; Ludwig Bieler, trans., *The Works of St. Patrick*, Ancient Christian Writers 17 (London, 1953), 21–40; Allan B. E. Hood, ed. and trans., *St. Patrick: His Writings and Muirchu's "Life"* (Chichester, 1978), 41–54; Richard P. C. Hanson, trans., *The Life and Writings of the Historical Saint Patrick* (New York, 1983), 76–125; Daniel Conneely, trans., *St. Patrick's Letters: A Study of Their Theological Dimension* (Maynooth, 1993), 63–76; and Thomas O'Loughlin, trans., *Saint Patrick: The Man and His Works* (London, 1999), 52–89.

Modern editions and translations of Patrick's Letter to the Soldiers of Coroticus include Bieler, *Libri Epistolarum*, 1:91–102; Hanson with Blanc, *Saint Patrick*, 134–53; Howlett, *Book of Letters*, 25–39; Bieler, *Works of St. Patrick*, 41–47; Hood, *St. Patrick*, 55–59; Hanson, *Life and Writings*, 58–75; Conneely, *St. Patrick's Letters*, 77–81; and O'Loughlin, *Saint Patrick*, 93–105.

Several monographs and edited volumes on Saint Patrick have been published since the beginning of the twentieth century. Chief among them are J. B. Bury, *The Life of St. Patrick and His Place in History* (London, 1905); Eoin MacNeill, *Saint Patrick: Apostle of Ireland* (London, 1934); Ludwig Bieler, *Life and Legend of St. Patrick* (Dublin, 1948); Richard P. C. Hanson, *Saint Patrick: His Origins and Career* (Oxford, 1968); James Carney, *The Problem of St. Patrick* (Dublin, 1973); E. A. Thompson, *Who Was Saint Patrick?* (Woodbridge, UK, 1985); David N. Dumville, *Saint Patrick: A.D. 493–1993*, with Lesley Abrams, T. M. Charles-Edwards, Alicia Corrêa, K. R. Dark, K. L. Maund, and A. Orchard (Woodbridge,

UK, 1993); Philip Freeman, *St. Patrick of Ireland: A Biography* (New York, 2004); and Thomas O'Loughlin, *Discovering Saint Patrick* (London, 2005). Two important article-length studies that consider the historiography on Patrick are D. A. Binchy, 'St Patrick and his biographers: ancient and modern', *Studia Hibernica* 2 (1962): 7–173; and Colmán Etchingham, 'Conversion in Ireland', in *The Introduction of Christianity into the Early Medieval Insular World*, vol. 1 of *Converting the Isles*, ed. Roy Flechner and Máire Ní Mhaonaigh (Turnhout, 2016), 181–207. On the Book of Armagh, see R. Sharpe, 'Palaeographical considerations in the study of the Patrician documents in the Book of Armagh', *Scriptorium* 36 (1982): 3–28; E. A. Lowe, *Codices Latini Antiquiores: A Palaeographical Guide to Latin Manuscripts prior to the Ninth Century*, 12 vols. (Oxford, 1934–72), 2:42 (no. 270); and Marvin L. Colker, *Trinity College Library Dublin: Descriptive Catalogue of the Medieval and Renaissance Latin Manuscripts* (Aldershot, 1991), 93–97. On education, literacy, and rhetoric in the later Roman Empire and late antiquity, see Pierre Riché, *Éducation et culture dans l'Occident barbare, 6e–8e siècles* (Paris, 1962), trans. John J. Contreni as *Education and Culture in the Barbarian West from the Sixth through the Eighth Century* (Columbia, SC, 1976), 17–38; W. V. Harris, *Ancient Literacy* (Cambridge, MA, 1989), 285–321; Robin Lane Fox, 'Literacy and power in early Christianity', in *Literacy and Power in the Ancient World*, ed. A. K. Bowman and G. Woolf (Cambridge, UK, 1994), 126–48; Yitzhak Hen, *Roman Barbarians: The Royal Court and Culture in the Early Medieval West* (Basingstoke, 2007); and Matthew Kempshall, *Rhetoric and the Writing of History, 400–1500* (Manchester, 2011), esp. 229, 343–45, 350–427 (on 'deliberative rhetoric', falsehood, fiction, and the contribution of Cicero and Quintilian). On the impact of the Bible and exegesis in late antiquity and the early Middle Ages, see Mark Stansbury, 'Early-medieval biblical commentaries: their writers and readers', *Frühmittelalterliche Studien: Jahrbuch des Instituts für Frühmittelalterforschung der Universität Münster* 33 (1999): 49–82; D. James, 'The world and its past as Christian allegory in the early Middle Ages', in *The Uses of the Past in the Early Middle Ages*, ed. M. Innes and Y. Hen (Cambridge, UK, 2000), 102–13; Kempshall, *Rhetoric and the Writing of History*, 52–81. The body of studies that consider Patrick's literary background and rhetorical ingenuity is considerable and continues to grow. The best and best known are Peter Dronke, 'St. Patrick's reading', *Cambridge Medieval Celtic Studies* 1 (1981): 21–38; Joseph Falaky Nagy, *Conversing with Angels and Ancients: Literary Myths of Medieval Ireland* (Ithaca, NY, 1997), 23–39 (quotation from 28); Máire B. De Paor, *Patrick, the Pilgrim Apostle of Ireland: An Analysis of St. Patrick's Confessio and Epistola* (Dublin, 1998), 9–21; E. MacLuhan, '"*Ministerium seruitutis meae*": The metaphor and reality of slavery in Saint Patrick's *Epistola* and *Confessio*', in *Studies in Irish Hagiography: Saints and Scholars*, ed. J. Carey, M. Herbert, and P. Ó Riain

(Dublin, 2001), 63–71; P. Lynch, "*Ego Patricius, peccator rusticissimus*": The rhetoric of St. Patrick of Ireland', *Rhetoric Review* 27 (2008): 111–30; D. Bracken, 'Rome and the Isles: Ireland, England and the rhetoric of orthodoxy', in *Anglo-Saxon/Irish Relations before the Vikings*, ed. J. Graham-Campbell and M. Ryan (Oxford, 2009), 75–98, at 76–77; D. F. Melia, 'The rhetoric of Patrick's Letter to the Soldiers of Coroticus', *Proceedings of the Celtic Studies Association of North America Annual Meeting 2008* (2011): 96–104; Howlett, *Book of Letters*, 11; and T. M. Charles-Edwards, 'Perceptions of pagan and Christian, from Patrick to Gregory the Great', in Flechner and Ní Mhaonaigh, *Introduction of Christianity*, 259–78. For a brief discussion of literary antecedents of the *Confessio*, see C. Stancliffe, 'Patrick', in *Oxford Dictionary of National Biography*, ed. H.C.G. Matthew and B. Harrison, 60 vols. (Oxford, 2004), 43:69–80. Insofar as there is a scholarly consensus on the late antique sources that Patrick's *Confessio* and Letter echo, it is that no such sources can be identified with certainty, with the possible exception of Victorinus of Pettau, on which see chapter 5. For a summary of the debate, see Dronke, 'St. Patrick's reading', 22–23. For a comprehensive list of Patrick's biblical allusions and citations, see Bieler, *Libri Epistolarum*, 113–16. The quotation regarding Patrick's 'barbarous Latin' is in D. A. Binchy, 'St Patrick and his biographers: Ancient and modern', *Studia Hibernica* 2 (1962): 7–173, at 34. For Dumville's metaphorical interpretation of Coroticus's Roman citizenship, see his *Saint Patrick*, 108: 'It is unwise to press the word *cives* to a specific association with Roman citizenship; the clue is provided by the *sancti romani*, the Roman saints'. Hanson, in *Saint Patrick*, 114, offered a similar hypothesis, which he reached via a more complicated route. The principle established by Jerome of reiterating *opinio vulgi* according to the *vera lex historiae* has been debated in relation to Bede by Charles W. Jones, *Saints' Lives and Chronicles in Early England* (Ithaca, NY, 1947), 80–93; Roger Ray, 'Bede's *Vera Lex Historiae*', *Speculum* 55 (1980): 1–21; and Walter Goffart, 'Bede's *Vera lex historiae* explained', *Anglo-Saxon England* 34 (2005): 111–16.

For comparanda of autobiographical self-praise by a modern missionary, see Tim Jeal, *Livingstone*, rev. ed. (New Haven, CT, 2013); and Meriel Buxton, *David Livingstone* (Houndmills, 2001). The former holds a more judgmental view of Livingstone's self-congratulatory remarks and fabrications.

On freeing slaves in Roman law, a custom that was permitted through manumission but entailed a series of restrictions on freedmen, who remained in a relationship of dependence to their former owners, now patrons, potentially including the provision of services and labour tasks, see Paul du Plessis, *Borkowski's Textbook on Roman Law*, 5th ed. (Oxford, 2015), 105–7. Instances of slavery as metaphor in the first four centuries AD are collected by Isobel A. H. Combes, *The Metaphor of Slavery in the Writings of the Early Church: From the New Testament to the Beginning of* the *Fifth Century* (Sheffield, 1998). Christ's parables involving slavery are discussed by Jennifer A. Glancy, *Slavery in Early Christianity* (Oxford, 2002), 102–29. Although Irish law acknowledged that slaves could be freed, it strongly discouraged masters from freeing them. See Fergus Kelly, *A Guide to Early Irish Law* (Dublin, 1988), 96–97.

On Patrick as the instigator of a 'national conversion', see George Stokes, *Ireland and the Celtic Church: A History of Ireland from St. Patrick to the English Conquest in 1172* (London, 1893), 23. On a folkloric tradition about Patrick's having had a wife, see Olivia Kelleher reporting on research in progress by Shane Lehane of the Department of Folklore at University College Cork: 'St Patrick had a wife, and her name was Sheelah', *Irish Times*, 16 March 2017.

Chapter 1: Patrick's Britain

On Roman and post-Roman Britain, see Charles Thomas, 'St Patrick and fifth-century Britain', in *The End of Roman Britain*, ed. P. J. Casey (Oxford, 1979), 81–101; Stephen Johnson, *Later Roman Britain* (London, 1980); I. N. Wood, 'The fall of the Western Empire and the end of Roman Britain', *Britannia* 18 (1987): 251–62; A. S. Esmonde Cleary, *The Ending of Roman Britain* (London, 1989); Michael E. Jones, *The End of Roman Britain* (Ithaca, NY, 1996), esp. 108–43; David Mattingly, *An Imperial Possession: Britain in the Roman Empire, 54 BC–AD 409* (London, 2006) (for the definition of 'villa', 370; and for maps showing the distribution of villa sites in Britain, 262, 380–81, 481); Robin Fleming, *Britain after Rome: The Fall and Rise, 400–1070* (London, 2010), 1–60; and T. M. Charles-Edwards, *Wales and the Britons, 350–1064* (Oxford, 2013). On the date AD 410, Honorius's rescript, and the debate on its intended addressees, see E. A. Thompson, 'Zosimus on the end of Roman Britain', *Antiquity* 30 (1956): 163–67; E. A. Thompson, 'Fifth-century facts?', *Britannia* 14 (1983): 272–74; and Jones, *End of Roman Britain*, 249n19. The dating of the earliest Irish settlement in western Britain to the 'barbarian conspiracy' of 367 is considered by T. M. Charles-Edwards, *Early Christian Ireland* (Cambridge, UK, 2000), 160. And for the possibility that some Roman troops remained at Hadrian's Wall after 410, though perhaps not as part of an official military network, see Rob Collins, *Hadrian's Wall and the End of Empire: The Roman Frontier in the 4th and 5th Centuries* (New York, 2012).

On slavery in the Roman Empire and its aftermath, see Kyle Harper, *Slavery in the Late Roman World, AD 275–425* (Cambridge, UK, 2011); and Alice Rio, *Slavery after Rome, 500–1100* (Oxford, 2017). Early Christian attitudes to slavery are explored by Jennifer A. Glancy, *Slavery in Early Christianity* (Oxford, 2002). The question of Paul's joint ownership of Onesimus is debated by Ulrike Roth, 'Paul, Philemon, and Onesimus: A Christian design for mastery', *Zeitschift für die neutestamentliche*

Wisenschaft 105 (2014): 102–30. Prices of slaves are considered by A.H.M. Jones, *The Later Roman Empire, 284–602: A Social, Economic and Administrative Survey*, 3 vols. (Oxford, 1964), 2:852; and Kyle Harper, 'Slave prices in late antiquity', *Historia* 59 (2010): 206–38. On the manner in which the papacy concerned itself with slaves owned by churches, see Gregory the Great's letters 1.38a, 6.36, 9.30, in *Sancti Gregorii Magni Registrum Epistularum Libri I–XIV*, ed. D. Norberg, CCSL 140–140A (Turnhout, 1982); John Martyn, trans., *The Letters of Gregory the Great*, 3 vols. (Toronto, 2004). On Clovis's conversion and attempts to date Patrick's *floruit* with reference to his mention of 'pagan Franks', see Simon Young, 'St Patrick and Clovis', *Peritia* 16 (2002): 478–79. The selling of liturgical utensils for redeeming captives is mentioned in A.H.M. Jones, *Later Roman Empire*, 2:854.

The identity of the slaver and warlord, or perhaps British king, Coroticus has been the subject of much debate, with his name alone inviting a great deal of linguistic speculation and comparison with tenth-century Welsh royal pedigrees, whose testimony was applied retrospectively. Among the more influential discussions are Richard P. C. Hanson, *Saint Patrick: His Origins and Career* (Oxford, 1968), 22–27; E. A. Thompson, *Who Was Saint Patrick?* (Woodbridge, UK, 1985), 125–43; David N. Dumville, *Saint Patrick: A.D. 493–1993*, with Lesley Abrams, T. M. Charles-Edwards, Alicia Corrêa, K. R. Dark, K. L. Maund, and A. Orchard (Woodbridge, UK, 1993), 107–16; and Charles-Edwards, *Early Christian Ireland*, 227–30.

The archaeology of Roman Britain in its twilight years continues to generate a significant amount of scholarship, of which a selection follows. For general works on the periods of concern to the present study, see Lindsay Allason-James, ed., *Artefacts in Roman Britain* (Cambridge, UK, 2010); and James Gerrard, *The Ruin of Roman Britain: An Archaeological Perspective* (Cambridge, UK, 2013). On towns and settlements, see Fleming, *Britain after Rome*, esp. 9 (on the number of villas in late antique Britain), 15 (on villas with agriculture); and Adam Rogers, *Late Roman Towns in Britain* (Cambridge, UK, 2011). On the proximity of pagan temples of the fourth century and villas: T. W. Potter and C. Jones, *Roman Britain* (London, 1992), 204. On villas and the rural aristocracy of Roman Britain, see Mattingly, *Imperial Possession*, 369–75, 453–71; and T. W. Potter, *Roman Britain* (London, 1983), 25, for the quotation on villas as impressive places. There is no consensus on the location of the town on whose council Calpornius served, of Patrick's family's *villula*, or of Bannavem Taburniae. The quoted suggested identifications are by Thomas F. O'Rahilly, *The Two Patricks: A Lecture on the History of Christianity in Fifth-Century Ireland* (Dublin, 1942), 33–34; and Charles Thomas, *Christianity in Roman Britain to AD 500* (London, 1981), 310–14. A couple of more recent speculative suggestions for the villa are Southern Dorset and the Cotswolds. See K. R. Dark, 'St Patrick's *villula* and the fifth-century occupation of Romano-British villas', in Dumville, *Saint Patrick*, 19–24. On inscriptions in Roman Britain, see Mark Handley, 'The origins of Christian commemoration in late antique Britain', *Early Medieval Europe* 10 (2001): 177–99. The most recent edition of the corpus of Roman inscriptions in Britain is R. G. Collingwood, R. P. Wright, et al., *The Roman Inscriptions of Britain*, 3 vols. (Oxford, 1995–2009); the standard, earlier edition is by E.W.E. Hübner, *Inscriptiones Britanniae Latinae*, Corpus Inscriptionum Latinarum 7 (Berlin, 1873), available at https://arachne.uni-koeln .de/books/CILvVII1873.

Christianity in Roman Britain was first explored in a book-length study from a chiefly archaeological perspective by Thomas, *Christianity in Roman Britain*. A synthesis of mainly archaeological finds attesting Christianity in Roman Britain is David Petts, *Christianity in Roman Britain* (Stroud, 2003) (on converted *basilicae* and house churches, see 56–83). On the spread of Christianity in Britain and its correlation with social status, see Dorothy Watts, *Christians and Pagans in Roman Britain* (London, 1991), 217–19. On identifying churches in the landscape in late Roman Britain and on the social status associated with paganism and Christianity, see K. R. Dark, *Civitas to Kingdom: British Political Continuity, 300–800* (Leicester, 1994), 38–39. For the distribution of churches in Roman Britain, see Barri Jones and D. Mattingly, *An Atlas of Roman Britain* (Oxford, 1990), 296, 298. The latest on the implications of Christianity more generally for wealth, its distribution, and the patronage of churches, is Peter Brown, *Through the Eye of a Needle: Wealth, the Fall of Rome, and the Making of Christianity in the West, 350–550 A.D.* (Princeton, NJ, 2012).

The question of Patrick's dates received much attention from scholarship. A survey of the debate is provided by Dumville, *Saint Patrick*, 13–18. On his obits in the annals, see Dumville, *Saint Patrick*, 29–33, 59–64. For the history of the Chronicle of Ireland, whence these annalistic entries derive, see T. M. Charles-Edwards, *The Chronicle of Ireland*, 2 vols. (Liverpool, 2006), 1:7–9. On dating Patrick before the fifth century, see, e.g., M. Esposito, 'The Patrician problem and a possible solution', *Irish Historical Studies* 10 (1956/7): 131–55. Esposito's speculative arguments were followed up by J. T. Koch, who tested them linguistically, in '*Cothairche*, Esposito's theory, and Neo-Celtic lenition', in *Britain 400–600: Language and History*, ed. A. Bammesberger and A. Wollmann (Heidelberg, 1990), 179–202. For a critique of his method, see Roy Flechner, 'Patrick's reasons for leaving Britain', in *Tome: Studies in Medieval History and Law*, ed. Fiona Edmonds and Paul Russell (Woodbridge, UK, 2011), 125–34, 126n11. On objections to a pre-fifth-century date, see Ludwig Bieler, 'Der Bibeltext des heiligen Patrick', *Biblica* 28 (1947): 31–58, 236–63; and Dumville, *Saint Patrick*, 15–16. But for later insertions from the Vulgate Bible into Patrick's writings, which suggest that the biblical quotations cannot be used as a secure contemporary dating criterion, see also Ludwig Bieler, *Libri*

Epistolarum Sancti Patricii Episcopi, 2 vols. (Dublin, 1952), 1:35, who draws on previous work by Newport J. D. White, '*Libri Sancti Patricii*: The Latin writings of Saint Patrick', *Proceedings of the Royal Irish Academy* 25C (1905): 201–326, at 216–19. Scottish traditions regarding Patrick's place of birth are discussed by Thomas Owen Clancy, 'The cults of Saints Patrick and Palladius in early medieval Scotland', in *Saints' Cults in the Celtic World*, ed. Steve Boardman, John Ruben Davies, and Eila Williamson (Woodbridge, UK, 2009), 18–41.

The discussion of decurions and trafficking in imperial offices is based primarily on A.H.M. Jones, *Later Roman Empire*, 738–46; C. Rapp, 'The elite status of bishops in late antiquity in ecclesiastical, spiritual, and social contexts', *Arethusa* 33, no. 3 (2000): 379–99; G. Mousourakis, *The Historical and Institutional Context of Roman Law* (Aldershot, 2003), 65; C. Kelly, *Ruling the Later Roman Empire* (Cambridge, MA, 2004), 160–63; and C. Wickham, *Framing the Early Middle Ages* (Oxford, 2005), 68, 167. Among the historians who speculated on Patrick's father's wishes to avoid curial obligations were J. B. Bury, *The Life of St. Patrick and His Place in History* (London, 1905), 20; Eoin MacNeill, *Saint Patrick: Apostle of Ireland* (London, 1934), 6–7; Hanson, *Saint Patrick*, 176–78; David R. Howlett, ed. and trans., *The Book of Letters of St. Patrick the Bishop* (Dublin, 1994), 116; Máire B. De Paor, *Patrick, the Pilgrim Apostle of Ireland: An Analysis of St. Patrick's Confessio and Epistola* (Dublin, 1998), 127; and Flechner, 'Patrick's reasons for leaving Britain', 131–32.

Chapter 2: Patrick's Ireland

The best on early Ireland in the historical period are T. M. Charles-Edwards, *Early Christian Ireland* (Cambridge, UK, 2000) (see 136–44 for honour and status and 220–21 for gift giving in the *Confessio*, including the quotation on the accusation that Patrick hoped to enrich himself in Ireland); and Clare Downham, *Medieval Ireland* (Cambridge, 2018). Preliterate Ireland is only reported in texts by outsiders, whose accounts were collated by Philip Freeman, *Ireland and the Classical World* (Austin, 2001). Archaeology is our primary source of evidence for Ireland in the Iron Age and up until the early Middle Ages, when literacy arrives. General surveys of this period include Barry Raftery, *Pagan Celtic Ireland: The Enigma of the Iron Age* (London, 1994); Barry Raftery, 'Iron-Age Ireland', in *A New History of Ireland*, vol. 1, *Prehistoric and Early Ireland*, ed. D. Ó Cróinín (Oxford, 2005), 134–81; and Lloyd Laing and Jennifer Laing, *Celtic Britain and Ireland, AD 200–800: The Myth of the Dark Ages* (Blackrock, 1990). Raftery has also explored issues relating to identifying La Tène culture in Ireland in his *La Tène in Ireland: Problems of Origin and Chronology* (Marburg, 1984). On farming in early Ireland, see Fergus Kelly, *Early Irish Farming* (Dublin, 1997). On cattle in early Ireland, see

Michael O'Connell, Fergus Kelly, and James H. McAdam, eds., *Cattle in Ancient and Modern Ireland: Farming Practices, Environment and Economy* (Newcastle, 2016). On proprietary churches and land alienation in medieval Ireland, see Susan Wood, *The Proprietary Church in the Medieval West* (Oxford, 2006), 140–47 (quotation in the present chapter is from 146). An anthropological perspective on the alienation of land to the church is Jack Goody, *The Development of the Family and Marriage in Europe* (Cambridge, UK, 1983). And on the ambiguities of Patrick's legal status, see T. M. Charles-Edwards, 'The social background to Irish *peregrinatio*', *Celtica* 11 (1976): 43–59, at 54–55; and Clare Stancliffe, 'Kings and conversion: Some comparisons between the Roman mission to England and Patrick's to Ireland', *Frühmittelalterliche Studien* 14 (1980): 59–94, at 63–64.

Connections between Roman Britain and Ireland are crucial to any study of Saint Patrick, who benefitted from them. In the Roman period and early post-Roman period, Ireland can be conceptualised as an imperial frontier zone, on which see Elva Johnston, 'Ireland in late antiquity: A forgotten frontier?', *Studies in Late Antiquity* 1 (2017): 107–23; and Elva Johnston, 'Religious change and frontier management: Reassessing conversion in fourth- and fifth-century Ireland', *Eolas* 11 (2018): 104–19. Once more, archaeology is the key primary source for this period. On Irish votive offerings at Anglesey, see Anne Ross, *Druids* (Stroud, 1999), 39. On Roman objects in Ireland, see J. D. Bateson, 'Roman material from Ireland: A re-consideration', *Proceedings of the Royal Irish Academy* 73C (1973): 21–97; N. Edwards, *The Archaeology of Early Medieval Ireland* (London, 1990), 1–5; and Ewan Campbell, *Continental and Mediterranean Imports to Atlantic Britain and Ireland, AD 400–800* (York, 2007), 14–26 (on fourth- and fifth-century Mediterranean pottery and its distribution); Edel Bhreathnach, 'Transforming kingship and cult: The provincial ceremonial capitals in early medieval Ireland', in *Landscapes of Cult and Kingship*, ed. Roseanne Schot, Conor Newman, and Edel Bhreathnach (Dublin, 2011), 126–48, at 127 (on Tara's Rath of the Synods). A table of all sites in Ireland in which sherds of Late Roman amphorae (B-ware) were found is Aidan O'Sullivan, Finbar McCormick, Thomas R. Kerr, and Lorcan Harney, *Early Medieval Ireland, AD 400–1100: The Evidence from Archaeological Excavations* (Dublin, 2014), 438–40. The Roman predecessors of Irish brooches are discussed by Niamh Whitfield, '"More like the work of fairies than human beings": The filigree on the "Tara" Brooch: A masterpiece of late Celtic metalwork', *ArchaeoScience, Revue d'Archéométrie* 33 (2009): 235–41. On the ambiguity between the Roman or Irish identity of a good number of pins that were previously believed to be Irish and the implications for identifying 'Celtic' motifs, see Fiona Gavin and Conor Newman, 'Notes on Insular silver in the "Military Style"', *Journal of Irish Archaeology* 16 (2007): 1–10. Seán Daffy's formidable but unpublished PhD thesis on the cultural context of Roman finds from Southeast Ireland, "Irish and Roman

Relations: A Comparative Analysis of the Evidence for Exchange, Acculturation and Clientship from Southeast Ireland" (PhD diss., National University of Ireland Galway, 2013), offers an up-to-date survey of Roman deposits at Megalithic tombs (160–99), discusses the *lar* in the river Boyne (now at the National Museum of Ireland; 258), and stresses throughout the significance of votive offerings. It can be accessed at https://aran.library.nuigalway.ie/handle/10379/4450.

Some of the linguistic evidence mentioned in the chapter that may afford insights on international trade is discussed by Damian McManus, 'A chronology of the Latin loan-words in early Irish', *Ériu* 34 (1983): 21–71; Damian McManus, 'The so called *Cothrige* and *Pátraic* strata of Latin loan-words in early Irish', in *Ireland and Europe: The Early Church / Irland und Europa: Die Kirche im Frühmittelalter*, ed. Próinséas Ní Chathain and Michael Richter (Stuttgart, 1984), 179–96; and Jean-Michel Picard, 'The Latin language in early medieval Ireland', in *The Languages of Ireland*, ed. Michael Cronin and Cormac Ó Cuilleanáin (Dublin, 2003), 44–56, esp. 45.

On finds of precious metals and their later use as currency in Ireland, see H. Mattingly and J. W. E. Pearce, 'The Coleraine hoard', *Antiquity* 11 (1937): 39–45; C. Etchingham and C. Swift, 'English and Pictish terms for brooch in an 8th-century Irish law text', *Medieval Archaeology* 48 (2004): 31–50; and L. Breatnach, 'Forms of payment in early Irish law tracts', *Cambrian Medieval Celtic Studies* 68 (2014): 1–20. On votive offerings in the Rath of the Synods, see L. Allason-Jones, 'Appendix A: The small finds', in *The Rath of the Synods, Tara, Co. Meath*, ed. Eoin Grogan (Dublin, 2008), 107–12.

There is some evidence for trading activity between Ireland and Britain, on which see Amanda Kelly, 'The discovery of Phocean Red Slip Ware (PRSW) Form 3 and Bii Ware (LR1 amphoae) on sites in Ireland', *Proceedings of the Royal Irish Academy* 110C (2010): 35–88; and Christopher Loveluck and Aidan O'Sullivan, 'Travel, transport and communication to and from Ireland: An archaeological perspective', in *The Irish in Early Medieval Europe*, ed. Roy Flechner and Sven Meeder (London, 2016), 19–37, at 21–23.

On the possibility that Irish soldiers served in the Roman army, see Catherine Swift, *Ogam Stones and the Earliest Irish Christians* (Maynooth, 1997), 6–9; and Jacqueline Cahill Wilson, 'Romans and Roman material in Ireland: A wider social perspective', in *Late Iron Age and "Roman" Ireland*, ed. Jacqueline Cahill Wilson, Discovery Programme Reports 8 (Dublin, 2014), 11–58, at 35–36.

The impact of Roman Britain on literacy in Ireland is best attested in the ogam script, on which the literature is extensive. There is a continually updated bibliography at the 'Ogham in 3D' project of the Dublin Institute for Advanced Studies, http://ogham.celt.dias.ie/menu.php?lang=en&menuitem=80. Select contributions include R.A.S. Macalister, *Corpus Inscriptionum Insularum Celticarum: The Ogham Inscriptions of Ireland and Britain* (Dublin, 1945); Damian McManus, *A Guide to*

Ogam (Maynooth, 1991); and Swift, *Ogam Stones*. There is a magisterial chapter on inscriptions in T. M. Charles-Edwards, *Wales and the Britons, 350–1064* (Oxford, 2013), 116–73. Challenges of dating ogam inscriptions are discussed by Anders Alqvist, *The Early Irish Linguist: An Edition of the Canonical Part of the Auraicept na n-éces* (Helsinki, 1983); and Anthony Harvey, 'Problems of dating the origin of the ogham script', in *Roman, Runes and Ogham: Medieval Inscriptions in the Insular World and on the Continent*, ed. John Higgitt, Katherine Forsyth, and David N. Parsons (Donington, 2001), 37–50. Both allow for a second-century dating of the invention of ogam. For more on the possibility of dating ogam script as early as the second century AD, see Anthony Harvey, 'Languages and literacy in mid-first-millennium Ireland: New questions to some old answers', in *Transforming Landscapes of Belief in the Early Medieval Insular World and Beyond*, vol. 2 of *Converting the Isles*, ed. Nancy Edwards, Máire Ní Mhaonaigh, and Roy Flechner (Turnhout, 2017), 53–64. On the earliest manifestations of script in Ireland in manuscripts, see Mark Stansbury, 'Conversion and the origin of Irish script', in Edwards, Ní Mhaonaigh, and Flechner, *Transforming Landscapes*, 65–78. That Patrick and Palladius were among those who introduced an 'uncomplicated' (*unkomplizierte*) script, which is likely to have been Roman, into Ireland has been suggested by Bernhard Bischoff, *Paläographie des römischen Altertums und des abendländischen Mittelalters*, 3rd ed. (Berlin, 2004), 113. And see D. Ó Cróinín, *Early Medieval Ireland, 400–1200* (London, 1995), 185, for an argument on direct Continental influence on the earliest form of the Irish half uncial. The survival of books from early medieval Ireland is discussed by Richard Sharpe, 'Books from Ireland, fifth to ninth centuries', *Peritia* 21 (2010): 1–55.

On 'Celtic' identity and material culture in Ireland, see Laing and Laing, *Celtic Britain and Ireland*. For a recent discussion of the historiography on Celtic Ireland in light of material evidence, see John Waddell, *Archaeology and Celtic Myth: An Exploration* (Dublin, 2014), 1–14. A study representative of more positivist views on the Indo-European inheritance is Myles Dillon's posthumously published *Celts and Aryans: Survivals of Indo-European Speech and Society* (Simla, India, 1975). Likewise, Alwyn D. Rees and Brinley Rees, *Celtic Heritage: Ancient Tradition in Ireland and Wales* (London, 1961), draws attention to similarities between Irish traditions and Indian mythology. On the hypothesis of Queen Medbh's Indo-European origins, see Thomas F. O'Rahilly, 'On the origin of the names *Érainn* and *Ériu*', *Ériu* 14 (1946): 7–28; Georges Dumézil, *Destiny of a King* (Chicago, 1973), 70–84; and Kim McCone, *Pagan Past and Christian Present in Early Irish Literature* (Maynooth, 1990), 109–10. On the question of a Celtic political identity, see Malcolm Chapman, *The Celts: The Construction of a Myth* (Basingstoke, 1992); Patrick Sims-Williams, 'Celtomania and Celtoscepticism', *Cambrian Medieval Celtic Studies 36*

(1998): 1–35; Simon James, *The Atlantic Celts: Ancient People or Modern Invention?*
(London, 1999); and John Collis, *The Celts: Origins, Myths and Inventions* (Stroud,
2003). For examples of euhemeristic hypotheses, see H. Munro Chadwick and
N. Kershaw Chadwick, *The Growth of Literature*, 3 vols. (Cambridge, UK, 1932–40);
Kenneth Hurlstone Jackson, *The Oldest Irish Tradition: A Window on the Iron Age*
(Cambridge, UK, 1964); E. Knott and G. Murphy, *Early Irish Literature* (London,
1966); and F. J. Byrne, '*Senchas*: The nature of Gaelic historical tradition', *Historical
Studies* 9 (1974): 157. For criticism and refinement of the euhemeristic approach,
see James Carney, *Studies in Irish Literature and History* (Dublin, 1955), 276–323 (the
title of the chapter that spans these pages is in itself telling: 'The external element
in Irish saga'); and Tomás Ó Cathasaigh, 'Pagan survivals: The evidence of early
Irish narrative', in Ní Chatháin and Richter, *Ireland and Europe*, 291–307, at 294–95.
On debating the validity of oral traditions and of the binary of oral versus written,
see McCone, *Pagan Past*; and Elva Johnston, *Literacy and Identity in Early Medieval
Ireland* (Woodbridge, UK, 2013) (the quotation in the present chapter is from 157).
Pertinent studies of Irish mythology and early medieval Irish Literature are Proinsias
Mac Cana, *Celtic Mythology* (Feltham, 1968; rev. ed., 1983); Joseph Falaky Nagy,
Conversing with Angels and Ancients: Literary Myths of Medieval Ireland (Ithaca,
NY, 1997); Tomás Ó Cathasaigh, 'The literature of medieval Ireland to *c.* 800', in
The Cambridge History of Irish Literature, ed. Margaret Kelleher and Philip O'Leary,
2 vols. (Cambridge, UK, 2006), 1:9–31; Tomás Ó Cathasaigh, 'Irish myths and
legends', *Studia Celtica Fennica* 2 (2005): 11–26; and Máire Ní Mhaonaigh, 'The
literature of medieval Ireland, 800–1200: From the Vikings to the Normans', in
Kelleher and O'Leary, *Cambridge History of Irish Literature*, 1:32–73. For a more
specialised treatment of the subject, see McCone, *Pagan Past*. The latest study on
the Finn Cycle is Kevin Murray, *The Early Finn Cycle* (Dublin, 2017); and on the
Mythological Cycle is John Carey, *The Mythological Cycle of Medieval Irish Literature* (Cork, 2018). On the fourfold division into 'cycles' being 'convenient', see Ó
Cathasaigh, 'Irish myths and legends', 13; Carey, *Mythological Cycle*, 2.
The literature on the development of the Irish language is vast. A few notable works,
as well as works used for the present chapter, are Rudolf Thurneysen, *Grammar of
Old Irish*, trans. D. A. Binchy and Osborn Bergin (Dublin, 1946); J. T. Koch, '*Cothairche*, Esposito's theory, and Neo-Celtic lenition', in *Britain 400–600: Language
and History*, ed. A. Bammesberger and A. Wollmann (Heidelberg, 1990), 179–202;
and Paul Russell, 'Latin and British in Roman and post-Roman Britain: Methodology and morphology', *Transactions of the Philological Society* 109, no. 2 (2011):
138–57.
On the hypothesis of the 'two Patricks', see Thomas F. O'Rahilly, *The Two Patricks:
A Lecture on the History of Christianity in Fifth-Century Ireland* (Dublin, 1942); D. A.

Binchy, 'St Patrick and his biographers: Ancient and modern', *Studia Hibernica* 2 (1962): 7–173 (quotations from 115, 143); and David N. Dumville, *Saint Patrick: A.D. 493–1993*, with Lesley Abrams, T. M. Charles-Edwards, Alicia Corrêa, K. R. Dark, K. L. Maund, and A. Orchard (Woodbridge, UK, 1993), 59–64. The disparaging quote by Allan B. E. Hood is from his *St Patrick: His Writings and Muirchú's Life* (London, 1978), 15.

Chapter 3: Captivity

On slavery in the Roman Empire and the transition to early medieval forms of unfreedom, see Marc Bloch, *La société féodale* (Paris, 1939), trans. L. A. Manyon as *Feudal Society* (London, 1965); Kyle Harper, *Slavery in the Late Roman World, AD 275–425* (Cambridge, UK, 2011); and Alice Rio, *Slavery after Rome, 500–1100* (Oxford, 2017). Attitudes towards slavery among early Christians are considered in Jennifer A. Glancy, *Slavery in Early Christianity* (Oxford, 2002); and Jennifer A. Glancy, 'Slavery and the rise of Christianity', in *The Cambridge World History of Slavery*, vol. 1, *The Ancient Mediterranean World*, ed. Keith Bradley and Paul Cartledge (Cambridge, UK, 2011), 456–81. On Gregory the Great's attitude to slavery and Jewish ownership of slaves, see Adam Serfass, 'Slavery and Pope Gregory the Great', *Journal of Early Christian Studies* 14 (2006): 77–103. On the legalities of resuming one's place in Roman society by means of *postliminium* after being taken captive and on selling freeborn people, see Paul du Plessis, *Borkowski's Textbook on Roman Law*, 5th ed. (Oxford, 2015), 89–91, 93–95, 157. Court cases involving *postliminium* in the late Roman Empire were identified by Harper, *Slavery*, 381–83. Conceptual difficulties of defining the states of freedom and unfreedom in late antiquity and the early Middle Ages are considered by Wendy Davies, 'On servile status in the early Middle Ages', in *Serfdom and Slavery: Studies in Legal Bondage*, ed. M. L. Bush (London, 1996), 225–46; and Alice Rio, ' "Half-free" categories in the early Middle Ages: Fine status distinctions before professional lawyers', in *Legalism: Rules and Categories*, ed. Paul Dresch and Judith Scheele (Oxford, 2015), 129–52. The captives were among Patrick's catechumens, on which see Paul F. Bradshaw, 'The gospel and the catechumenate in the third century', *Journal of Theological Studies* 50 (1999): 143–52.

The go-to place for legal aspects of slavery and captivity in early Ireland is Fergus Kelly, *A Guide to Early Irish Law* (Dublin, 1988), 95–97. On sexual exploitation of female slaves in Ireland and elsewhere in late antiquity, see Margaret Y. MacDonald, *Early Christian Women and Pagan Opinion* (Cambridge, UK, 1996), 224; T. M. Charles-Edwards, *Early Christian Ireland* (Cambridge, UK, 2000), 68–69; and Helen Oxenham, *Perceptions of Femininity in Early Irish Society* (Woodbridge, UK, 2016), 52–53.

On Patrick's precarious status as captive, see Clare Stancliffe, 'Kings and conversion: Some comparisons between the Roman mission to England and Patrick's to Ireland', *Frühmittelalterliche Studien* 14 (1980): 59–94, at 63–64. For the quotation concerning Patrick's defence against claims he left Ireland for financial gain, see Charles-Edwards, *Early Christian Ireland*, 220.

On social exclusion as the decisive defining criterion for unfreedom, see Orlando Patterson's *Slavery and Social Death* (Cambridge, MA, 1982), 35–76; and Alain Testart, *L'Esclave, la dette et le pouvoir* (Paris, 2001), 25, 42, 110. The model of a 'peasant-mode economy' was first applied to early Ireland by Chris Wickham, *Framing the Early Middle Ages: Europe and the Mediterranean 400–800* (Oxford, 2005), 535–47. For a counterthesis, see Wendy Davies, 'Economic change in early medieval Ireland: The case for growth', in *L'Irlanda e gli irlandesi nell' alto medioevo: Settimane di studio della fondazione centro italiano di studi sull' alto medioevo LVII, Spoleto 16–21 Aprile 2009* (Spoleto, Italy, 2010), 111–33.

On the ambiguity of the noun *gratia*, see, for example, *Dictionary of Medieval Latin from British Sources: Fascicule IV: F–G–H*, ed. David Howlett (Oxford, 1989). On interpreting the expression *sancti Romani* in Patrick's Letter, see David N. Dumville, *Saint Patrick: A.D. 493–1993*, with Lesley Abrams, T. M. Charles-Edwards, Alicia Corrêa, K. R. Dark, K. L. Maund, and A. Orchard (Woodbridge, UK, 1993), 108; and Richard P. C. Hanson, *Saint Patrick: His Origins and Career* (Oxford, 1968), 114.

On the hypothesis of ritual sucking at breasts of Irish kings and on the occurrences of men suckling others in Irish hagiography, see Eamonn P. Kelly, 'An archaeological interpretation of Irish Iron Age bog bodies', in *The Archaeology of Violence: Interdisciplinary Approaches*, ed. Sarah Ralph (Albany, NY, 2013), 232–40; and Dorothy Ann Bray, 'Suckling at the breast of Christ: A spiritual lesson in an Irish hagiographical motif', *Peritia* 14 (2000): 282–96.

Chapter 4: Religion in Britain and Ireland

Key general studies of paganism in late antiquity and the early medieval period have tended to concentrate on 'Germanic' rather than 'Celtic' Europe, but many findings are transferable nevertheless. Among the best are Ramsay MacMullen, *Christianity and Paganism in the Fourth to Eighth Centuries* (New Haven, CT, 1997); I. N. Wood, 'Pagan religion and superstitions east of the Rhine from the fifth to the ninth century', in *After Empire: Towards an Ethnology of Europe's Barbarians*, ed. G. Ausenda (Woodbridge, UK, 1995), 253–79; I. N. Wood, 'The pagans and the Other: Varying presentations in the early Middle Ages', *Networks and Neighbours* 1 (2013): 1–22; and Bernadette Filotas, *Pagan Survivals, Superstitions and Popular Cultures in Early Medieval Pastoral Literature* (Toronto, 2005).

Archaeology plays a crucial role in investigating religion in predominantly illiterate societies. The general reference works on archaeology used here are Barry Raftery, *Pagan Celtic Ireland: The Enigma of the Iron Age* (London, 1994); and Lloyd Laing, *Archaeology of Celtic Britain and Ireland c. 400–1200* (Cambridge, UK, 2006). On finds from Roman Britain associated with Christianity, see Charles Thomas, *Christianity in Roman Britain to AD 500* (London, 1981); David Petts, *Christianity in Roman Britain* (Stroud, 2003); and David Mattingly, *An Imperial Possession: Britain in the Roman Empire, 54 BC–AD 409* (London, 2006), 349. On Roman objects in prehistoric sites in Ireland and their interpretation as votive offerings, see Raftery, *Pagan Celtic Ireland*, 180; Laing, *Archaeology*, 271–76; J. D. Bateson, 'Roman material from Ireland: A re-consideration', *Proceedings of the Royal Irish Academy* 73C (1973): 21–97, at 31; and Catherine Swift, *Ogam Stones and the Earliest Irish Christians* (Maynooth, 1997), 20. On Tara, see Conor Newman, ed., *Tara: An Archaeological Survey* (Dublin, 1997); and L. Allason-Jones, 'Appendix A: The small finds', in *The Rath of the Synods, Tara, Co. Meath*, ed. Eoin Grogan (Dublin, 2008), 107–12. Burials in Ireland (especially *ferta*) have been the subject of a number of important studies by Elizabeth O'Brien, among them 'Burial practices in Ireland: First to seventh centuries AD', in *Sea Change: Orkney and Northern Europe in the Late Iron Age, AD 300–800*, ed. Jane Downes and Anna Ritchie (Balgavies, UK, 2003), 62–72; and, with Edel Bhreathnach, 'Irish boundary *ferta*, their physical manifestation and historical context', in *Tome: Studies in Medieval Celtic History and Law in Honour of Thomas Charles-Edwards*, ed. Fiona Edmonds and Paul Russell (Woodbridge, UK, 2011), 53–64. On the possible connection between prehistoric traditions associated with the Newgrange passage tomb and medieval Irish written mythology, see John Carey, 'Time memory, and the Boyne Necropolis', *Proceedings of the Harvard Celtic Colloquium* 10 (1990): 24–36 (quotation from 7). The inscription bearing the word DRVVIDES is discussed by Damian McManus, *A Guide to Ogam* (Maynooth, 1991), 61, 93–94, 97.

General studies on pagan religion and mythologies in Britain and Ireland from both a textual and archaeological perspective are Anne Ross, *Druids* (Stroud, 1999); Ronald Hutton, *Pagan Britain* (New Haven, CT, 2013); and Mark Williams, *Ireland's Immortals: A History of the Gods of Irish Myth* (Princeton, NJ, 2016). The classic port of call for Irish mythology is Proinsias Mac Cana, *Celtic Mythology* (Feltham, 1968; rev. ed., 1983). See also Kim McCone, *Pagan Past and Christian Present in Early Irish Literature* (Maynooth, 1990).

For an introduction to contemporary Irish literature, see Tomás Ó Cathasaigh, 'The literature of medieval Ireland to c. 800', in *The Cambridge History of Irish Literature*, ed. Margaret Kelleher and Philip O'Leary, 2 vols. (Cambridge, UK, 2006), 1:9–31; and Máire Ní Mhaonaigh, 'The literature of medieval Ireland, 800–1200: From the

Vikings to the Normans', in Kelleher and O'Leary, *Cambridge History of Irish Literature*, 1:32–73. The latest study on the Finn Cycle is Kevin Murray, *The Early Finn Cycle* (Dublin, 2017); and on the Mythological Cycle is John Carey, *The Mythological Cycle of Medieval Irish Literature* (Cork, 2018). For a relatively recent example of a search for correlation between myth and landscape, see Chris Lynn, Cormac McSparron, and Peter Moore, *Excavations at Navan Fort, Co. Armagh*, Data Structure Report 13 (Belfast, 2002), esp. 8. Irish sacral kingship is discussed by Bart Jaski, *Early Irish Kingship and Succession* (Dublin, 2000), 57–88. On the question of sun worship in Ireland, see Thomas F. O'Rahilly, *Early Irish History and Mythology* (Dublin, 1946), 58, 290–94; Mac Cana, *Celtic Mythology*, 30; and John Waddell, *Archaeology and Celtic Myth: An Exploration* (Dublin, 2014), 1–55. For a revised date range for the Martyrology of Óengus (replacing the previously accepted 828 × 833 proposed by Pádraig Ó Riain, 'The Tallaght martyrologies, redated', *Cambridge Medieval Celtic Studies* 20 [1990]: 21–38), see David Dumville, 'Félire Oengusso: Problems of dating a monument of Old Irish', *Éigse* 33 (2002): 19–48. An invaluable resource on 'Celtic' religion containing extracts from predominantly Greek and Latin sources in German translation, with commentary and cross-references, is Andreas Hofeneder, *Die Religion der Kelten in den antiken literarischen Zeugnissen: Sammlung, Übersetzung und Kommentierung*, 3 vols. (Vienna, 2005–11).

Investigations of aspects of the empire's transition towards Christianity are Ramsay MacMullen, *Christianizing the Roman Empire (A.D. 100–400)* (New Haven, CT, 1984); Michelle Salzman, 'The evidence for the conversion of the Roman Empire', *Historia* 42 (1993): 362–78; David Hunt, 'Christianising the Roman Empire: The evidence of the Code', in *The Theodosian Code*, ed. Jill Harries and Ian Wood (London, 1993), 143–58; Scott Bradbury, 'Constantine and the problem of anti-pagan legislation in the fourth century', *Classical Philology* 89 (1994): 120–39; Christopher Jones, *Between Pagan and Christian* (Cambridge, MA, 2014) (109–10, 186, for references to the *numen* of Christian emperors); and Greg Woolf, 'Only connect? Network analysis and religious change in the Roman World', *Hélade* 2 (2016): 43–58. An evaluation of the state of the art on Roman attitudes to *interpretatio Romana* is Clifford Ando, '*Interpretatio Romana*', *Classical Philology* 100 (2005): 41–51. The question of *interpretatio Romana* by early medieval clerics is considered in James Palmer, 'Defining paganism in the Carolingian world', *Early Medieval Europe* 15 (2007): 402–25.

Interpretations of contemporary terms and concepts are pivotal for any investigation of religion in antiquity and late antiquity. The Roman conceptions of *religio* and *superstitio* are elucidated in a classic study by Denise Grodzynski, '*Superstitio*', *Revue des études anciennes* 76 (1974): 36–60. For scholarly debates on the term *paganitas* in Roman times, see Robin Lane Fox, *Pagans and Christians in the Mediterranean*

World from the Second Century to the Conversion of Constantine (London, 1986), 30–31; Pierre Chuvin, *Chronicle of the Last Pagans* (Cambridge, MA, 1990), 7–9; and Christopher Jones, *Between Pagan and Christian*, 5. On Patrick's use of the expression *gentes* as distinct from *pagani*, see T. M. Charles-Edwards, 'Perceptions of pagan and Christian, from Patrick to Gregory the Great', in *The Introduction of Christianity into the Early Medieval Insular World*, vol. 1 of *Converting the Isles*, ed. Roy Flechner and Máire Ní Mhaonaigh (Turnhout, 2016), 259–78. The meanings of Hiberno-Latin *laicus*, among them 'lay tenant', 'layman', 'man', 'warrior', and 'brigand', are discussed by Richard Sharpe, 'Hiberno-Latin *laicus*, Irish *láech* and the devil's men', *Ériu* 30 (1979): 75–92, esp. 87–90. The important caveat concerning the interpretation of *magi* in Irish hagiography is made by Catherine McKenna, in *Identifying the 'Celtic'*, ed. Joseph Falaky Nagy (Dublin, 2002), 66–74.

The survey offered in the present chapter of the terms *gentiles* and *pagani* in Hiberno-Latin literature is based on the following texts, contained in the Royal Irish Academy's electronic Archive of Celtic Latin Literature: Saint Patrick's *Confessio* and Letter (probably fifth century, *CLH* § 216); penitentials and canon law (sixth, seventh century, *BCLL* §§ 598–609, 612–14); 'The Twelve Abuses' (seventh century, *CLH* §576); Lives of Patrick by Tírechán and Muirchú, *Additamenta, Liber Angeli* (seventh century, *BCLL* §§ 301, 303, 358, 360); *Patricius uenit in campo* (seventh century, *BCLL* § 355); Adomnán's Life of Columba and *De locis sanctis* (seventh/eighth century, *CLH* §§ 230, 568); the Irish Augustine's *De mirabilibus sacrae scripturae* (seventh century, *CLH* §574); the three seventh-century Lives of Brigit (*CLH* §§ 227 [*Vita Prima*], 228 [by Cogitosus], 248 [*Bethu Brigte*]); the ninth-century Metrical Life of Brigit (*CLH* § 229); the ninth-century Tripartite Life of Patrick (*CLH* § 246); and the ninth-century Life of Fursa (*CLH* § 236). Both expressions are absent from most texts. The texts that employ *gentilis* most frequently are Muirchú's Life of Patrick (twenty-six times), the *Hibernensis* (twelve times), Tírechán's *Collectanea* (eleven times), and Adomnán's Life of Columba (nine times). Only Cogitosus and the *Hibernensis* use *paganus*.

Recent explorations of the notions of 'Celtic' identity and religion are Bernhard Maier, *Die Religion der Kelten* (Munich, 2001); Bernhard Maier, *The Celts: A History from Earliest Times to the Present* (Edinburgh, 2003); Nagy, *Identifying the 'Celtic'*; Raimund Karl and David Stifter, eds., *The Celtic World: Critical Concepts in Historical Studies*, 4 vols. (London, 2007); Katja Ritari and Alexndra Begholm, eds., *Understanding Celtic Religion: Revisiting the Pagan Past* (Cardiff, 2015); Malcolm Chapman, *The Celts: The Construction of a Myth* (Basingstoke, 1992); and Joep Leerssen, 'Celticism', in *Celticism*, ed. Terence Brown (Amsterdam, 1996), 1–20. For a study that is largely a response to the latter two that upholds the thesis of a cultural

coherence among an ancient people that self-identified as 'Celtic', see Kim Mc-
Cone, *The Celtic Question: Modern Constructs and Ancient Realities* (Dublin,
2008). For references in chapter 4 relating to debates about the validity of the concept 'Celtic' and about continuities and connections across Celtic, European,
Mediterranean, and Atlantic cultures, see J. Vendryes, 'La religion des Celtes', in
Mana: Introduction à l'histoire des religions, 2 vols. (Paris, 1948), 2:239–320, at 272,
273; Mac Cana, *Celtic Mythology*, 20; and Julia Farley and Fraser Hunter, eds., *Celts:
Art and Identity* (London, 2015), 35 (quote from exhibition catalogue on absence of pan-European Celts).

On Georges Dumézil's 'three-functions model' of Indo-European cultures, see his
L'idéologie tripartie des Indo-Européens (Brussels, 1958). There is a discussion of the
theory in Mac Cana, *Celtic Mythology*, 60. For criticism, see C. Scott Littleton, *New
Comparative Mythology: An Anthropological Assessment of the Theories of Georges
Dumézil* (Berkeley, 1966; 3rd ed. 1982), 186–203. Barry Raftery's quotation regarding pan-Celtic deities is from his *Pagan Celtic Ireland*, 178. For the quotation setting
out the opposite view, see Patrick Sims-Williams, 'Celtic civilization: Continuity
or coincidence?', *Cambrian Medieval Celtic Studies* 64 (2012): 1–45, at 42.

Cultural continuity across Celtic and other cultures that Matthias Egeler explores is
discussed in his *Walküren, Bodbs, Sirenen: Gedanken zur religionsgeschichtlichen
Anbindung Nordwesteuropas an den mediterranen Raum* (Berlin, 2011); and Matthias Egeler, 'Death, wings, and divine devouring: Possible Mediterranean affini-
ties of Irish battlefield demons and Norse valkyries', *Studia Celtica Fennica* 5
(2008): 3–24. For scepticism in historiography about equating an Irish 'Celtic'
culture with Continental Iron Age La Tène culture and about the notion that La
Tène culture reached Ireland via migration rather than trade, see Laing, *Archaeology*, 271–72.

On the search for the origins of the Celts being 'perfectly meaningless', see Raimund
Karl, 'The Celts from everywhere and nowhere: A re-evaluation of the origins of
the Celts and the emergence of Celtic cultures', in *Celtic from the West: Alternative
Perspectives from Archaeology, Genetics, Language and Literature*, ed. Barry Cunliffe
and John T. Koch (Oxford, 2010), 39–64, at 62. And for the radically innovative
hypothesis of an origin in the Atlantic region, see Barry Cunliffe and John T. Koch,
introduction to *Celtic from the West*, ed. Cunliffe and Koch, 1–12 (quote from 1).
The idea of Atlantic origins was originally presented in Barry Cunliffe, *Facing the
Ocean: The Atlantic and Its Peoples 8000 BC–AD 1500* (Oxford, 2001), 293–97. Some
experts have expressed strong scepticism of the notion of 'Celtic from the West',
in particular criticising inconsistencies in the methodological approach. See, for
example, the review by Jürgen Zeidler in the *Bryn Mawr Classical Review* 2011.09.57;
the review of the sequel to the first volume (*Celtic from the West 2*, 2013) by

Joseph F. Eska in the *Bryn Mawr Classical Review* 2013.12.35; and the review by John
Collis in the *Archaeological Journal* 171 (2014), 405–6. Other experts have been
more receptive towards the radical linguistic hypotheses—for example, Colin
Renfrew in his review in the *Cambridge Archaeological Journal* 21 (2011), 327–28.
For the application of the theories of 'wave of advance' and 'elite transfer' to the history
of the formation of European peoples, see Peter Heather, *Empires and Barbarians*
(London, 2009), 22. On the hazards of identifying a discrete material culture with
a single race in late antiquity, see I. N. Wood, 'Barbarians, historians, and the construction of national identities', *Journal of Late Antiquity* 1 (2008): 61–81.

Chapter 5: The Missionary Life

The title of this chapter is a tribute to the best monograph on conversion through
missions in late antique and early medieval Europe: I. N. Wood, *The Missionary
Life: Saints and the Evangelisation of Europe 400–1050* (Harlow, 2001). Recent contributions on cultural, social, and economic aspects of the conversion of Britain
and Ireland can be found in the twin volumes emanating from the Converting the
Isles research network: Roy Flechner and Máire Ní Mhaonaigh, eds., *The Introduction of Christianity into the Early Medieval Insular World*, vol. 1 of *Converting the
Isles* (Turnhout, 2016); and Nancy Edwards, Máire Ní Mhaonaigh, and Roy Flech-
ner, eds., *Transforming Landscapes of Belief in the Early Medieval Insular World and
Beyond*, vol. 2 of *Converting the Isles* (Turnhout, 2017). Good accounts of the model
missionary saint of late antiquity, Martin of Tours, and his biographer continue
to be (despite their vintage) Clare Stancliffe, *St. Martin and His Hagiographer:
History and Miracle in Sulpicius Severus* (Oxford, 1983); and Raymond Van
Dam, *Leadership and Community in Late Antique Gaul* (Berkeley, 1985), 119–41.
On parallels between the conversion of the Irish and the conversion of the Carin-
thians, as well as echoes of the so-called double insurance policy, see Henry Mayr-
Harting, *Two Conversions to Christianity: The Bulgarians and the Anglo-Saxons*,
Stenton Lecture 1993 (Reading, 1994), 13–16. For a comparison between Patrick's
mission and Augustine's mission to Anglo-Saxon England, see Clare Stancliffe,
'Kings and conversion: Some comparisons between the Roman mission to
England and Patrick's to Ireland', *Frühmittelalterliche Studien: Jahrbuch des Instituts
für Frühmittelalterforschung der Universität Münster* 14 (1980): 59–94.
Patrick's eschatology and apocalyptic worldview have been mentioned in a number
of publications, among them the following: Richard P. C. Hanson, *Saint Patrick:
His Origins and Career* (Oxford, 1968), 201; Thomas O'Loughlin, *Discovering Saint
Patrick* (London, 2005), 84–91; T. M. Charles-Edwards, *Early Christian Ireland*
(Cambridge, UK, 2000), 215–16; and James Palmer, *The Apocalypse in the Early
Middle Ages* (Cambridge, UK, 2014), 81–83.

On the linguistic evidence for British ecclesiastical influence on Ireland, see Kenneth Jackson, *Language and History in Early Britain* (Edinburgh, 1953), 122–48. The hypothesis was refined by Damian McManus, 'A chronology of the Latin loan-words in Early Irish', *Ériu* 34 (1983): 21–71. An assessment of the history of scholarship in light of more recent views is provided by Paul Russell, 'Latin and British in Roman and post-Roman Britain: Methodology and morphology', *Transactions of the Philological Society* 109, no. 2 (2011): 138–57, esp. 139–41. Linguists would be especially sceptical about attempts to map the relative chronological progression suggested by the phonological changes on an absolute timeline. For using the linguistic evidence as proof of early British missions in Ireland, see Thomas F. O'Rahilly, *The Two Patricks: A Lecture on the History of Christianity in Fifth-Century Ireland* (Dublin, 1942), 42–44 (who draws on earlier work by Christoph Sarauw); T. M. Charles-Edwards, 'Britons in Ireland, c. 550–800', in *Ildánach ildírech: A Festschrift for Proinsias Mac Cana*, ed. John Carey, John T. Koch, and Pierre-Yves Lambert (Aberystwyth, 1999), 15–26; and Charles-Edwards, *Early Christian Ireland*, 184.

On Palladius, see T. M. Charles-Edwards, 'Palladius, Prosper, and Leo the Great: Mission and primatial authority', in *Saint Patrick: A.D. 493–1993*, by David N. Dumville, with Lesley Abrams, T. M. Charles-Edwards, Alicia Corrêa, K. R. Dark, K. L. Maund, and A. Orchard (Woodbridge, UK, 1993), 1–12; D. Ó Cróinín, 'Who was Palladius "First Bishop of the Irish"?', *Peritia* 14 (2000): 205–37. The assertions that Palladius's mission was a fulfilment of an injunction in Celestine's fourth letter and that Ireland is implied in Leo's Sermon 82 were first made by Charles-Edwards, *Early Christian Ireland*, 205, 6.

The latest monograph on Pelagius and Pelagianism, which challenges much of the received wisdom, including the mere existence of an organised Pelagian movement, is Ali Bonner, *The Myth of Pelagianism* (Oxford, 2018). A recent study that allows for the possibility that Germanus's mission was also meant to preempt Pelagianism from establishing a base in Ireland is Colmán Etchingham, 'Conversion in Ireland', in Flechner and Ní Mhaonaigh, *Introduction of Christianity*, 181–207, at 185. For older hypotheses on Pelagians in Ireland and speculations on Pelagius's possible Irish identity, see James F. Kenney, *The Sources for the Early History of Ireland: An Introduction and Guide*, vol. 1, *Ecclesiastical* (New York, 1929), 161–62; and E. A. Thompson, *Who Was Saint Patrick?* (Woodbridge, UK, 1985), 57. That the Irish observance of Easter was mistaken in the seventh century for Pelagianism was shown by D. Ó Cróinín, '"New heresy for old": Pelagianism in Ireland and the papal letter of 640', *Speculum* 60 (1985): 505–16. For a recent succinct appraisal of the theology of the debate concerning Pelagianism, see John Marenbon, *Pagans and Philosophers: The Problem of Paganism from Augustine to Leibniz* (Princeton, NJ, 2015), 33, 37, 64–65. On Pelagius's surviving writings, see *BCLL* §§ 2–20.

On the identity of Victoricus, whom Patrick says inspired him to preach in Ireland, see Allan B. E. Hood, ed. and trans., *St. Patrick: His Writings and Muirchu's "Life"* (Chichester, 1978), 3–4. The latest discussions of Victricius are Dennis Trout, *Paulinus of Nola: Life, Letters and Poems* (Berkeley, 1999), 60–61, 238–39; and Gillian Clark, 'Translating relics: Victricius of Rouen and fourth-century debate', *Early Medieval Europe* 10 (2001): 11–76. On the idea that he was a fellow Briton, see Philip Freeman, *St. Patrick of Ireland: A Biography* (New York, 2004), 50.

That Patrick held converts who took monastic vows in exceptionally high regard was observed by Charles-Edwards, *Early Christian Ireland*, 223, who argues that, for Patrick, 'the appearance of monastic life among his converts was the culmination of his mission'. The possibility that Patrick had a portable altar with him in his missionary work gains support from a contemporary portable altar found at Vindolanda on Hadrian's Wall, on which see Robin Birley, *Vindolanda: Everyday Life on Rome's Northern Frontier* (Greenhead, 2008), 107. The parallels between Patrick's creed and Victorinus's commentary on the Apocalypse of John were first noted by John E. L. Oulton, *The Credal Statements of St. Patrick as Contained in the Fourth Chapter of His Confession* (Dublin, 1940). For Peter Brown's quotation regarding the implications of revering widowhood and celibacy, see his *Through the Eye of a Needle: Wealth, the Fall of Rome, and the Making of Christianity in the West, 350–550 A.D.* (Princeton, NJ, 2012), 270.

Introductory literature on the rise of monasticism and its introduction to the Latin West includes Marilyn Dunn, *The Emergence of Monasticism from the Desert Fathers to the Early Middle Ages* (Oxford, 2000); and C. H. Lawrence, *Medieval Monasticism: Forms of Religious Life in Western Europe in the Middle Ages*, 4th ed. (London, 2015).

Chapter 6: Imagining Patrick in the Middle Ages

The bibliography on the cult of saints is vast, and so I only offer two important titles: Peter Brown, *The Cult of the Saints: Its Rise and Function in Latin Christianity* (Chicago, 1981; 2nd ed., 2015); and Robert Bartlett, *Why Can the Dead Do Such Great Things? Saints and Worshippers from the Martyrs to the Reformation* (Princeton, NJ, 2013). The cult of saints was inseparable from hagiography and the veneration of relics. On relics generally and their social, religious, and economic significance, see Patrick Geary, *Furta Sacra: Thefts of Relics in the Central Middle Ages* (Princeton, NJ, 1978); Michael McCormick, *Origins of the European Economy: Communications and Commerce, A.D. 300–900* (Cambridge, UK, 2001), 283–318; and Julia M. H. Smith, 'Portable Christianity: Relics in the medieval West (*c.* 700–1200)', *Proceedings of the British Academy* 181 (2012): 143–67. The most recent study of relics in Ireland is Niamh Wycherley, *The Cult of Relics in Early Medieval Ireland* (Turnhout,

2015). On surviving books from early Ireland and the relic status of some of them, see Richard Sharpe, 'Books from Ireland, fifth to ninth centuries', *Peritia* 21 (2010): 1–55. Another important manifestation of saintly cult that corresponded to hagiography was veneration in the landscape. On the converted landscape in Tírechán's *Collectanea*, see T. M. Charles-Edwards, *St. Patrick and the Landscape of Early Christian Ireland*, Kathleen Hughes Memorial Lecture 10 (Cambridge, UK, 2012).

On Patrick's hagiographers and their motives, especially the promotion of Armagh, but also, perhaps, of Donaghpatrick (County Meath) and Domnach Mór (County Mayo), see R. Sharpe, 'St Patrick and the see of Armagh', *Cambridge Medieval Celtic Studies* 4 (1982): 33–59; Kim McCone, *Pagan Past and Christian Present in Early Irish Literature* (Maynooth, 1990), 244–48; Charles Doherty, 'The cult of St Patrick and the politics of Armagh in the seventh century', in *Ireland and Northern France AD 600–850*, ed. Jean-Michel Picard (Dublin, 1991), 53–94; Catherine Swift, 'Tírechán's motives in compiling the *Collectanea*: An alternative interpretation', *Ériu* 45 (1994): 53–81; Elizabeth Dawson, 'The *Vita Patricii* by Tírechán and the creation of St Patrick's nationwide status', in *Civis Patrocinio Tota Gaudet Regio: Saints' Cults and the Dynamics of Regional Cohesion*, ed. Stanislava Kuzmová, Ana Marinkovič, and Trpimir Vedriš (Zagreb, Croatia, 2014), 1–20; and David E. Thornton, 'Tírechán [St Tírechán] (fl. c. 690)', in *Oxford Dictionary of National Biography* (Oxford, 2004), http://www.oxforddnb.com/view/article/27473.

Armagh's patronage of Sleaty is discussed by Francis John Byrne, 'A note on Trim and Sletty', *Peritia* 3 (1984): 316–19. On the appearance of Áed and Muirchú in the Law of Innocents, see M. Ní Dhonnchadha, 'The guarantor list of *Cáin Adomnáin*, 697', *Peritia* 1 (1982): 178–215.

Various early Irish customs, practices, and beliefs have been mentioned in this chapter. On fosterage in early Ireland, see Fergus Kelly, *A Guide to Early Irish Law* (Dublin, 1988), 86–90. On the physical perfection required of Irish kings, see Bart Jaski, *Early Irish Kingship and Succession* (Dublin, 2000), 82–87. On keening and lamenting in early medieval Ireland, see Kaarina Hollo, 'Laments and lamenting in early medieval Ireland', in *Medieval Celtic Literature and Society*, ed. Helen Fulton (Dublin, 2005), 83–94. On the *Túatha Dé Danann*, see Mark Williams, *Ireland's Immortals: A History of the Gods of Irish Myth* (Princeton, NJ, 2016). The latest on the veneration of holy wells in Ireland is Celeste Ray, *The Origins of Ireland's Holy Wells* (Oxford, 2014).

The starting point for any discussion of the social and legal status of the *filid* is a legal text regulating their profession, *Uraicecht na Ríar*: Liam Breatnach, ed., *Uraicecht na Ríar: The Poetic Grades in the Irish Church* (Dublin, 1987), 102–15. For a more recent assessment of the place of *filid* in early Irish society, see Elva Johnston,

Literacy and Identity in Early Medieval Ireland (Woodbridge, UK, 2013), esp. 131–56, 170–75. On the poets' being a discrete strand within Irish aristocracy, see T. M. Charles-Edwards, 'The context and uses of literacy in early Christian Ireland', in *Literacy in Medieval Celtic Societies*, ed. Huw Pryce (Cambridge, UK, 1998), 62–82.

The latest monograph to explore the Irish phase of the Easter Controversy in context is Caitlin Corning, *The Celtic and Roman Traditions: Conflict and Consensus in the Early Medieval Church* (New York, 2006). On the centrality of Rome to the Easter Controversy, see R. Sharpe, 'Armagh and Rome in the seventh century', in *Ireland and Europe: The Early Church / Irland und Europa: Die Kirche im Frühmittelalter*, ed. Próinséas Ní Chatháin and Michael Richter (Stuttgart, 1984), 58–72 (quotation from 68). His designation of the term *Romani* in Ireland follows observations made by W. Ullmann, 'On the use of the term *Romani* in the sources of the earlier Middle Ages', *Studia Patristica* 2 (1957): 155–63.

Aspects of the literary ingenuity of the hagiographers are explored by John Hennig, 'The literary tradition of Moses in Ireland', *Traditio* 7 (1949–51): 233–61; Joseph Falaky Nagy, *Conversing with Angels and Ancients: Literary Myths of Medieval Ireland* (Ithaca, NY, 1997), 40–134; McCone, *Pagan Past*, 179–97; Aideen M. O'Leary, *Trials and Translations: The Latin Origins of the Irish Apocryphal Acts of the Apostles*, 2 vols. (Aberdeen, 2013), 1:146–56 (who attempts to argue on circumstantial evidence that Muirchú drew on apocryphal biographies of the apostles); and Katja Ritari, 'From pagan to Christian in the 7th century Irish hagiography', *Studia Celtica Fennica* 1 (2004): 14–23. For echoes of an early version of the *Táin* story in seventh-century Armagh hagiography, see John Carey, 'Muirchú and the Ulster Cycle', in *Ulidia 3: Proceedings of the Third International Conference on the Ulster Cycle of Tales*, ed. Gregory Toner and Séamus Mac Mathúna (Berlin, 2013), 121–26. Other comparisons with vernacular literature were explored by Kim McCone, 'An introduction to early Irish saints' Lives', *Maynooth Review* 11 (1984): 26–59.

The textual history of the early medieval Patrician hagiography and its influence on later medieval accounts is crucial for the development of the myth of Patrick. On the hypothesis of a 'primitive Life' underpinning a number of the medieval Lives of Patrick, see Ludwig Bieler, ed., *Four Latin Lives of St. Patrick* (Dublin, 1971), 9. On the dating of the *Vita Secunda* and *Vita Quarta*, see Bieler, *Four Latin Lives*, 12 (and 220 for the confusion Armuircc Letha/Letha). For a translation, see F. J. Byrne and Pádraig Francis, 'Two Lives of Saint Patrick: *Vita Secunda* and *Vita Quarta*', *Journal of the Royal Society of Antiquaries of Ireland* 124 (1994): 5–117, at 17–64. On the background to the *Vita Tertia* and its dating, see Byrne and Francis, 'Two Lives', 8 (for its possible connection to Landévennec); Bieler, *Four Latin Lives*, 26 (reinforcing Bury's hypothesis of a date in or after the eighth century); *BCLL* § 367 (date and bibliography); and *CLH* § 219 (date and bibliography). The association of Patrick with Glastonbury is investigated by Lesley Abrams in David N. Dumville, *Saint Patrick: A.D. 493–1993*, with Lesley Abrams, T. M. Charles-Edwards, Alicia Corrêa, K. R. Dark, K. L. Maund, and A. Orchard (Woodbridge, UK, 1993), 233–44. On the Life by Probus, see Byrne and Francis, 'Two Lives', 8; *BCLL* § 1184; and *CLH* § 221 (the last two of which date it to the eleventh century but add a question mark). For a recent study concentrating primarily on the textual history and sources of the Life by Jocelyn, see Helen Birkett, *The Saints' Lives of Jocelin of Furness: Hagiography, Patronage and Ecclesiastical Politics* (Woodbridge, UK, 2010), 25–58. Another interesting case of intertextuality is the curious appearance of Patrick in the Irish normative tradition, usually alongside the poet Dubthach, which has received a good deal of attention. The most recent contribution, referencing many of the important earlier studies, is Patrick Wadden, 'The pseudo-historical origins of the *Senchas Már* and royal legislation in early Ireland', *Peritia* 27 (2016): 141–58.

Epilogue: Remembering Saint Patrick

There is a good deal of popular work on the veneration of Patrick in the early modern and modern eras. There is also work emanating from academic research, of which here are a few titles: G. Montague, 'History of the feast of St Patrick', *Irish Ecclesiastical Record* 70 (1949): 278–82; Jeanne Sheehy, *The Rediscovery of Ireland's Past: The Celtic Revival, 1830–1930* (London, 1980), 9–12; Alannah Hopkin, *The Living Legend of St. Patrick* (London, 1989); Seosamh Ó Dufaigh, 'Saint Patrick and how he was remembered', *Seanchus Ardmhacha* 16 (1995): 69–82; Bernadette Cunningham and Raymond Gillespie, '"The most adaptable of saints": The cult of St Patrick in the seventeenth century', in *Archivium Hibernicum* 49 (1995), 82–104; Mike Cronin and Daryl Adair, *The Wearing of the Green: A History of St. Patrick's Day* (London, 2002); and John McCafferty, 'The communion of saints and Catholic Reformation in early seventeenth-century Ireland', in *Community in Early Modern Ireland*, ed. R. Armstrong and T. Ó hAnnracháin (Dublin, 2006), 199–215. For commemorations of Patrick by wells and for the shamrock, see Bridget McCormack, *Perceptions of St Patrick in Eighteenth-Century Ireland* (Dublin, 2000), 37–39, 80; and Celeste Ray, *The Origins of Ireland's Holy Wells* (Oxford, 2014). The earliest Saint Patrick's Day celebration in America is discussed by John Crimmins, *St. Patrick's Day: Its Celebration in New York and Other American Places, 1737–1845* (New York, 1902), 15. On celebrations of Saint Patrick's Day in the eighteenth century being primarily a Catholic affair, on the competition between the Williamite and saintly anniversaries, and on the changing attitudes in Dublin Castle, see Jacqueline R. Hill, 'National festivals, the state and the Protestant Ascendancy in Ireland, 1790–1829', *Irish*

Historical Studies 24 (1984): 30–51, at 30, 46–48. On the early modern rediscovery of the seventh-century Patrician hagiography, see Ludwig Bieler, ed., *Libri Epistolarum Sancti Patricii Episcopi*, 2 vols. (Dublin, 1952), 1:30.

On Saint Patrick's Purgatory and some of the literature associated with it, see Carol G. Zaleski, 'St. Patrick's Purgatory: Pilgrimage motifs in a medieval otherworld vision', *Journal of the History of Ideas* 46 (1985): 469–70; Michael Haren and Yolande de Pontfarcy, eds., *The Medieval Pilgrimage to St Patrick's Purgatory: Lough Derg and the European Tradition* (Enniskillen, 1988); and, most recently, Giovanni Paolo Maggioni, Roberto Tinti, and Paolo Taviani, *Il Purgatorio di San Patrizio: Documenti letterari e testimonianze di pellegrinaggio (secc. XII–XVI)* (Florence, 2018). A study of the cults of Palladius and Patrick, especially in Scotland, is Thomas Owen Clancy, 'The cults of Saints Patrick and Palladius in early medieval Scotland', in *Saints' Cults in the Celtic World*, ed. Steve Boardman, John Ruben Davies, and Eila Williamson (Woodbridge, UK, 2009), 18–41.

On relics and material culture associated with Patrick and saintly veneration in Ireland, see Charles Doherty, 'The use of relics in early Ireland', in *Ireland and Europe: The Early Church*, ed. Próinséas Ní Chatháin and Michael Richter (Stuttgart, 1984), 89–101; Cormac Bourke, 'The shrine of St Patrick's hand', *Irish Arts Review* 4 (1987): 25–27; M. Ronan, 'St Patrick's staff and Christ Church', in *Medieval Dublin: The Living City*, ed. Howard B. Clarke (Dublin, 1990), 12–131; Peter Harbison, *Pilgrimage in Ireland: The Monuments and the People* (London, 1991); Cormac Bourke, *Patrick: The Archaeology of a Saint* (Belfast, 1993); Niamh Wycherley, *The Cult of Relics in Early Medieval Ireland* (Turnhout, 2015); and Rachel Moss, 'The staff, the snake and the shamrock: St Patrick in Art', Saint Patrick's *Confessio*, accessed 30 July 2018, http://www.confessio.ie/more/article_moss#. The concluding quotation, by Daniel Binchy, is from his 'St Patrick and his biographers: Ancient and modern', *Studia Hibernica* 2 (1962): 7–173, at 173.

INDEX

abbot, office of, 187–88

Abraham (biblical figure), 19

absentee landowners, 53–54

Acallam na Senórach, 149

accusations, against Patrick, 11, 101,
107, 179–180, 233. *See also* defence,
Patrick's; elders, Patrick's conflict
with; trial, Patrick's

Acts of Union, 227

Adair, Daryl, 232

Additamenta, 186, 197, 206

Adelphius of Lincoln, 33, 127

Adomnán, 185, 188, 204, 206, 213

Adversus Hilvidium (Jerome), 25–26

Adversus Jovinianum (Jerome), 77

Áed of Sleaty, 186, 187, 188

Æthelberht, 162

Agar (biblical figure), 19

Agricola, 61, 77, 78, 137

Ailerán, 206

Airgíalla (group of dynasties), 195

Alcuin, 120

Alexandrian school, 20

allegorical exegesis, vs. literal
understanding, 24–26. *See also*
exegesis, biblical

altars: portable, 177; throwing gifts at,
170

Amalek (biblical people), 19

amicitia, 78

Ammianus Marcellinus, 41, 42,
76, 79

Amolngid dynasty. *See* Uí Amolngid

ancestors, veneration of, 148, 204

Antiochene school, 20, 51

apocalypse. *See* eschatology

apostasy, 97, 162, 174

appearance, 200, 201

archaeology, xvi; Boyne sites, 142–43;
evidence for cult practices and
religion, 138–140, 142–49; evidence
from Ireland, 68–72; ritual sites in
Ireland, 140

argumentum, 12, 13

aristocracy: hereditary, 191–92; Irish,
201–2; Roman, 166–67

Armagh, 7; absence of Patrick's relics
at, 194–95; claims of supremacy,
185; Patrick's patronage of, 186–87;
Patrick's request for, 193; relics at,
194–95; subjection of churches to,
205

Armorica, 208

artefacts, Irish, 68–72, 138, 144–45

Astérix comic books, 129

attacks, during Christian festivals,
110

Attacotti, invasions of Britain, 41–42

Attila the Hun, 126
Augustine, Saint, 48, 159
Aurelian, 124

Ballymacaward, 148–49
Bank Holiday (Ireland) Act, 230
Bannavem Taburniae, 31, 32
baptism, 109, 159–160; commitment to
    faith and, 203; compensation for,
    168–69, 180; conversion and,
    172–73; creed used in, 173; of druids,
    204; preparing for, 174–75 (see also
    catechumens)
barbarians, Irish referred to as, 2
Basil of Caesarea, 47
basilica, basilicae, 33, 128. See also
    churches
Battle of the Boyne, 230
Bede, 26, 184, 209, 213, 214
Benedictine Rule, 167
bereavement, 204
Bergin, Osborn, 91
betrayal, of Patrick, 101. See also
    accusations, against Patrick
Bhreathnach, Edel, 144
Bible: interpretation of (see exegesis,
    biblical) Latin translation, 34–35;
    Patrick's use of, 20–26; as
    prescriptive text, 22; as prophetic
    text, 23
Biblical allusions, 21, 99–100, 105
Bieler, Ludwig, 5, 20, 34, 36, 207,
    210–11
Binchy, Daniel, 16, 90–91, 233
biography, Patrick's: previous works
    of, 5–6; sources for, 4–6 (see also
    writings, Patrick's) standard
    narrative of, 7–26. See also
    hagiography, of Patrick

Birdoswald (Banna), 31
birthplace, Patrick's, 30, 31, 32
Bischoff, Bernhard, 74
bishop, office of, 187–88
bishops, 158, 178; consecration of,
    164–65; Palladius, 90–91, 157, 189,
    194, 209. See also clergy
Boniface, Saint, 77
Book of Armagh, 7, 9, 89, 194; Life of
    Patrick, 44; Martin's hagiography
    in, 176; texts in, 186
Book of Revelations (Peter of Cornwall),
    223
Boyne sites, 142–43
Brendan, Saint, 219
Brían Bórama (Brian Boru), 9
Brigantes, 32, 75, 129, 133
Brigit, Saint, 122, 146, 185, 209, 219,
    222, 226
Britain: assimilation of native elites
    into Roman society, 37, 38;
    churches in, 32–33; connection with
    Ireland, 69–71; contrast with
    Ireland, 2; departure of legionaries
    from, xv, 43; diversity in, 43–44;
    invasions of, 41–42, 79; land market
    in, 53–54; in Patrick's adult life, 53;
    Patrick's life in relation to, 33–36;
    as refuge for Pelagian exiles, 160;
    religion in, 127–131; Roman
    occupation of, 33–36; romanitas in,
    57; slavery in, 43–49; taxes in,
    50–51; third-century crisis and, 38;
    towns in, 37; understanding of, 5;
    United Kingdom of Britain and
    Ireland, 227–28. See also Roman
    Empire
British, indigenous, 132
Brown, Peter, 166

burial, 147–49; *ferta*, 148–49; of
  Patrick, 194, 226
burial sites, 151
Bury, J. B., 5, 52, 210
Butler, James, 226
Byrne, F. J., 66, 187, 210

Caelestius, 159, 160
Caesar, Julius, 68, 75–76, 124, 129–130,
  131, 133, 134, 136–37, 140
Cáilte, 150
calendars, 184; Irish legal, 228;
  liturgical, 208–9. *See also* Easter
  Controversy
Calpornius (father of Patrick), 30, 32,
  33, 34, 37, 38, 41, 45, 46, 50, 52,
  209–10
cannibalism, 76, 77
captives: freeing of, 114; women,
  sexual exploitation of, 112. *See also*
  captivity; converts, abducted;
  Coroticus; slavery
captivity: Christian captives, 113–15; in
  Confessio, 94, 108–17; discussed
  generally, 101–9; in Letter to the
  Soldiers of Coroticus, 94, 108–17;
  rehabilitation and, 103–4; Roman
  law and, 103–4. *See also* captives;
  Coroticus; slavery
captivity, Patrick's, 10–11, 15, 25,
  79–80, 94, 97–108; doubts about,
  101–7; Patrick's account of, 11;
  rehabilitation and, 103–4;
  shepherding during, 97. *See also*
  slavery
Carey, John, 66, 143, 200
Carlisle, 31, 32, 37
Carney, James, 5, 65
Cassiodorus, 12

catechumens, 110, 174–75. *See also*
  converts, abducted
Catholic Counter-Reformation,
  219–220, 222
Catholic Relief Act, 230
Catholic-Protestant relations,
  227–232
Catholics, Irish, 220, 227–232
Celestine, Pope, 89, 157, 158, 160, 162,
  189
celibate lifestyle, 166–67
Celtic culture, 62–64; language and,
  134–36; material culture, 62;
  problem of uniformity across,
  132–36
Celtic deities, 129–130
Celtic from the West (Cunliffe and
  Koch), 136
Celtic identity, xvii, 63–64, 134–35.
  See also Gauls
Celtic Iron Age, 62
Celts, distinguished from Irish, 63
cemeteries, 147–49, 204
Chadwick, Henry, 65
Chadwick, Nora, 65
Charlemagne, 82, 120
Charles-Edwards, Thomas, 43, 82–83,
  92, 158, 161, 192
childhood, Patrick's, 36–58
children: fosterage of, 200, 201–2;
  Law of Innocents and, 188; raising
  of, 78
chrism, 109
Christ: genealogies of, 25; as true sun,
  141
Christian, acceptance as, 203
Christian community, in Ireland, 158
Christian festivals, attacks during, 110
Christianitas/paganitas, 121

Christianity: assimilated into existing system, 151; conversion to (*see* conversion) of Coroticus's soldiers, 111–12; Nicene Creed, 202–3; relation with paganism, 132, 189–190; in Roman Empire, 29, 123–27, 144; slavery and, 45–49; social changes and, 29; suppression of, 125

Chrysostom, Dio, 137

"church," in Patrick's writings, 177

church, Irish, relation with Roman Catholicism, 221

churches: construction of, 177, 204–5; conversion and, 177; by entrance to Purgatory, 223; income of, 86; landholding by, 86–88; pledging of, 187; proprietary, 88, 187; in Roman Britain, 32–33, 128; slave ownership by, 48–49, 86; in Tírechán's narrative, 197, 198; at well of Clébach, 205

Chuvin, Pierre, 122

Cicero, 12, 121, 137

cimbid, 103

circumstances, 86

citizens, Roman: captivity and, 103–4; Coroticus's identification as, 44; identification as, 57; Patrick's identification as, 31, 33

citizenship, Roman, 44–45

civitas, civitates, 37

Clébach, 199, 204, 205

clergy: admittance of slaves into, 49; ecclesiastical hierarchy, 178–79; exemption from serving on council, 50; freeing of captives, 114; ordained by Patrick, 178–79; Patrick's ordination of, 164–65; roles of, 179;

slave ownership by, 46. *See also* bishops; ordination

clericus, 178–79

client-patron relationship, 78–79

Clovis, 35

Cogitosus, 122, 185

coins, Roman, 70–71, 124, 139–140, 143–44

Colgan, John, 219

Collectanea, 196, 201–2. *See also* Life of Patrick (Tírechán)

Colman, Saint, 219

colonia, 37

Colum Cille. *See* Columba, Saint

Columba, Saint, 185, 188, 194, 204, 206, 213, 222, 226

Combes, Isobel, 24

commemoration of Patrick, 228–232

Concessa (legendary mother of Patrick), 207, 209

Conchad, 186, 187–88

concubines, 112

Confessio (Patrick), 3, 7, 9, 10, 54, 218; on accusations against Patrick, 11; attempt to date Patrick from, 34–36; autobiographical details in, 30–31; biblical allusions in, 21, 99–100, 105; captivity in, 94, 108–17; compared to Letter, 10; conflict with elders in, 54–56; conversion in, 109, 163–66; eschatology in, 154–55; exegesis of, 23–26; first mention of Ireland in, 79; gifts in, 82; interpretation of, 99–100; on Irish religious practice, 141; objective of, 25; Patrick's childhood in, 31; Patrick's family's wealth in, 49; on Patrick's Latin, 16; on Patrick's mission, 154; profession of faith in, 173; readers of, 36; on return to Ireland, 14; rhetoric and, 16; slavery in, 23–24; suckling in, 98–99; thematic framework, 21; understanding of, 23; use of Bible as prophetic text, 22–23; Vulgate in, 34–35; widows in, 170–71. *See also* defence, Patrick's

Congal Cáech, 201

Connacht, 196

Constantine, 29, 30, 42, 51, 123, 124, 127, 141, 144

Constantius, 42, 144

contribution, 2

conversion, 119; attraction to, 175; baptism, 172–73; catechumens, 174–75; churches and, 177; in *Confessio*, 109; durable, 174; idea of, 158; of Irish Catholics, 220; kings and, 85–86; lapse back into paganism, 162; in Letter to the Soldiers of Coroticus, 109; metaphors for, 22; of slave women, 172; successful, 172. *See also* Christianity; mission, Patrick's; religion

conversion, of Ireland, 154; Bede's narrative of, 214; daughters of Lóegaire and, 198–205; focus on children of kings, 165–66 (*see also* monastic communities/life) in Life of Patrick, 189–193; Lóegaire and, 192–93; Palladius and, 160–61; Patrick omitted form narrative of, 214; Patrick's role in, 1. *See also* mission, Patrick's

converts, abducted: freeborn status of, 109; motivations for taking, 179. *See also* Letter to the Soldiers of Coroticus

Coroticus, 10, 30, 44–45, 57, 72, 80, 81, 111–12, 179, 180; excommunication of, 115–16; identification as Roman citizen, 44–45. *See also* Letter to the Soldiers of Coroticus

council. *See* curia; *curiales*

Council of Constantinople, 158

Council of Nicaea, 29, 30

Counter-Reformation, 219–220, 222

crannogs, 69

creeds, 172–74

Cronin, Mike, 232

Crúachain, 145–46, 147, 199

Cú Chulainn, 202

cult of Patrick, 211, 218–19

cult sites, 142–44, 176–77, 199. *See also* pagan sites

cultic practices, 137–152

cults: described by Patrick, 177; of saints, 218–19

cultural transmission, 136–37

culture, Ireland's: as Celtic, 62; daily life, 68–70; kin groups, 87–88; knowledge of, 91–92; literacy, 73–74; marriage, 85–86; Patrick's status in, 82–83; reciprocal gift giving in, 81–84; shepherding in, 79–80; sources on, 64 (*see also* mythology, Irish literary)

cumal, 85, 112. *See also* slave women

Cummène, 184

Cummène Fota, 184

Cunliffe, Barry, 136

curial obligations, 49–52, 107

curia, 32, 38, 50, 51, 53

curiales, 15, 33, 49–53. *See also* decurions

Cycle of Kings, 66–67, 149

Cyprian of Carthage, 174

Daffy, Seán, 71
Dagda, the, 141
Dark, Kenneth, 39
David Mattingly, 32
De antiquitate Glastoniensis ecclesiae (William of Malmsbury), 210
De inventione (Cicero), 12
De locis sanctis (Adomnán), 188
De Paor, M. B., 52
deacons, 179
death: Patrick's, 89; ritual lamentation and, 204
decurions, 15, 33, 49–53. *See also* *curiales*
defence, Patrick's, 13–14, 25, 107. *See also* accusations, against Patrick; elders, Patrick's conflict with; trial, Patrick's
deities, plurality of, 130–32
demigods, 201
derbfine, 87
Díarmait mac Cerbaill, 146
Diocletian, 37, 46, 123
diversity, in Britain, 43–44
Donnchadh (son of Flan Sinna), 9
druids, 68, 189–191, 192, 193, 202, 204, 205
Dublin Castle, 229
Dubthach maccu Lugair, 191, 192
Dumézil, Georges, 135
Dumville, David N., 5, 15, 34, 89
Dún Ailinne, 145–46

Eadbald, 162, 174
Easter, 110, 157, 185, 189–190
Easter Controversy, 183–85, 188
Easter uprising, 231
Eborius of York, 33, 127
ecclesiastical hierarchy, 178–79

Ecclesiastical History (Bede), 184
economy, slaves and, 96
education: Christian, 18; Patrick's, 12–14, 35–36
Egeler, Matthias, 135
elders, Patrick's conflict with, 54–56. *See also* accusations, against Patrick; defence, Patrick's; trial, Patrick's
Elijah (biblical figure), 125
Elizabeth (biblical figure), 25
Emain Macha, 145, 146, 147
emancipation, Patrick's, 21–22
emperor, Roman, 124, 126
end of time, anticipation for, 180. *See also* eschatology
Éndae, 198
England: cult of Patrick in, 31, 210, 211. *See also* Britain; Roman Empire
Erc mac Dego, 190
Eriugena, John Scottus, 150
Esau (biblical figure), 47
escape, Patrick's, 10–11, 102–3. *See also* emancipation, Patrick's
eschatology, 154–56, 173, 180
Etchingham, Colmán, 161
Ethne, 150, 199–205
ethnic diversity, 43–44
ethnic identity, 62–64
etiological tales, 198, 205. *See also* princesses, conversion of
evidence. *See* archaeology; sources; writings, Patrick's
exclusion, 116–17
excommunication, 115–16
exegesis: biblical, 18–26; of *Confessio*, 23–26
exegetical reflex, 18
Exodus, book of, 25, 189

fabula, 12

faith: Nicene Creed, 202–3; Patrick's, 205; Patrick's profession of, 173; profession of, 203

falsehoods, in rhetoric, 13

fame, Patrick's, 208–14

familia, 196

family, Patrick's, 30–31. *See also* Calpornius; Concessa

father of Patrick (Calpornius), 30, 32, 33, 34, 37, 38, 41, 45, 46, 50, 52, 209–10

Fedelm, 150, 199–205

Ferdomnach, 7, 186

ferta, 148–49, 204

Fíacc (poet), 191

filid, 191–92

Finn Cycle, 66, 149–150

Finn mac Cumaill, 66

Fith Fio, 170, 171

Flan Febla, 186, 187

Flan Sinna, 9

flight of *curiales*, 51, 52–53

fosterage, 77, 200, 201–2

Fox, Robin Lane, 122

Francis, Pádraig, 210

Franks, 35, 114

free status: of abducted converts, 109; Patrick's, 11

free will, 159–160

freedom: exclusion and, 116–17; in Letter, 108

Freeman, Philip, 6

fuidir, 96

Gaelic League, 231

Gallic War, 75, 129

Gallus, Saint, 209

Gaul, 63; captives in, 114; Gallic associations attributed to Patrick, 207; Patrick in, 164; religion in, 129–130

Gauls: plurality of cults among, 133; religion of, 134. *See also* Celtic identity

gelfine, 87

Génair Patraicc in Nemthur (hymn), 31

genealogy: of Patrick, 209–10; of saints, 219

generosity, Patrick's, 106

gentilis, 122, 123, 140–41

gentlide, 122

geographical overviews of Ireland, 74–76

George, Saint, 227–28

Gerald of Wales, 77, 211, 213, 226

Germanus of Auxerre (Saint Germanus), 160, 161, 189, 207

gift giving, reciprocal, 73, 81–84

gifts: of land, 171; for monasteries, 170; Patrick's attitude towards, 105; Patrick's refusal to accept, 168–69, 171–72; thrown on altar, 170

Gilbert (monk), 223

Glastonbury, 31, 210

Goody, Jack, 86

Goody thesis, 86–88

Goscinny, René, 129

government in Ireland, 67–68. *See also* kings; kingship

grace, divine (*gratia*), 97–98, 159

grandfather, Patrick's. *See* Potitus

Gratian, 126

graves, 147–49

Great Witcombe, villa, 38–39

Gregory the Great, Pope, 9, 49, 178

Hadrian's Wall, 41, 42

Hagar, 20

hagiography: genealogies of saints, 219; of Martin of Tours, 176; Patrick in, 3, 4; property claims in, 197–98; purposes of, 185; relation with mythology, 150; saints' Lives, 185; templates for, 176. *See also individual Lives of saints*

hagiography, of Patrick: influences on, 205–8; Palladius written out of, 162; social context of, 200, 204–5; sources for, 185–86. *See also* Lives of Patrick; *individual Lives of Patrick*

Hallstatt culture, 62

Hanson, Richard, 5, 52

Harvey, Anthony, 73

Helios, 125, 141

Henry of Saltry, 223

heresies, 158–160. *See also* Pelagianism

Herod (biblical figure), 146, 190

Herodotus, 76

Hibernensis (canon law text), 86

Hibernia, 75. *See also* Ireland

Higbald of Lindisfarne, 120

hillforts, 138–39

historia, 12–13

Holy Trinity, 221

Honorius, Pope, 42, 160, 183–84

honour price, 84

Hood, Allan B. E., 90, 164

Howlett, David, 52

humility, 16

Hutton, Ronald, 139

Icelandic saga tradition, 66

ideas, Plato's theory of, 17–18

identity: language and, 134–35; politics of, 232; reuse of cemetery sites and, 148

immigration, 2

imperial offices, 15, 33, 49–53. *See also curiales*

income, church's, 86

Innocent I, Pope, 160

Innocent XI, Pope, 222

inscriptions, 73

interpretatio Romana, 129–132, 134

interpretation, biblical. *See* exegesis

Iona, 184, 185, 188

Ireland: Christian community in, 158; connection with Roman Britain, 61, 69–71; contacts with Rome, 157; contrast with Britain, 2; cultural changes in, 74; described, 61–92; first mention of in *Confessio*, 79; as frontier zone, 74; geographical overviews of, 74–76; material culture in, 62, 63; Patrick's initial departure to, 52–53, 55; Patrick's return to, 14–15, 55, 101; religion in (*see* religion) slavery in, 80–81, 85; start of Patrick's missionary work in, 56 (*see also* mission, Patrick's) strategic importance of, 61; understanding of, 5; wealth in, 14. *See also* conversion, of Ireland

Irish language, 64; as Celtic, 62; Latin and, 72, 73, 80, 156; Patrick's knowledge of, 80; Q-Celtic, 80; script, 73–74

Irish people: contact with Romans, 61; distinguished from Celts, 63; indigenous, religion of, 132–152; invasions of Britain, 41–42, 79

Irish Times, 231–32

Irish Volunteers, 231

Isaac, 19, 20

Isidore of Seville, 213–14

Jackson, Kenneth, 65
Jacob, 47
James II, 229
Jerome, Saint, 24, 25–26, 34, 77, 160,
    161, 162, 166, 167
Jews, 122, 208
Jocelyn of Furness, 207, 211–12,
    226
John (biblical figure), 48
John Cassian, 167
John de Courcy, 226
Johnston, Elva, 65, 73, 74
Jones, Catherine, 39
Jones, Christopher, 122, 126
Joseph (biblical figure), 25, 26
jubilee, 104–5
Julian the Apostate, 42, 123, 125, 141
Justinian, 46, 49

keenings, ritual, 204
Kenny, Enda, 2
kidnapping. See converts, abducted
Kildare, 185
kin group, Irish, 87–88
kings (reges, reguli), 165, 189; children
    of, Patrick's focus on, 165–66 (see
    also monastic communities/life)
    conversion and, 85–86; Patrick's
    dealings with, 151; sacral status,
    151–52. See also kingship; Lóegaire
    mac Néill; individual dynasties
kingship, 67–68, 78–79; gift giving
    and, 82; physical perfection and,
    201. See also kings
Knott, Eleanor, 65
Koch, John T., 136

La Tène culture, 62
láech, 123

laicus, 123
lamentation, ritual, 204
lamia, 150
land: ancestral, 148; gifted to church,
    171–72; monastic communities
    and, 168, 170. See also property
    interests
land market in Roman Britain, 53–54
land transfers, 197–98
landholding, 86–88
landowners, absentee, 53–54
language: identity and, 134–35. See also
    Irish language
Latin: Bible translated into, 34–35
    (see also Vulgate) Irish language
    and, 72, 73, 80, 156; names for
    Irish/Ireland, 75; Patrick's, 15–16,
    35–36
law, canon: Hibernensis, 86; marriage
    and, 87; slavery in, 105
law, Irish, 83, 105; on captives, 103;
    foster children in, 202; on honor
    prices, 191–92; Law of Innocents,
    186; penal laws, 230; reconciliation
    with church law, 192; on slavery, 103,
    104
law, Old Testament, 104–5
law, Roman, xv, 36, 105; captivity
    and, 103–4; on concubines, 112;
    religion and, 121; on slavery, 103–4,
    106–7, 109; Theodosian Code, 113,
    126
law, spiritual, 19–20
Law of Innocents, 186, 188
lawsuits, 51, 106
Legenda Aurea, 224
legends. See mythology, Irish literary
Leo the Great, Pope, 161, 162
leodgeld, 84

Letter to the Soldiers of Coroticus (Patrick), 3, 7, 9, 15, 218; biblical references in, 21; captivity in, 108–17; citizenship in, 44–45; compared to *Confessio*, 10; conversion in, 109; description of converts in, 174; Franks in, 35; motivations for, 179; objective of, 94; Roman features of, 44; understanding of, 23; Vulgate in, 34. *See also* converts, abducted; soldiers of Coroticus

Libanius, 51

Liber Angeli (The Book of the Angel), 186, 194–95

Life of Brigit (Cogitosus), 122

Life of Columba (Adomnán), 188, 204, 213

Life of Patrick (anonymous), 211

Life of Patrick (Jocelyn of Furness), 207, 211–12, 226

Life of Patrick (Muirchú), 44, 186–196, 211

Life of Patrick (Probus), 210–11

Life of Patrick (Tírechán), 196–205

Life of Saint Patrick (William of Malmsbury), 210

Life of Saint Wilfrid of York (Stephanus), 198

literacy, 73–74

literary tradition. *See* mythology, Irish literary

Littlecote villa, 40

Lives, of saints, 185; *Legenda Aurea*, 224. *See also* hagiography; hagiography, of Patrick; Lives of Patrick; *individual Lives of Patrick*; *individual saints*

Lives of Patrick: influences on, 210; published by Colgan, 222; Tripartite

Life of Patrick, 205, 219; *Vita Quarta*, 207–8; *Vita Secunda*, 207; *Vita Tertia*, 210. *See also* hagiography, of Patrick; *individual Lives of Patrick*

Livingstone, David, 17, 163

Lochru, 190, 191

Lóegaire mac Néill, 68, 146, 189, 190, 192–93, 198; conversion of daughters of, 198–205, 206

lóg n-enech, 84

Losack, Marcus, 208

Lucan, 129

Lucet Máel, 190, 192

Mac Cana, Proinsias, 134, 141

MacNeill, Eoin, 6, 52

Madhavi, 63–64

Magnus Maximus, 42

Maiden Castle, 138–39

Malachy, Saint, 1

manuscripts, as relics, 9, 194

March 17, 222. *See also* St Patrick's Day

marriage, 85–88, 166–67

Martin of Tours, Saint, 164, 167, 175–76, 207

Martyrology of Óengus, 145

Mary (biblical figure), 25, 26, 48

material culture, 62, 63, 151

Mattingly, David, 32, 127

Mayr-Harting, Henry, 166

McCafferty, John, 222

McCormack, Bridget, 221, 229

McKenna, Catherine, 137

McManus, Damian, 137

Medbh, 63–64, 200

meekness, Patrick's reputation for, 81

Melania the Elder, 167

Melania the Younger, 53–54, 167

Melchizedek, 19

Melia, Daniel, 12

Middle Ages: cult of Patrick in, 218–19; Patrick's fame in, 208–14

miracles, 206

mission, Patrick's, 81; baptism, 168–69; call to, 164; challenge to idea of, 158–160; in *Confessio*, 154, 163–66; eschatology and, 154–56, 180; focus on children of kings in, 165–66; insults/persecution and, 175; lack of information on, 156; motivations for, 154–56; opposition to, 85; ordination of clergy and, 164–65, 178–79; practicalities of, 156. *See also* conversion, of Ireland

missionaries: compensation for, 169; in Ireland, 156, 158; Livingstone, 163; Martin of Tours, 175–76; narratives of, 16–17; Palladius, 74, 89, 90–91, 151, 157–58, 160, 161, 162, 163, 164, 189, 194, 209; as storytellers, 163; Victricius, 164; Willibrord, 208–9

missions, xvii; churches and, 177–78; failure of, 162; relics and, 178. *See also* mission, Patrick's

monastic communities/life, 165; circumstances for joining, 85–86; early, 167; gifts for, 170; in Ireland, 167; land and, 170; opposition to, 168; at Saint Patrick's Purgatory, 223–26; women and, 166–67. *See also* monks; nuns

Monesan, 199

monks, 166. *See also* monastic communities/life

Morrígan, 150

mosaics, 39, 128

Moses (biblical figure), 19, 125, 189, 208

mother of Patrick, legendary (Concessa), 207, 209

mourning, 204

Muirchú, 9, 31, 44, 162, 164, 185–196; influence of, 211; influences on, 205–6; Moses analogy by, 208; on Patrick's sojourn with Germanus, 207; sources of, 200; tale of Monesan, 199

municipia, 37

Murphy, Gerard, 65

Mythological Cycle, 66, 149

mythology, Irish literary, 64, 141; cycles, 66–67, 149; euhemeristic interpretation of, 64–65, 66; influences on Lives of Patrick, 206–7; Irish religion and, 149–150; Ulster Cycle, 63–64, 65, 147, 149, 150, 199–200

myths/legends, associated with Patrick, 1

Nabuchodonosor (king), 190

Nagy, Joseph, 21, 65

narrative: of missionaries, 16–17; of Muirchú's Life of Patrick, 188–196; Patrick's (*see Confessio*; Letter to the Soldiers of Coroticus) in rhetoric, 12

National Volunteers, 231

nationalism, 232

Nemthor, 31

Newgrange, Neolithic site, 71, 142–43

Nicaea, first ecumenical council in, 183

Nicene Creed, 202–3

nipples, removal of, 98–99

nobility, 52, 53. *See also* aristocracy

noncombatants, 188
nuns, 85–86, 166. *See also* monastic
    communities/life

obits, Patrick's, 34, 89
oblates, 86, 170
O'Brien, Elizabeth, 148
Ó Cathasaigh, Tomás, 65, 66
Ó Cróinín, Dáibhí, 74
Óengus the Culdee, 145
ogam inscription, 73–74
Oisín, 150
Ólaf Tryggvason, Saint, 66
Old Testament: jubilee laws, 105;
    slavery in, 95
O'Loughlin, Thomas, 6
O'Mara, James, 230
omnes gentes, 154
Onesimus, 48
O'Rahilly, Thomas, 31, 90–91, 141
ordination: compensation for, 169; by
    Patrick, 178–79
Origen, 20
original sin, 159–160
Orosius, 122, 160
Orthodox Nicene Creed, 172–73
Orthodoxy, Patrick's, 205
Ostia, 130

pagan sites, converted to Christian
    worship, 205
págánach, 122
paganism, 119; before Christian era,
    120–21; in Christian era, 120, 121–23;
    cult sites, 199; destruction of sites,
    176–77; end of, 203, 205; imagined
    past of, 199; in Ireland, 145–46;
    lapsing back into, 162 (*see also*
    apostasy) in Life of Patrick, 189–190;

relation with Christianity, 132; sun
    worship, 125; in Theodosian Code,
    126; Túatha Dé Danann, 201
pagans, terms for, 122–23, 140–41
paganus, 121–22
Palladius, 74, 89, 90–91, 151, 157–58,
    160, 161, 162, 163, 164, 189, 194,
    209
pantheon, in early Irish culture, 201,
    203
Pantheon, Roman, 178
parades, Saint Patrick's Day, 231–32
Patrick, Saint, 1, 214; burial of, 194;
    dating of, 33–36, 53, 193–94; death
    of, 193; fame of, 208–14; Gallic
    associations attributed to, 207;
    genealogy of, 209–10; in hagiogra-
    phy, 3, 4; historical, 2–3; historical
    context of, 9; Jewish origins
    attributed to, 208; lack of informa-
    tion about, 3–4; legacy, 119;
    legendary, 3; Q-Celtic phase
    pronunciation of, 80; remains of,
    226; Roman bias of, 2; Romano-
    British phase, 30–58; status in
    Ireland, 82–83; as topical, 2
Paul, Saint, 19, 48, 131–32, 161; address
    to the Athenians at the Areopagus,
    131–32; First Epistle to the
    Corinthians, 169; Letter to the
    Philippians, 173; letter to Titus, 24
Peada, 165
Pelagianism, 159–160, 161–62
Pelagius, 159–160, 161–62
penal laws, 230
Penda, 165
Peter, Saint, 161
Peter of Cornwall, 223
Philemon, 48

Philo, 20

physical perfection, 201

Picard, Jean-Michel, 72

Picts, invasions of Britain, 41–42, 79

Pilate (as biblical figure), 146

pilgrimages, 219, 222–26

Plato, 17–18, 77

Pliny the Younger, 48

poets, 191–92, 193

political organisation, Irish, 67–68.
   See also kings; kingship

politics, Irish, 227–232

politics of identity, 232

pope. *See individual popes*

Posthumus, 42

postliminium, 103–4, 106–7

Potitus, 10, 30, 46

Potter, Timothy, 39

preaching, 175

presbyter, 178, 179

priests, 179

princely conversions, 165–66

princesses, conversion of, 198–205,
   206

Priscus of Panium, 126

Probus, 210–11

property interests, hagiography and,
   186–87, 197–98. *See also* land

prophecy, Patrick's ability to receive,
   23

Prosper of Aquitaine, 151, 157, 158,
   160–61, 162, 189

Protestant Reformation, 219–220,
   226

Protestant-Catholic relations, 227–232

Ptolemy, 75, 133

Quebec Chronicle Telegraph, 230

Quintilian, 12, 13, 17

Raftery, Barry, 135

raiding: between Britain and Ireland,
   70–73; on holy days, 110

Reformation. *See* Protestant
   Reformation

relics, 177–78, 194–95, 204–5, 213;
   curing snakebite with, 214;
   destruction of, 226; of Erc mac
   Dego, 190; manuscripts and, 9;
   Patrick's, 194–95, 211, 226;
   veneration of, 191

religio, 121

religion: archaeology and, 142–49; in
   Britain, 127–131; Celtic, 132, 134–36;
   Christianitas/paganitas binary, 121;
   Christianity assimilated into
   existing system of, 151; cultic
   practices, 137–152; druids, 68,
   137–38, 189–191, 192, 193, 202, 204,
   205; Gallic, 129–130, 134; *gentes*, 122;
   of indigenous British and Irish,
   132–152; *interpretatio Romana*,
   129–132; Irish religious practice in
   Patrick's time, 141; non-Christian
   Other, 122–23; offerings, 144–45;
   plurality of deities, 130–32; *religio/
   superstitio* binary, 121; reuse of cult
   sites, 142–44; rival cults, 119–120
   (*see also* paganism) in Roman
   Empire, 121, 123–134, 144; sacral
   status of kings, 151; sun worship,
   124–25, 141–42; syncretism, 124–27,
   128–29, 151; transmission of
   concepts with potential religious
   connotations, 150–51; Túatha Dé
   Danann, 201, 203; wealth/status
   and, 39; written sources on,
   149–150. *See also* Christianity;
   conversion; paganism

religion in Ireland: indigenous, 132–152; material culture and, 151; mythology and, 149–150; Patrick's writings as source on, 140–42

reptiles, venomous, 211–14

Restitutus of London, 33, 127

rhetoric: classical, 11–14; *Confessio* and, 16; falsehoods in, 13; truth and, 17

Rhoda (biblical figure), 48

rí túaithe, 165. *See also* kings

Richardson, John, 219–220

ritual sites: association with ceremonial political centres, 151; association with heroic tales, 149; in Ireland, 140; reuse of, 151

Roman Catholicism, relation with Irish church, 221

Roman Empire: assimilation of native elites into, 37, 38; citizenship in, 44–45 (*see also* citizens, Roman) Constantine III's coup, 42; decline of, 41–43; religion in, 121; slavery in, 45, 94–96; third-century crisis, 37, 38. *See also* Britain

romanitas, in Britain, 57

Romano-British phase, Patrick's, 30–58

Rome: contacts with Ireland, 157; conversion of Ireland and, 161; Irish delegation to, 157, 184; submission to, 183. *See also* Roman Catholicism

Roth, Ulrike, 48

Rufinus, 167

saga, 65–66. *See also* mythology, Irish literary

Saint George and Saint Patrick (anonymous), 227–28

Saint Patrick's Bell Shrine, 226–27

Saint Patrick's Day, 221, 228–232

Saint Patrick's Purgatory, 222–26

saints: cults of, 218–19; genealogies of, 219; Irish, 1, 2, 222; local traditions about, 219; revocation of feast days, 229. *See also* hagiography; relics; *individual saints*

Sarah (biblical figure), 20

Saxons, 41–42

scholars, their legal status in Ireland, 191–92

Scotti, 41–42, 75

script, 73–74

Scythians, 76–77

Second Coming. *See* eschatology

Ségéne of Armagh, 186, 187

Ségéne of Iona, 184

self-identification, 45

Seneca, 121

serfs, 96

serpents, 211–14

servitude, xvii, 45, 95–96. *See also* captivity; slavery

settlements, in Ireland, 68–69

sexual impropriety, 77

shamrock, 221, 230

Sharpe, Richard, 7, 183

Sheelah (legendary wife of Patrick), 4

shepherding, 79–80, 97

shrines, pagan, 178

Sims-Williams, Patrick, 135

slave economy, 45, 95

slave raiding, 44

slave trade, 45, 72–73, 110

slave women: conversion of, 172; value of, 112

slavery, 94; in Britain, 43–49; Christianity and, 45–49; Christians serving non-Christian masters, 113–14; in *Confessio*, 23–24; in Ireland, 80–81; Irish law on, 103, 104; in Old Testament, 95, 104–5; Roman law on, 103–4, 109; in Roman world, 94–96. *See also* captivity; captivity, Patrick's; servitude; slaves

slavery metaphors, 23–24

slaves: admittance of into clergy, 49; church's ownership of, 48–49, 86; cost of, 46–47; economy and, 96; escaped, 102–3; in Ireland, 85; ownership of, 85; papal protection of, 113; Patrick's father's, 45; *postliminium*, 103–4; Roman law on, 106–7; value of, 112; wealth and, 49, 84–85. *See also* captivity; captivity, Patrick's; servitude; slavery

Sleaty, 187–88

Snorri, 66

Sol Invictus, 124, 141

soldiers, 231

soldiers of Coroticus, 15; Christianity of, 111–12; excommunication of, 115–16. *See also* Letter to the Soldiers of Coroticus

Solinus, 214

sources, xvi. *See also* archaeology; writings, Patrick's

Stancliffe, Clare, 83

Stanley, Henry Morton, 163

Station Island, 223–26

status: in Ireland, knowledge about, 95; religious differences and, 39

Stephanus, 198

Stilicho, 42

Stokes, George, 1

storytellers, 163

Strabo, 63, 76, 77

suckling, 98–99

Sulpicius Severus, 9, 175–76, 178

sun worship, 124–25, 141–42

superstitiones, 121, 130

Symmachus, 126

syncretism, 124–29, 151

Tacitus, 61, 68, 72, 77, 78, 79, 137

Táin Bó Cúailnge (epic), 202

Tara, 144, 145, 147

Tara brooch, 70

taxes, 50–51, 106

temples, 147

tenants, rent-paying, 96

Testart, Alain, 81

texts, shift in critical approach to interpreting, 5

Thanet (island), 213

Themistius, 45

Theodosian Code, 113, 126

Theodosius II, 30, 123, 126, 128

Thomas, Charles, 31, 32

Thompson, E. A., 5

Threlkeld, Caleb, 221, 230

time, end of. *See* eschatology

Tírechán, 9, 162, 185–86, 194–95, 196–205, 208

Topographia Hiberniae (Gerald), 211

Torbach, Abbot, 7

town council. *See* curia

towns, in Britain, 37

Tractatus de purgatorio Sancti Patricii (Henry of Saltry), 223

trade, 70–73

travel tales, 163

trial, Patrick's, 14–15, 54–56. *See also*
    accusations, against Patrick;
    defence, Patrick's; elders, Patrick's
    conflict with
Tricorii, 133
Tripartite Life of Patrick, 205, 206–7,
    219
trivium, 12
Trump, Donald, 2
truth, 13–14, 16, 17
túath, 67, 78
Túatha Dé Danann, 201, 203
Two Patricks, The (O'Rahilly), 90
two Patricks tradition, 89–91, 194

Uí Amolngid dynasty, 196, 197, 198
Uí Bairrche dynasty, 187
Uí Dúnlainge dynasty, 187
Uí Néill dynasty, 185, 188, 195, 197
Ulster Cycle, 63–64, 65, 66, 147, 149,
    150, 199–200
Ulster Volunteers, 231
Ultán, 196, 206
uncial, Roman, 74
United Kingdom of Britain and
    Ireland, 227
Ussher, James, 196, 218

Valentinian I, 126
Vendryes, Joseph, 133
veneration of Patrick, 220; pilgrimage
    to Saint Patrick's Purgatory, 222–26;
    references to, 183, 184, 185; relics,
    226; Saint Patrick's Day, 221,
    228–232
Victoricus, 164
Victorinus of Pettau, 174
Victricius, 164
Vikings, 110

villas, 31, 32, 37–41, 128
violence, over relics/ecclesiastical
    settlements, 194–95
virgin birth, of Mary, 26
virginity, 166–67. *See also* monastic
    communities/life; nuns
Vita Quarta, 207–8
Vita Secunda, 207
Vita Tertia, 210
Vulgate, 34–35

Waddell, John, 141–42
Wadding, Luke, 221
war, 188
Ware, James, 218
water features, 199. *See also* wells
wealth: administrative roles and,
    49–50 (*see also curiales*) in Ireland,
    14; Patrick's, 84, 106–7; of Patrick's
    family, 49–50, 52; religious
    differences and, 39; in Roman
    Empire, 49–50; slaves as, 49, 84–85;
    women as potential alienators of,
    171
wells, 199, 205, 219, 220
wergeld, 84
widows, 166–67, 170–71. *See also*
    monastic communities/life; nuns
wife, Patrick's legendary, 4
Wilfrid of York, Saint, 198
William III (of Orange), 229
William of Malmsbury, 210
Williamite anniversaries, 229–230
Willibrord, 208–9
Wilson, Jacqueline Cahill, 71
women: burial sites of, 149; captive,
    sexual exploitation of, 112; celibate
    lifestyle and, 166–67; freeborn, as
    concubines, 112; gifts given by, 170;

Irish, sharing of, 78; Law of
Innocents and, 188; slave, 85; wealth
and, 171

Wood, Susan, 88

Wood of Voclut, 10, 197

worship, in Ireland, 67–68

writings, Patrick's, 3, 9, 233–34;
churches in, 177; in context, 4–5;
eschatology in, 154–55; historical
context, 233–34; Muirchú's use of,
189; publication of, 218; rediscovery
of, 218; rhetorical traditions in,
11–14; as source of information,
140–42; use of "church" in, 177. *See
also Confessio*; Letter to the Soldiers
of Coroticus

Zosimus, Pope, 160

A NOTE ON THE TYPE

This book has been composed in Arno, an Old-style serif typeface in the classic Venetian tradition, designed by Robert Slimbach at Adobe.